FOUR COMEDIES

FOUR COMEDIES

by Pedro Calderón de la Barca

Translated with an Introduction by

KENNETH MUIR

With notes
to the individual plays by

Ann L. Mackenzie

THE UNIVERSITY PRESS OF KENTUCKY

Library of Congress Cataloging in Publication Data

Calderón de la Barca, Pedro, 1600-1681.
    Four comedies.

    Bibliography: p.
    CONTENTS: From bad to worse.--The secret spoken
aloud.--The worst is not always certain.--The
advantages & disadvantages of a name.
    I. Muir, Kenneth.
PQ6292.A1M35   1980   862'.3   80-14570
ISBN 0-8131-1409-8

Scholarly publisher for the Commonwealth
serving Berea College, Centre College of Kentucky,
Eastern Kentucky University, The Filson Club,
Georgetown College, Kentucky Historical Society,
Kentucky State University, Morehead State University,
Murray State University, Northern Kentucky University,
Transylvania University, University of Kentucky,
University of Louisville, and Western Kentucky University.

Editorial and Sales Offices: Lexington, Kentucky 40506

To Geoffrey Ribbans *and* Harold Hall

Preface

These four translations were drafted some years ago. My version of *Casa con dos puertas mala es de guardar (A House with Two Doors Is Difficult to Guard)* had appeared in the *Tulane Drama Review* in 1963, when Eric Bentley was encouraging a series of new translations. This appearance led to two successful productions: the first by the Drama Department at the University of Pittsburgh, and the second by the Department of Dramatic Art and Speech at the University of California, Davis. My aim (as with my versions of Racine and Corneille) had been to produce a text that actors could speak naturally, and that audiences with little or no knowledge of the originals could hear with pleasure. This meant avoiding the rhymed alexandrines of French classical tragedy and the characteristic metres and assonances of the writers of the Golden Age of Spanish drama. Judging by the enthusiasm of audiences I had succeeded in my limited aim; and this encouraged me to translate four more of the comedies. Then came a series of commissioned projects that appeared more seemly for a Shakespeare scholar. So, while I edited Shakespeare and Wyatt and wrote a number of books on tragedy and comedy, the Calderón translations were put to one side. I was aware at the same time that there were scholars on both sides of the Atlantic who could produce more accurate translations, even if my long experience of acting and directing gave me one advantage — knowing how the lines would sound on the stage.

My interest in Spanish drama was revived in 1978 when Professor Joseph Jones, who had somehow heard of my translations — some of which had been circulating among friends — invited me to put into verse his own prose translation of Luis Vélez de Guevara's *Reinar después de morir*. He was so pleased with the result that I looked again at the translations contained in the present volume and, at his suggestion, I submitted them to the University Press of Kentucky.

These versions are based on the Aguilar edition, but I have frequently consulted the French prose translations of M. Damas Hinard (1903–1906). I have also sought the help of my colleagues in the Department of Hispanic Studies at Liverpool, and they have been generous with their time and

charitable to my ignorance. In particular I wish to thank
my friend of thirty-years standing, Professor Harold Hall,
for saving me from numerous mistakes. He is not responsible for those that remain. The headnotes and footnotes to
the individual plays have been provided by Miss Ann L. Mac-
kenzie.

K.M.

Introduction

These four plays, although excellent, are not positively
Calderón's best, but I decided to confine my efforts to the
production of *actable* versions of comedies and to avoid any
play that was already available in English.[1] Translators
have fought shy of the comedies, although they comprised a
third of Calderón's huge output. Moreover, I could not see
much chance of a revival of interest in the theatre or in
churches of the *autos* — "flowery and starry" as Shelley
called them[2] — for they need an audience of believers. It
is true that there has been at least one successful modern
production of *El gran teatro del mundo* and that fine actor
Miles Malleson had been translating another just before he
died. Several of the tragedies were available in Roy Camp-
bell's admirable versions.[3] The comedies, therefore, seemed
to provide an untapped reservoir of plays for theatres anxious to extend their repertoires, whether off Broadway, on
campuses in England or America, or in the subsidized reper-
tory theatres of England, from the National Theatre down-
wards. During the last few years we have had the opportunity of seeing comedies by Aristophanes, Jonson, Middleton,
Machiavelli, Molière, Dryden, Wycherley, Congreve, Vanbrugh,
Farquhar, Goldoni and Sheridan — but no Calderón, who is a
better comic writer than some of those listed.

Naturally enough critics have been tempted to write
books and articles on Calderón's more serious plays — *La
vida es sueño, El príncipe constante, El mágico prodigioso,
A secreto agravio, secreta venganza* — and to treat the comedies as of secondary importance, with Madariaga even stat-
ing that they were negligible. So one might say that *As You
Like It* was negligible beside *King Lear*. Edward M. Wilson
in his chapter on the dramatist[4] spent only one-tenth of his
space on the comedies; and, to give a last example, R. B.
Heilman in his comprehensive book on comedy entitled *The
Ways of the World* (1978) has space for the discussing of
such minor dramatists as Barrie, Levy, Katev, Kaufman, and
Osborne, but has only a single reference to Calderón, and
this to the tragicomedy *La vida es sueño*.

There are several other comedies as good as the four I
have included, e.g., *Mañanas de abril y mayo* and *No hay bur-*

las con el amor. The principle of not including plays already available has meant that I could not include *La dama
duende,* which Edwin Honig translated for his Dramabooks collection (1961). It is often regarded as Calderón's best
comedy and it certainly contains a lively plot and some good
scenes. But it suffers from a number of defects that make
it less satisfying than several of the other comedies. Don
Manuel, even though he deduces that there is a secret entrance to his department through which "the phantom Lady"
comes, has no suspicion that the cupboard conceals this entrance. Ángela finds the portrait of a lady in his luggage,
which she assumes to be of his mistress, but the audience is
never told the solution. We are not told how Beatriz is
reconciled to her father; and when the final duel between
Manuel and Luis is interrupted by his being disarmed, Manuel, instead of handing back Luis's sword (possibly damaged)
lets him go off to find another — a clumsy device on the
part of the dramatist to get him off the stage. Such flaws
are less evident in other comedies.

A good deal has been said of Calderón's serious view of
life as exemplified in the comedies, and obviously one
should not overlook the fact that he was a man of deep religious convictions and that most of his plays, not merely
the *autos,* are firmly based on moral principles. Nevertheless, even some of the best critics are inclined to treat
the comedies more solemnly than the case demands. Professor
Wilson, for example, remarks:

> [The comedies,] though they are intended as entertain-
> ment, did not merely serve to "amuse an idle moment in
> their day." They were based on certain strict conven-
> tions of manners and upheld them: be polite, keep your
> word, protect the helpless, help your friends, and so
> forth. They also show...that mistakes in conduct and in
> the interpretation of the circumstances in which we are
> placed, can, and do, have disagreeable consequences....
> Insight and prudence are valuable qualities that help
> men and women in their difficulties. Rashness, impuls-
> es, hunches, are dangerous traps for the unwary. These
> plays almost deserve the title of entertaining moral
> allegories.[5]

This account of the comedies is difficult to square with the
plays themselves. Of course prudence is a good thing and
rashness dangerous. Of course one should keep his word,
help his friend, and so forth; but these are not "strict
conventions of manners" but rather the ordinary code of de-
cent people in any society. They can be taken for granted;
and no audience watching these plays would regard them
as moral allegories. There are good moral lessons to be

learned from any of Shakespeare's comedies, more probably
than from Calderón's.

It is true that there are strict conventions, a promi-
nent one being the way the honor of a parent or guardian is
affected by the behavior of a girl in his charge. Some
critics believe that Calderón upheld such conventions, but
there is some evidence that he was critical of them. I cannot believe that any audience was expected to deplore the
behavior of the charming heroine of *Casa con dos puertas* who
sallies out to meet her brother's guest and so gains a husband. I think Edwin Honig is right to suggest that *La dama
duende* is a criticism of the code of honor; and when Don
Pedro in *The Worst Is Not Always Certain*[6] exclaims

> Woe to the first who made so harsh a law,
> A contract so unjust, a tie so impious,
> Which deals unequally to man and woman,
> And links our honor to another's whim —

we are meant to approve this sentiment of a wise and sympathetic character. Calderón was as aware of the absurdities
of the code of honor as we must be. This is equally apparent in the three plays in which honorable men murder their
wives — *El pintor de su deshonra, El médico de su honra,*
and *A secreto agravio, secreta venganza* — and in Shakespeare's *Othello.*[7]

The four plays in this volume are all *comedias de enre-
do,* comedies of intrigue; one of them, *El secreto a voces,*
because it treats of dukes and duchesses, is usually called
a *comedia palaciega,* and *Dicha y desdicha* could also be
placed in the same category; *Peor está* and *No siempre* are
capa y espada (cloak-and-sword) comedies. But the bound-
aries between the genres are not very precise. The characteristics of the cloak-and-sword comedies have been summar-
ized by Norman Maccoll:[8]

> Not only does Calderón confine these plays to one sec-
> tion of society, but he also adheres to one type of
> plot; and his characters are strictly limited in number,
> and bear a strong resemblance to one another. The in-
> trigue in the comedies always turns upon the love-
> affairs of two or three young gentlemen and two or three
> young ladies, a father or guardian or two being added,
> whose watchfulness the lovers endeavour to circumvent.
> They are aided by their serving man...and by the maids
> of the ladies. These *dramatis personae,* who number from
> ten to twelve, reappear in every comedy and the national
> custom of going about masked furnishes the machinery of
> the plot.... The young ladies who figure in them are in-
> variably motherless. [The same thing is true of Shake-
> speare's comic heroines]. They either live with a fath-

er who is a widower, or, if they are orphans, they are
under the charge of a brother who is always a bachelor.
... Even the appearance in her father's house of a male
visitor who is not a relative is usually the signal for
a young lady's withdrawal to her own apartment.

Add to this the absurdity that after a prolonged courtship of months or years, the lady condescends to talk to her
admirer through the window and, after the lapse of time,
even to allow him into the house. Of course, says Maccoll,
"in all the comedies one of these stolen interviews is the
moment chosen for the reappearance of the master of the
house...an additional complication is given to the plot when
the interview takes place at the abode of a friend of the
heroine who has been persuaded to lend her house for that
purpose. In that case the lovers are invariably surprised
by the lover of the accommodating friend; he at once suspects a rival, and quarrels with his mistress on the grounds
of her infidelity."
    A house is lent in *Casa con dos puertas* with the results
indicated. In *From Bad to Worse* César kills a man in a
duel, wrongly assuming him to be Flérida's lover; and in *The
Worst Is Not Always Certain* Carlos assumes that the man hidden in Leonor's room is there with her knowledge and consent.
    Although Maccoll gives a fair idea of the general atmos-
phere of the plays, there is rather more variety than he
suggests. For example, most of the complications and misunderstandings in *The Advantages and Disadvantages of a Name*
are caused by the hero's assuming his friend's name; in
other plays they are caused by disguise; and in others again
by the actual structure of the house. In all the plays
there are mysteries, quarrels, and jealousies. In the end
all is explained. The women recover their jeopardized honor
by suitable marriages and honor is thereby restored to their
parents or guardians.
    The plays do not depend on subtlety of characterization.
Goethe, with some exaggeration, said that the heroes were as
like as so many leaden bullets. They are all easily jealous
and as prone to duel as Tybalt in *Romeo and Juliet*. Even
the names of heroes and heroines are repeated in play after
play — Félix, Juan, Carlos, Flérida, Laura, etc. Nevertheless, although the characters are types, the best of them
are sufficiently differentiated. No one would confuse Laura
and Marcela in *Casa con dos puertas,* or Leonor with Beatriz
in *The Worst Is Not Always Certain*. But the effectiveness
of the plays depends less on character — there is no heroine
as enchanting as Rosalind or Viola, no man as interesting as
Jaques or Shylock — than on the sparkle of the dialogue and

the quality of the poetry (inevitably dimmed in translation), and also on the ingenuity of the plots.

Not everyone has approved of Calderón's style. When Edward Fitzgerald translated six of the plays, he remarked:[9]

> I do not believe an exact translation of this poet can
> be very successful; retaining so much that, whether real
> or dramatic Spanish passion, is still bombast to English
> ears; and confounds otherwise distinct outlines of char-
> acter; conceits that were a fashion of the day;...viola-
> tions of the probable, nay possible, that shock even
> healthy romantic licence; repetitions of thoughts and
> images that Calderón used (and smiled at) as so much
> stage properties — so much, in short, that is not Calde-
> rón's own better self, but concession to private haste
> or public taste by one who so often relied upon some
> striking dramatic crisis for success with a not very ac-
> curate audience.

In conformity with these opinions, Fitzgerald, "while
faithfully trying to retain what was fine and efficient,
sunk, reduced, altered, and replaced much that seemed not."
Even as late as 1926 a learned editor complained of Calderón's conceits, his quibbles, and his excessive use of rhetorical devices, as Victorian critics complained of the same
things in Shakespeare's early plays, or blamed the ground-
lings, as Fitzgerald blamed Calderón's "not very accurate
audience."

Students of iterative imagery are not likely to complain
of Calderón's repetition of images; and admirers of Jacobean
drama and of metaphysical poetry are unlikely to find Calderón's style repellent.

If some of the poetic quality of the plays is inevitably
lost in translation, Calderón's mastery of stagecraft is
everywhere apparent. He is as expert as Feydeau in develop-
ing dramatic complications from initial situations. One of
Calderón's contemporaries praised him for having given to
drama the logical form of the syllogism, and Micheline Sauvage actually applies a kind of algebraic notation to *Casa
con dos puertas*.[10] When that play was performed at Davis in
1965, three reviewers actually referred to it as a farce,
rather surprised that it was so funny; but since farce depends entirely on situation and plot, it is surely unjust to
Calderón to put his comedies in this category. His cleverly
developed situations depend on the social conventions of the
day, and his plays are the comments on them. Moreover the
dialogue of the plays is essentially poetical. No one in
his senses would refer to *Twelfth Night* as a farce although
the confusions arising from mistaken identity (caused by

Viola's disguise as Cesario) are often as farcical as the
situations in *The Comedy of Errors*.

We should also bear in mind that although all four plays
end happily, there are passages of pathos and heartbreak;
and Calderón does not always let the audience into the secret, so that we cannot be sure (as we always are with
Shakespeare's comedies) that all will come right in the end.
Lisarda's marriage to Juan in *From Bad to Worse* is somewhat
reluctant, and we may have doubts about some of the pairings
in other plays.

Notes

1. I have since discovered that *El secreto a voces* was translated, as *The Secret in Words,* by D. F. McCarthy (*Dramas of Calderon* [London, 1853]), and that there is an inaccurate prose version
of *Peor está que estaba* by Fanny Holcroft (*The Theatrical Recorder*
[London, 1805], vol. 1).

2. *Letters,* ed. F. L. Jones (1964).

3. Some are included in Eric Bentley's *The Classic Theatre*
(1959), vol. 3.

4. Edward M. Wilson and Duncan Moir, *The Golden Age: Drama 1492-
1700* (London and New York, 1971).

5. Ibid., p. 106.

6. See below p. 170.

7. Professor Wilson himself gave a radio talk on *Othello* from
this point of view.

8. Published in 1888; reprinted in the Dramabook Calderón. Maccoll, of course, is giving a generalized view which does not precisely fit any particular play. The servants, both male and female,
provide plenty of physical and verbal humor. The custom of going
about masked was only at times of carnival. Women, however, did
often wear veils.

9. *Eight Dramas of Calderón* (London and New York, 1906).

10. *Calderon: Dramaturge* (Paris, 1959).

Peor está
que estaba

D. PETRVS CALDERON
DE LA BARCA.

Peor está que estaba was published in Calderón's *Primera
parte*...of 1636 but was evidently written several years before that date. A somewhat corrupt edition of the text,
wrongly attributing it to a certain Luis Alvarez, and dated
1630, once formed part of the library of Ludwig Tieck.[1] The
play, then, might well have been written in 1629, the same
year as Calderón's *La dama duende,* to which indeed the playwright alludes in *Peor está que estaba.*[2] It seems to have
been almost as popular in the Spain of its day as was the
famous *Dama duende.* An otherwise unimportant manuscript
copy of *Peor está que estaba,* preserved in the Biblioteca
Nacional, Madrid, contains a note by the Madrid censor, An-
tonio de Nanclares, dated April 1657, in which he gives permission for its performance and comments that he himself had
seen it performed many times. Nor was its popularity confined to Spain itself. In seventeenth-century France it inspired two different adaptations, by De Brosse in 1645 and
by Bois-Robert ten years later. In England in the early
1660s, the comedy caught the attention of George Digby, earl
of Bristol. He translated it together with its "sister"
play, *Mejor está que estaba,* as *Worse and Worse* and *'Tis
Better Than It Was.* Unhappily, these translations have not
survived. But Samuel Pepys tells us in his *Diary* that he
attended a performance of *Worse and Worse* in 1664, and "very
pleasant it was."

And a "very pleasant" stage-play it is, by any standards. The entire action takes place in or near Gaeta, so
that there is a sense of unity of location, yet, not at the
expense of visual variety, for scenes change from a country
garden to a prison tower, and to different rooms of the Governor of Gaeta's mansion. In act 3 in particular the scene
in Carlos's prison could be made to provide in performance
a striking visual contrast to the scenes that follow, set in
Juan's luxuriously appointed guest room in the Governor's
house. Calderón offers detailed stage directions as to how
the guest room should be furnished; offers them indirectly,
in Lisarda's comments and exclamations as she looks around
the room and sees a desk, pictures, a mirror, tapestries,
and so on.[3] The playwright also provides opportunities for
changes in costume, and not only as far as the ladies are
concerned. When Don Juan first comes on stage we learn that
he has just returned from fighting in Flanders, and that before he visits his betrothed he intends to buy some fine new
clothes, more befitting a bridegroom. And indeed when he
arrives at the Governor's house in act 2 for his first meeting with Lisarda, his attire is so splendid, complete with
plumes and spurs, that the Governor himself remarks upon it
in admiring terms.

Shakespeare demonstrated in *Hamlet* that "when sorrows

come, they come not single spies, but in battalions," and so
added a new saying to the English language. It is this same
idea that Calderón develops in *Peor está que estaba,* but of
course in a much lighter and less profound way. Also, far
from creating a new Spanish proverb in the process, Calderón
limits himself to exploiting to the full the dramatic possi-
bilities of one already in existence: the saying that "peor
está que estaba." This saying is not only used for the
title, but is repeated several times at key points in the
action: by César, for example, toward the end of act 1; by
the Governor in act 3, and in the same act, by the heroine,
Lisarda herself.[4] The general result is an admirable impression of thematic unity; though one might perhaps have
wished that Lisarda's allusion to the proverb had been made
more concisely, without those references to Camoen's ode
on a similar theme, and without so much recapitulation of
events of the previous two acts. Yet, such recapitulation,
which seems superfluous to us, was doubtless necessary in
Calderón's own day, when audiences tended to be rowdy and
inattentive, and when the one-act farces, put on to entertain them during the intervals, were liable to make them
forget act 1 before the actors had begun act 2.

The play evidences not only unity of theme but also re-
markable unity of action, with carefully orchestrated en-
trances, exits, concealments, and interruptions. Sometimes
a dramatist so tightly controls his medium that dramatic
unity comes to signify dramatic monotony. Not so Calderón:
his play is full of variety in mood, pace, and incident.
There are tender, self-searching dialogues of love between
César and Lisarda. There are sudden moments of high excitement, as when César's pistol goes off unexpectedly during
his secret visit to Lisarda's room. There are scenes of
sustained tension and suspense, such as that in act 2, where
Lisarda, wrongly imagining that her father already knows of
her meetings with César, tries to throw herself upon his
mercy. Any audience would surely sit with nerves on edge
through a whole series of misunderstandings between father
and daughter, which somehow, despite her confessions and
explanations, manage to keep the Governor unaware of his
daughter's guilty secret. Not least, there are the comic
exchanges between Camacho and Celia, in parody of the love
affair between their master and mistress. This parody is at
its best in act 1, when Camacho tries in vain to persuade
Celia to lift her veil, and, again, in act 2, when the *gracioso* goes into a huff, so that it is Celia now, perversely
feminine, who even resorts to bribery in an attempt to en-
tice the disgruntled Camacho to look beneath her mantle at
her face.

All the main characters of the play are in certain re-

spects interesting: Juan, something of a dandy and more in
love with Lisarda's beauty and position than with Lisarda as
a person; César, with emotional and moral commitments to one
woman, yet genuinely and deeply attracted to another; the
Governor, a typical Golden Age father in the way in which he
worries about his honor, yet curiously untypical, in that he
does not threaten or attack his daughter when he finds her
in a compromising position.[5] But it is the heroine, Lisarda, who is the most memorable character. She displays the
same love of romantic mystery shown by Ángela in *La dama
duende*. But she is a much more vulnerable person than Ángela. In act 3, for example, she is very frightened at the
thought of a confrontation with Juan. It is true that when
this confrontation takes place she manipulates the opposing
forces with great ingenuity. Nevertheless, hers, unlike
Ángela's, is not natural ingenuity. Rather, it is the product of her very desperation. Fear inspires her to feign a
different emotion, indignation, and to forestall any charge
her betrothed might bring against her, by accusing him of
using her house for an assignation with another woman.[6]
Lisarda also differs from Ángela in that her love for César
impresses us as being much more profound than Ángela's for
Manuel.

　　Still, whereas Ángela in fact marries Manuel at the end
of *La dama duende* no such happy outcome awaits the heroine
of *Peor está que estaba,* surely one of Calderón's most serious comedies. Instead, Lisarda must witness the marriage of
the man she loves to Flérida, the woman whose honor César
had compromised before ever he met Lisarda. And then she in
turn must marry Don Juan, her father's choice, for whom she
herself has never displayed the least affection. Lisarda
tries to console herself with the sad reflection that things
are surely now as bad as they could ever be. But, with the
gracioso's final comment ringing in our ears that "now is
the time, since they are being wed,/ to apply the saying
'From bad to worse,'" we might suspect that poor Lisarda's
future life with Juan will often give her cause to exclaim:
"peor está que estaba."[7]

Notes

　　1. See E. Cotarelo y Mori, *Ensayo sobre la vida y obras de D.
Pedro Calderón de la Barca* (Madrid, 1924), pp. 143-44.
　　2. See note 3, p. 279.
　　3. See act 3, scene 3.
　　4. See pp. 26, 50, 52, and 61.
　　5. See act 2, scene 3.
　　6. See p. 63.
　　7. For notes to the text of *From Bad to Worse* see pp. 279-81.

From Bad to Worse

ԶԶ

DRAMATIS PERSONAE

Don César Ursino
Don Juan
The Governor
Camacho ⎱
Fabio ⎰ servants
Félix

Flérida
Lisarda, the Governor's daughter
Celia ⎱
Nise ⎰ servants
A jailer
Guards and servants

The scene is laid in and around Gaeta

ԶԶ

ACT ONE

Scene 1: A Room in the Governor's House

[Enter the GOVERNOR and FÉLIX]

GOVERNOR: *[Reading]* "It is only to you, to you alone, my
dear lord and friend that I would dare to confide freely
the misfortune that crushes me, because even if you are
not in a position to bring a remedy for it, I have at
least the certainty that you will keenly sympathize with
me. A gentleman (whose name the servant who brings this
letter will disclose) has disappeared from this town,
after having killed a man. He took with him a daughter
of mine, who had been his accomplice, and who to this
initial fault has added a second. I am told that they
intend to cross over into Spain. If by any chance they
seek asylum in Gaeta, will you keep them in custody and
treat them as my children? Although they have gravely
compromised my honor, act in such a way, I beseech you,
that I do not lose it entirely."[1]
[To FÉLIX] Yes, I feel keenly this disgrace of his;
And I am glad Alonso does remember
My friendship for him even in his sorrow.
I hope this gentleman takes refuge here:

> I'd give the richest of my jewels for that...
> If it should happen, I swear that I'll arrange
> The honor of my friend will be preserved;
> For it's a great responsibility
> When one is told so intimate a secret.
> May I display my gratitude to him
> For all the kindnesses which I've received
> Since we were comrades in the fields of Flanders!
> Tell me but this — the name of the gentleman
> Who has so compromised the life and honor
> Of Don Alonso.

FÉLIX: My lord, the man in question
> Who killed a man and took away Flérida
> Is named Don César. We can hardly doubt it,
> Because my mistress's beauty was the cause
> Of the duel; and he and my mistress disappeared
> On the same day. I know the man by sight,
> And if you want me to concern myself
> With searching for him, will you authorize me
> In virtue of your office now to visit
> All the town's hostelries? I have some clues
> Which make me think that he is hidden here.

GOVERNOR: I will myself join in the search with you.
> What is this clue?

FÉLIX: Arriving at my lodging,
> I saw one of his servants pass this morning
> (One who must surely have set off with him);
> That made me think Don César must be here.

GOVERNOR: Did you follow him?

FÉLIX: He knows me too well, my lord.
> But I have charged a fellow who is with me
> To follow him, and let me know the place
> Where he is staying.

GOVERNOR: Good. Go and find out
> All that your fellow knows. When I am given
> Sufficient information, I will go
> Myself to apprehend him. We must be careful.
> For were a magistrate to cause commotion
> Without more knowledge, it would upset the town,
> Let César know that we are searching for him,
> And put him on his guard.

FÉLIX: The precautions
> Are full of prudence. When I have found, my lord,
> What you require, I will return at once.

[Exit]

GOVERNOR: Ah! Honor! Honor! To what dreadful dangers
> You are exposed by women's frailty!

[Enter LISARDA and CELIA]

LISARDA: My lord?
GOVERNOR: Where are you going, my child?
LISARDA: I came to see you
    To know in what my love and my respect
    Have forfeited esteem that you should leave
    The house without a greeting. What is it, sir?
    You appear sad.
GOVERNOR: Don't be surprised, my dear,
    To see this sadness, however strange it is.
    I am a father, and I fear... Consider:
    The lonely traveler, lost at dead of night,
    Who meets a passenger despoiled by brigands,
    Should he not fear? Should not the seaman tremble
    Who sails across a bay where another ship
    Was broken on a treacherous rock? The hunter,
    Who finds upon his path at break of day
    A man all torn to pieces by the tooth
    Of some wild beast, may he not tremble too?
    Well, by this letter, I myself am now
    The traveler whose path is perilous,
    The seaman who perceives a dangerous shoal,
    The hunter who has seen a savage beast
    Waiting to leap upon me. Honor indeed
    To those who recognize the risk involved,
    Is even a hunt, a journey, and a ship,
    And one must watch out for the shoal, the danger,
    And death itself.
                              [Exit]

LISARDA: I'm ill at ease and tongue-tied,
    Celia, perhaps my father has been told
    Something about me; and, in speaking so,
    He wants to warn me he's not unaware
    Of threats to his honor.
CELIA: Señora, I do not know,
    But certainly he seems to have intended
    (Beneath his words) a sermon aimed at you.
    I do not doubt that he has some suspicion;
    And, to be frank, I do not think he's wrong
    To preach to you like this, since with some scorn
    For your renown, you are a heretic
    Who wish to start a novel sect of love.
    For if you loved as your ancestors did —
    You would not now experience those torments
    Which you have suffered since you chose to love
    In secret, in despite of honor, a man
    Who does not know your real identity.
LISARDA: You would be right to scold me for my love
    Had you not known it from the start; but since
    You blame me and feign ignorance, now listen.

The reputation that my father gained
Deserved the appointment by His Majesty
As Governor of this town. He settled here;
And naturally I came to live with him.
Soon I became the cynosure of all,
So much observed that I was vexed by it.
I was no longer, Celia, my own mistress:
Wherever I went, I heard to right and left
The whispered words "There is the Governor's daughter."
In church, there was a murmur when I entered;
And when I left I found myself surrounded
By people who knew me. I could not take a step
Without being spied upon or pointed at.
If I cried or laughed, they would debate the cause
Of smile or tears. How vexing it became!
At last fatigued by this officiousness
(For though at first one's vanity is flattered,
One becomes tired at last) wishing to flee
From this perpetual surveillance, and be
Myself incognito, I would go for walks,
Accompanied by my maidens to those gardens
Outside the town. Wrapped in my mantle there
I could converse with them and freely see
All that I wished. One day as I was walking
Beside the sea, I saw my father coming.
O heavens! there is no way to foresee Misfortune's
     stroke.
I fled from him, and in a country house
Took refuge. There I found a gentleman,
Who, seeing me afraid, and doubtless thinking
My plight was worse than in reality,
Offered me his protection, and prepared
Forthwith to defend me. Thanking him for his offer,
I reassured him on my danger, talked
Some minutes with him, and I found him witty
As well as brave, with an attractive mind.
(I do not speak of his nobility,
For when one says a man is brave and courteous,
That means that he is noble.) He demanded
To know my name; to which I answered him
That if he purposed to return some afternoon
To the same place, I would be there to meet him
On these conditions: — that he would not seek
To follow me, that he would not entreat
To see my face uncovered, and that, lastly,
He would not ask my name. To this he agreed,
Swearing a limitless discretion. Now
What more shall I confess? I went to see him
On several afternoons. He never seems

To leave the villa — whether he's a prisoner,
Or hiding there, I know not: all I know
Is that his name is Fabio. And now to end,
I sought an innocent pastime in these meetings,
But now I find at the bottom of my heart
A feeling for this gentleman, new and strange.
Dare I say love? Oh no, it is not love,
But whether it be love or not, I warn you,
Celia, that all the sermons of my father
Will not succeed in stopping me from going
To see this gentleman.   This folly bodes not well.

CELIA: This folly bodes not well.
Do you forget your marriage contract's drawn?
That even now your father expects your betrothed
To come at any time? And don't you know
That yesterday he ordered that a room
On the ground floor (the one that's next to yours)
Should be prepared?

LISARDA: Ah! Celia, that gives me
A greater reason to complain of fate!

[Enter NISE]

NISE: Señora, a fine lady, who appears
To be a stranger, asks permission now
To speak with you.

LISARDA: Did she not give her name?

NISE: No, señora. She asked me to inform you —
"A woman."

LISARDA: Well, let her come in.

                                        [Exit NISE]

Who can this be?

NISE: *[Within]*   You may come in.

[Enter FLÉRIDA, her face veiled]

FLÉRIDA: Your house,
Señora, will be a happy haven to my fortune,
If I am worthy on that snow-white hand
To plant a kiss.

    [Kneels and uncovers her face]

LISARDA: Rise, I beseech you.
It is not fitting that a heavenly star
Should thus prostrate herself.

    [Raises FLÉRIDA]

FLÉRIDA: Alas, señora,
Even if my feeble beauty did deserve
The name that you too kindly give to it,
I should yet bow before a greater star.
Kneeling before you, with your shining beauty,
I would be, pale with sorrow, like a moon

Dimmed by the presence of the radiant sun.
CELIA: *[Aside]* The lady's witty.[2]
LISARDA: I thank you for the well-turned compliment,
    Although I don't deserve such flattery.
    But to come down to facts, how do you wish
    That I should serve you?
FLÉRIDA: I desire, señora,
    That you would grant your generous protection
    To an unhappy woman.
LISARDA: If you wish
    To speak to me in secret, we will go
    Where we can talk alone.
FLÉRIDA: As for me, madam,
    If it suits you, it matters little to me
    If what I have to tell is known today,
    Which will be common knowledge before long.
LISARDA: Speak, then, since that is so.
FLÉRIDA: I will be brief.
    Most beauteous lady, whose beauty is enhanced
    By a noble mind, I am — but vain it is
    For me to vaunt my birth or noble line,
    My father's fame; for what's the use of boasting
    Of these advantages, when through my plight
    They have been called in question. Let me say
    Simply that I'm a woman most unlucky:
    That title will suffice me to procure
    The meed of pity that a heart like yours
    Never refused to the unfortunate.
    What though I have not brought a token with me
    To prove I speak the truth — these flowing tears
    Will validate my story. I was born
    Of noble parents, but for their dear sakes
    I will not breathe their names: it is enough
    That there my faults dishonored them, without
    Destroying their renown in this place too.
    I was young, courted by many. Among the rest
    A cavalier, who was by birth my equal,
    Equal in fortune, cast his eyes on me.
    Our stars would have it so. When we had met
    Two or three times, he began to haunt my street
    From dusk to dawn. As soon as Day arose
    And dressed her golden locks with flowers, until
    She sank to rest in her cold bed of waves,
    He turned the street into a myriad colors
    With his bright plumes. In daylight, like the sun-
        flower,
    He turned toward my window; and at night,
    When the bright sun was muffled up in darkness,
    He was an Argus watching o'er his treasure.

His assiduity was pleasing to me,
And, touched by his attentions, I gave up
My liberty to him. I do not doubt,
Since you're a woman, that you will excuse me:
You know how well our vanity is touched
By secret adoration. Before long,
Screened by the night, my suitor was allowed
Within our garden. It was there we passed
Some happy moments talking heart to heart
Among the jessamine and myrtles. Though
We met with difficulty, the danger lent
A charm for both of us, though beset by fears.
These soon proved justified, for while we sailed
Joyously on the ocean of our love,
Quite reassured by a deceiving calm,
The tempest was at hand. A valiant soldier
Against my wishes fell in love with me,
And stalked before my window. Finding in me
Only indifference and disdain, he saw
It was not wisdom kept me still aloof
But love for another man. Wounded and angry,
He wished to avenge himself. One night — a night
Of sadness, sadder than the others, since
The moon displayed her frowning face behind
Black clouds — he came into my street the first,
Knocked like his rival; I admitted him
Just as my lover came upon the scene.
He, seeing another man before him there,
Came at his heels, demanding what he sought.
He did not answer; but muffling up his face,
He drew his sword; and, as for me, I watched,
More dead than alive, and saw them cross their swords,
From which there came a rapid clash and sparks
Flashed as comets. God willed — my fate willed
Our foe should be struck first. "I'm dead," he cried;
Then stumbling fell among the wilting flowers,
Which had been born to deck a bridal bed,
And died to deck a funeral. Then my lover
Approaching me, said in a voice that shook
With anger: "Rejoice, ungrateful woman. This
Is your doing. Look upon this man
Who came to seek you at this guilty hour!
Bathed there in his own blood, he breathes no more.
But, dead though he is, my heart is not at peace;
One victim's not enough for jealousy!"
Stunned and confused, I answered as I could.
He would not deign to hear — for jealousy
Is like a sacred book which will admit
No contradiction — but he left the garden,

Mounted his horse which stood not far away,
And swift as a bird in flight was carried off.
                    I stayed in the same place
Half dead, till I was wakened from my trance
By noises coming nearer — first our neighbors
Collecting in the streets, and then our servants
Who poured out from the house in great alarm.
Then my unlucky father, informed of me,
Called out my name; but I had not the strength
Nor yet the courage to reply to him.
Then the thought came to me that my best plan
To avoid his anger was to flee. I left
The house, and full of terror and of anguish
I sought a refuge at the house of a friend.
I hid there for some days; and then I learned
My lover meant to journey into Spain.
Meaning to justify myself to him,
I went to seek him; but till now, alas,
I've found no trace of him; and realizing
That I was going alone and weak, among
All kinds of dangers, I wished to drown my hope,
The foolish hope of finding him. I've heard
Your reputation, madam; everyone
Has praised your generosity of heart,
And therefore I presumed to come to you.
You have numerous servants — let me serve you too.
    [Kneels]
You'll hardly notice that you have one more.
Protect my reputation; dissipate
My fears; señora, lend your kind assistance
To my distress. You are a woman. Take
Pity upon a woman. May you be spared
The assaults of love, but if you love at all,
May you be happy in it.

LISARDA: Pray, señora,
Dry your tears. It is not for you to weep.
It is the dawn's prerogative to shed
The dew, and she will be offended with you
If you usurp her office. I have no need
Of other witnesses besides your beauty
To be convinced of the sincerity
Of your discourse. Tell me: what is your name?

FLÉRIDA: "Laura."

LISARDA: Well, Laura, since you wish it,
From this time forth I'll keep you by my side:
Not to serve me (as you request) but rather
For me to serve you. Enter. It would not do
For you to be seen by my father, till I've obtained
Permission from him.

FLÉRIDA: May the heavens preserve you.
   [Aside] O Fate! if only you at last would cease
   To hound me!

                                                [Exit]

CELIA: I am very far from blaming
   Your pity; but yet, madam...
LISARDA: Yet what, Celia?
CELIA: I do not know if it is wise of you
   To take her in: there is in the world
   More than one woman who is maid and widow,
   A peasant and great lady all at once;
   And who beneath an innocent appearance
   Conceals a wide experience; who puts on
   The art of lying to strip her mistress bare.

                                        [Exeunt]

Scene 2: The Garden of a Country House near Gaeta

[Enter DON JUAN and DON CÉSAR, in traveling dress]

JUAN: It is a great happiness for me, Don César
   That I have come now to this country villa,
   Since you are here. I did not hope for it.
CÉSAR: It was my lucky star which brought you here.
   Let us embrace afresh.
JUAN: My arms will hold you
   So closely, that not even Death can part us.
   What are you doing here?
CÉSAR: Oh! it would be
   Too long a tale to tell you, and too sad.
   It's obvious you have just arrived from Flanders
   Since you are ignorant of what has happened.
JUAN: I have already heard that you have suffered
   Some great misfortune; so I was surprised
   To find you here so calm.
CÉSAR: I'm not so calm
   As you suppose me, Juan. I live in the midst
   Of ceaseless cares. Had I not recognized you,
   I would not have ventured out. I'm hidden here,
   Waiting the chance of setting out for Spain.
   The owner of this villa has placed it now
   At my disposal, and I look on it
   As an asylum. If anyone should chance
   To seek me out, I have a boat in readiness,
   Which I would leap into, and then by rowing
   I'd quickly reach the sea, where I'd be safe.
JUAN: I'm glad that I've arrived at the very moment
   When I can be of service. You know, my friend,

That I am not without some influence
In Gaeta. Lucky in love, I've come
To wed the famed Lisarda, young and rich,
Lovely and charming, it is said. What's more
She is the only daughter of Don Juan
Of Aragón. My future father-in-law
Is Governor of this country; and his power
Will surely let me, in one way or another,
Be useful to you.

CÉSAR: It will not be the first time
You've done me a service. I have not forgotten
All that I owe you. May this marriage prove
As happy as I wish; and may you find
When the first raptures of your passion fade
Long years of peace and love! But, cutting short
Wishes of which my heart is prodigal,
Tell me, my friend, what brings you to this place.

JUAN: I wished to pass the day here. I have come
To Gaeta, somewhat ill provided now
With jewels and dress, and too much like a soldier:
And though a soldier's uniform is prized,
One does not marry in it. That is why,
Till I am furnished with some finery,
Suitable for a call on my betrothed,
I'll stay for two days in retirement here.

CÉSAR: My luck is better than I had supposed,
Since I will have you here for two whole days
Hidden with me.

JUAN: I would have liked that well:
But in Gaeta I have a friend,
Commander of the Castle, whom I've warned
Of my arrival. I'm taking my ease now
In this pleasant garden while I await
His answer. For the same reason I must leave you,
For doubtless he will come to meet me soon,
And ought not to discover that you're here.

CÉSAR: That's a precaution worthy of a friend —
A friend like you.

JUAN: God be with you, César.
I'll come and see you secretly, and promise
To serve you all I can. Adieu!

CÉSAR: Juan, adieu!

                              [Exit DON JUAN]

[Enter CAMACHO]

CAMACHO: I wager, sir, that you were soliloquizing just now,
that you catechized your soul and your five senses, and
made your thought dog your memory and your intelligence
as persistently as the devil in the play. Which is the

woman, sir, if I may make so bold, who now reigns in
your heart? Is it the absent Flérida, or the mysterious veiled woman who wants to be another Phantom Lady?[3]

CÉSAR: Although I've never been very keen on your jests,
Camacho, I assure you that they've never been so unseasonable as they are now!

CAMACHO: Why are you so annoyed, sir?

CÉSAR: Because you asked me which woman now reigns in my
heart. Can it be concerned with anyone but the lovely
Flérida?

CAMACHO: If you're madly in love with her, how is it you are
now amusing yourself with another?

CÉSAR: Because, alas, I'm far away from her.

CAMACHO: So you'd fill the vacancy — everyone's liable to do
it.

CÉSAR: In a single night I've lost both my country and the
woman I love.

CAMACHO: And you've committed a fault for which everyone
will blame you.

CÉSAR: My fight, you mean?

CAMACHO: No, another.

CÉSAR: Which do you mean?

CAMACHO: That you should have left Flérida behind, without
thought of her safety.

CÉSAR: Very well; but if those who accuse me love too, tell
them to go to their mistress's house and find her with
another man — if they act as they should in such a cruel
situation, and restrain their grief or preserve their
presence of mind, then let them blame me.... If it were
to do again, I would doubtless behave differently, because one doesn't make the same mistake twice: but I
hadn't then had my dreadful experience. But what can
have become of Flérida?

CAMACHO: Didn't you hear from a traveler when you came here
that they think at Naples that she has retired to a convent? But after what we've said about the lady errant,
here she comes. This will be a case of the old proverb
about the wolf in the fable who....[4]

*[Enter LISARDA and CELIA, their faces hidden by their
mantles]*

CÉSAR: When I beheld the radiant sun appear
Above the horizon, I had a presentiment
That you would come here, madam; and here you are,
A sun disguised; may you come to bring delight
To the flowers of the field, who worship you indeed
As their divinity, though you hide your light,
Burst into blossom, and on every side
Whisper to you of love.

LISARDA: I'd like to think,
    Lord Fabio, for politeness, that the flowers
    Would tell me pretty things, if they should listen
    To you, my flatterer; for your gallantry
    Is so refined, that even the very flowers
    Would learn love's language from you.
CESAR: On the contrary
    Señora; that language I have learned from them,
    Since you came here. It would have been absurd
    To pretend that *I* taught *them*. There's not a flower,
    Which having been in love before I came here,
    Would not know how to speak; and since they have loved
    I have learned their flowers of speech.
LISARDA: O you are,
    A dreadful flatterer.
CESAR: Why do you say so?
LISARDA: Since
    You love me without seeing me.
CESAR: But is it not
    True love where one has not beheld one's love?
LISARDA: No.
CESAR: But I'll prove it to you.
LISARDA: In what manner?
CESAR: Thus: can a blind man love?
LISARDA: Yes.
CESAR: Very well.
    I love like one who's blind.
LISARDA: Impossible.
    The blind man loves by what is in his mind
    And as he does not hope to see the loved one,
    Neither does he desire it. If he could see
    He would not love a thing he could not see.
    And so, contrariwise, since you're not blind,
    You cannot love the thing you cannot see.
CESAR: Señora, you're deceived; this love you speak of
    In me, as in the blind man, is more lofty
    Than you allow.
LISARDA: Have you a way to prove it?
CESAR: Yes, señora — thus.
                          The chief object
    Of a rational soul is the light of understanding.
    That's what I love in you, with that I love you.
    If I beheld your beauty's rays, that instant
    My soul and eyes would have to share my love,
    Which therefore would be less, being so shared.
    I leave it you to judge if it would be
    Proper to rob the soul of half its love
    And give it to the eyes.
LISARDA: Even though the soul

    Should share with the eyes its love, which is its light,
    The soul would not love less, but there would be
    Merely more love.
CÉSAR: I don't quite understand.
LISARDA: If when there is a light, another spark
    Is brought against it, it communicates
    Its flame, but does not thereby cease to burn.
    Love is a fire which can inflame the soul,
    Unless communicated through the eyes,
    Yet does not cease to be as bright a fire
    When this occurs. The very eyes, which once
    Were sad and dull, shine with a sudden radiance!
    You see, the fire has entered in the eyes
    Without departing from the soul.
CAMACHO: *[To CELIA]*   And you,
    Adorable Abigail, are you adopting
    The fashion of your mistress. Tell me, now
    Will you not let me see your face?
CELIA: No.
CAMACHO: You're not going to see me either:
    I've also got a reputation to lose.
CELIA: How right you are!
CAMACHO: *[Covering his face with a handkerchief]* Zounds!
    It's now a double masquerade. And may the Devil carry
    you off if ever you show your face! And may he drag you
    by your cloak into some diabolic corner! May you always
    go around with a big cloak to hide this big figure of
    yours, so that you'll be wooed only by the giant Gara-
    mantle! And when you get to hell may your punishment be
    to be mantled eternally by the furious Radamantle.[5]
CÉSAR: Señora, I am convinced by what you've said:
    I was quite wrong, wrong a thousand times,
    To sustain against you such an argument:
    But since there's no true love unless one sees,
    It won't be impolite of me to raise
    Your mantle just a little.
       [He tries to lift her veil]
LISARDA: Think what you're doing.
CÉSAR: You will forgive me: I must see your face.
LISARDA: You have the power: but if you do it, you risk
    Never to see me after.
CÉSAR: Truly it is
    The tale of Cupid and Psyche in reverse:
    For Cupid went to Psyche in disguise:
    Now Psyche is disguised, and it's my love
    That is revealed. I beg of you, madam,
    Remove that dark veil and dispel the cloud
    That covers you. If beauty is heaven itself,
    Then let that heaven, your face, reveal its glory.

      If while on earth I saw your beauty veiled,
      Now I'm in heaven I desire to enjoy
      Your beauty to the full, for otherwise
      This heaven will be a kind of hell to me.
LISARDA: Since you employ
      Such wit to persuade me, and since you compare me
      To goddesses, I must remind you, sir,
      That on occasion they surround themselves
      With filmy clouds; and if you were to press me,
      I'd prove to you I know a goddess's duties,
      For I would disappear into my cloud
      And nevermore return.
CÉSAR: Whether you do
      Or not, I still must see you.
LISARDA: *[Uncovering]*   Well, do you see me?
CÉSAR: Yes, and I'm dazzled by your beauty's brightness;
      Why did you keep it from me? *[Noise off]* What is that
          noise?
LISARDA: I hear a sound of voices.

      [Enter FABIO]

CÉSAR: What is it, Fabio?
FABIO: Fly, fly at once, my lord, toward the sea.
      The Governor comes to seek you.
CÉSAR: He has been warned
      That I was here.
LISARDA: *[Aside]*   My father! Heaven protect me!
      For when he spoke this morning about honor,
      It was a warning.
CÉSAR: What is to be done?
CAMACHO: Fly to the sea, and plow the glassy waves.
CÉSAR: Farewell, señora, I dare not stay here longer.
      I must fly disaster.
LISARDA: If you go, my lord,
      My own will be upon me.
CÉSAR: What do you ask?
LISARDA: If you're a gentleman, as your behavior
      And speech proclaim, do not in such a way
      Abandon one who risks her life and honor
      In coming thus to see you. My rank is higher
      Than you imagine. If you leave me here
      Without assistance, I will give the world
      A notable lesson by my death. It's I,
      Not you, they seek. I am the daughter of...
      I cannot finish... The door is broken open...
      Alas! Alas!
CÉSAR: *[Aside]*   I go *from bad to worse,*
      And I thought it could not be. I have no choice.
      The same fault should not be committed twice.

They must not say that always I desert
Ladies in danger. *[Aloud]* I give you my word,
That they shall rather kill me ere your life
And honor should be compromised. Go in and hide.
Go quickly, while I stay to guard the door.
You've naught to fear, señora. When they find me,
They will not search for you. It's me they seek.
LISARDA: *[Fleeing]* Come, Celia, follow me.
                                                          [Exit]
CELIA: *[Losing her chopines]*   O heavens! My shoes!
                                                          [Exit]
CÉSAR: Pick up those shoes.
CAMACHO: Here's a fine mess we're in!
                                                [Exit with shoes]

    [Enter the GOVERNOR, accompanied by GUARDS and SERVANTS]

GOVERNOR: Are you not Don César Ursino?
CÉSAR: A gentleman never denies his name.
GOVERNOR: Surrender yourself to go to prison.
CÉSAR: I obey
    I only beg you to remember that I am
    Of noble birth.
GOVERNOR: I know well who you are.
    There is no need for you to resign your sword.
    Keep it, although you are a prisoner.
    There should be a lady with you. Kindly see
    That she presents herself without delay
    She will be treated with respect — but yet
    She too must be arrested.
CÉSAR: A lady, you say?
GOVERNOR: Yes, a lady.
CÉSAR: A lady here?
GOVERNOR: It's useless
    For you to deny it, for I'm well informed.
    I know that she is here — and here with you.
    Search the house.
                                        [Exeunt GUARDS]
CÉSAR: O heavens! Who can be
    This woman who's landed me in such a fix?

    [A GUARD enters, bringing CAMACHO]

GUARD: This man was hidden there, my lord.
GOVERNOR: Who are you?
CAMACHO: I am the footman of this errant knight.
GOVERNOR: Why are you hiding?
CAMACHO: It's a weakness of mine.
    My lord; I do it without ill intent.
GOVERNOR: What are you holding?
CAMACHO: Shoes, my lord.

GOVERNOR: I see
    Clear indications of the one I seek.
    Where is the person to whom these belong?
CAMACHO: Before you. It is me.
GOVERNOR: You don't wear those?
CAMACHO: I do, my lord; although cork shields are prohibited
    by the just laws of the kingdom, it's not the same with
    cork-heeled slippers. On the contrary. There's a very
    fine proverb which says: "Where would a sick man be
    without the comfort of a dainty pair of legs" — I mean
    "slippers" — "about the place." Well, my master being
    indisposed, I am wearing a dainty pair of slippers to
    comfort him in his misfortune.[6]

*[Two GUARDS bring in LISARDA: her face is covered by her
cloak]*

GUARD: We have found this lady in the inner room.
    Uncover, madam.
GOVERNOR: Let her alone. Señora,
    You need not show your face. I know that I
    Should show this courtesy; pardon me, then,
    That I have come to take you.
CÉSAR: Pardon me, rather:
    That she does not go with you. I'm resolved
    To perish rather than permit such outrage.
GOVERNOR: Don César Ursino, do not speak
    So arrogantly; for, despite your courage,
    It will not be so easy for you to free her
    As to declare it. But I pardon you
    This interference because of the respect
    I entertain for her. I know who she is,
    And I presume as much as you to bring
    Her reputation back to high esteem.
    Her father is so much my friend that I regard him
    As another self. I keenly feel his grief,
    And it's for his sake that I overlook
    Your words, for though I do not know you, sir,
    I am obliged for his sake to protect
    Your honor as best I may.
LISARDA: *[Aside]*   He has no need
    To express himself more clearly. My misfortune
    Is but too plain.
CÉSAR: If I had said, my lord,
    That I would save this lady, in spite of you
    And all your soldiers, you would have the right
    To think me arrogant; but I did not say so.
    I do not think to free her. As for me
    I only wish to die; and it is easy
    For a cavalier to die!

GOVERNOR: It would be better
   For us to settle matters amicably;
   With prudence and with wisdom, we shall do it.
   But rest assured that rather than as judge,
   You have in me a mediator, who'll
   Resolve your difficulties. I've received
   All necessary information.
CÉSAR: But if, my lord
   I am the guilty one and go to prison,
   What fault has she committed?
GOVERNOR: You underrate
   My wisdom. I know who she is, I tell you.
   Don César Ursino, follow me
   To the fortress. As for this lady, I promise her
   That she'll be entertained in my own house,
   As though she were my daughter.
LISARDA: *[Aside]*   There's now no doubt:
   He must have recognized me. The safest thing
   Is to invoke his pity. *[To CÉSAR]* I submit.
CÉSAR: *[To LISARDA]* Then since you are content, señora,
   I have no more to say. *[Aloud]* I accept, my lord,
   The plan which you propose. The lady will stay
   In your house.
GOVERNOR: That is understood. Hola!
GUARD: My lord?
GOVERNOR: Conduct this lady to my carriage
   And take her to the palace. Tell my daughter
   To bear her company till I return.
   [To CÉSAR] And now I'm going to take you to the Tower.
CÉSAR: I'll go with you, both honored and contented.
                [Exeunt all except CAMACHO]

   [Enter CELIA]

CELIA: They've gone?
CAMACHO: Yes.
CELIA: By running to the house,
   I'll get there first.
CAMACHO: By heavens, I'd love to know
   Who your mistress is!
                      [Exeunt]

ꙖꙖꙖꙖꙖꙖꙖꙖꙖꙖꙖꙖꙖꙖꙖꙖꙖꙖꙖꙖꙖꙖꙖꙖꙖꙖꙖꙖꙖꙖꙖꙖꙖꙖꙖꙖꙖꙖꙖ

ACT TWO

Scene 1: In the Governor's House

[Enter CELIA and NISE]

NISE: Celia, why have you returned alone?
    Where is our mistress? You do not reply.
    What is the matter?
CELIA: Ah! Nise, I'm half dead.
NISE: What has happened?
CELIA: You know we went together...
    There are people coming: I will tell you later.

[Enter two GUARDS and SERVANTS with LISARDA]

GUARD: Kindly inform Lisarda...
NISE: Heaven protect us!
    Is it not she?
GUARD: ...my mistress that we have
    A message from the Governor, and we crave
    Permission to speak with her.
CELIA: *[Aside]*   We must dissemble.
    [Aloud] My mistress is unwell. It is impossible
    For you to speak with her. I'll take a message.
GUARD: My lord, the Governor,
    Begs her to give a welcome to this lady,
    To entertain her well, and to be pleased
    At having found so good a friend.
CELIA: Be sure
    I'll tell her so in the same terms.
GUARD: A word
    In private. This lady is a prisoner here.
    Keep watch on her.
                        [Exeunt GUARDS and SERVANTS]
LISARDA: Are they gone?
CELIA: Yes, señora:
    They are outside.
LISARDA: Take off this mantle, Celia.
    Nise, fetch me some other clothes.
NISE: Señora,
    What is the meaning of such goings on?
    You a prisoner in your home? Appointed
    The jailer of yourself. Relate to me,
    I pray you, this adventure. I am dying
    To hear of it.
LISARDA: I am unfortunate.
    It is enough for me to tell you now
    That Love and Fortune have conspired against me.
    My father but this morning hinted to me
    With an afflicted air that he had stumbled

Upon the secret of my foolish love.
I did not wish to believe. In the evening,
When I went out, he followed me and found...
CELIA: A moment, señora. How can you imagine
Your father, who could make you stay at home
On some pretext or other, can have preferred
To have a troop of guards to search for you,
Catch you, red-handed, before everyone,
And make his injury public. No, señora,
It is not possible. My only fear
Had been that one would recognize you there
Before you reached the house. Now all is well.
But now I am afraid that he'll demand
The prisoner he has taken; for I'm sure
When he arrested you he must have thought
That you were someone else.
LISARDA: You are a fool.
You don't consider what he said to me:
"I hold her reputation and her honor
As if I were her father. It's for her sake
I treat her as I do." He recognized me;
He surely did not choose those words at random.
You say he would not wish me to be seen;
True, but he ordered me not to unveil.
Don't contradict me: I am sure he knew me.
CELIA: What are you going to do?
LISARDA: I'll throw myself
At his feet when he arrives, and confess to him...
To tell him I was sad, and therefore went
To walk in those pleasure-gardens. After all
A father does not kill one.

   [Enter FLÉRIDA]

FLÉRIDA: Welcome, madam.
LISARDA: *[Aside]*   Be careful now.
We're not yet sure if she's discreet or tactful.
   [To FLÉRIDA] I've been to visit one of my friends to-
      day.

   [Enter the GOVERNOR and FÉLIX in the other room]

GOVERNOR: You are to go to Naples, Félix, as speedily as you
   can, and tell Don Alonso that I have his daughter in my
   house and Don César in the Tower.
FÉLIX: Yes, my lord, I will go at once; but first let me
   confess a doubt. I didn't enter the villa with you, so
   that Don César and my young mistress should not suspect
   that I had informed you of them. While I was waiting
   outside, a woman came out. But it's possible that this
   woman was not my mistress; for it's easy to make a mis-

take about a woman when her face is covered with a cloak
and she does not speak. I saw her, but I'm not certain
she was my mistress; and to travel to Naples to tell her
father without being certain would be to run the risk of
committing an unforgivable fault.
GOVERNOR: I approve your prudence. Wait a moment. I'm going to call her, and you will assure yourself that it is
   she.
FÉLIX: I would be glad to do so, my lord, but I fear that if
   my mistress were to see me, she would guess that I've
   been tracking her down; she would complain of my fidelity and detest me; and I don't want to be detested by
   the person I have to serve. If there were a way, my
   lord, by which I could see her without being seen, my
   doubts would be dispersed without danger to myself.
GOVERNOR: So be it. Come with me. *[Goes to connecting*
   door] Look! my daughter is there; your mistress should
   be with her.
FÉLIX: Yes, my lord, that is my mistress, that's her...
   Flérida is on the left of your daughter.
GOVERNOR: Yes, she is the only one I do not know.
   The others are my daughter and two of her maids.
FÉLIX: I am satisfied. I leave for Naples at once.

                                                  [Exit]

[The GOVERNOR enters from the other room]

CELIA: *[Announcing]* My lord!
FLÉRIDA: If you speak to him, speak in
   my favor.
   Ask him to let you shelter me.
LISARDA: Yes, madam.
FLÉRIDA: Importune him.
LISARDA: Retire a little then.
                        [FLÉRIDA retires]
CELIA: *[Aside]* Now is the ticklish moment!
GOVERNOR: Well, Lisarda,
   You do not thank me for the friend I've sent you.
   Why are you silent?
LISARDA: *[Aside]*   I'm in a deadly fright.
   [Aloud] If you have any pity on your daughter...
GOVERNOR: I understand. You're fond of her already,
   And, full of compassion for her, you request
   That I should pardon her.
LISARDA: So slight a fault,
   My lord, deserves your pardon.
GOVERNOR: Not so slight.
FLÉRIDA: *[Aside]* He looks this way. She doubtless pleads
   for me.
LISARDA: Is it so bad to go into a garden

So long as one's face is hidden by a cloak?
GOVERNOR: Lisarda, you should know this lady had a father
    Who deserved more respect.
LISARDA: *[Aside]*   He speaks to me
    With so much wisdom and so much discretion,
    He stabs me to the soul. *[Aloud]* Don't shame me, sir,
    Don't shame me; I implore you on my knees
    For your indulgence.
       [Kneels]
GOVERNOR: I would not shame you, child,
    But yet I can't consent to what you ask.
LISARDA: I will not rise from off my knees until
    I have obtained your pardon.
FLÉRIDA: How much I owe her!
    She kneels to plead my cause.
GOVERNOR: Stand up, my child.
    [Raising her] But do not ask my pardon for this lady —
    That would be labor lost: she will not leave
    This house, except as wife.
LISARDA: Yes, it shall be so,
    My lord, and furthermore, if you so wish,
    She promises that she will not appear
    Upon the balcony, or at the window.
    All that I ask is the recovery
    Of your favor toward her.
GOVERNOR: I do not refuse her
    My favor: on the contrary, she has it
    Without reserve. To prove it, see, Lisarda,
    The way I treat her.
    [He goes toward FLÉRIDA]
    You're most welcome to this house: it will be yours
    As much as mine, señora. I'm not surprised
    At your ill luck in love. There are many tales
    Of similar occurrences, — as sad,
    And even sadder than yours; and I am lucky
    That after your shipwreck this my house can be
    A haven of refuge. Use it at your pleasure;
    And be assured that you will only leave
    Honest and satisfied. All will be settled
    Before long, as I hope, to the satisfaction
    Of all concerned. Meanwhile you shall dwell here.
    My life, if need be, is at your disposal.
    Even if I did not do this for your sake,
    Lisarda has so warmly pleaded for you
    That I would do it for hers.
LISARDA: *[Aside]*   Heaven help me!
    What do I hear?
CELIA: *[Aside]*   Madam, you see how wrong
    You were to believe your father recognized you:

    He thinks she was the captive.

LISARDA: *[Aside]*   You're right.
    But since so rarely evil turns to good
    I couldn't credit it. May the error last!

FLÉRIDA: *[Aside]* How good she is to tell him of my griefs
    To spare my shame in telling him myself!
    Sir...

CELIA: *[Aside]*   Let's hope she doesn't ruin everything.
    She had best be silent.

FLÉRIDA: One of your birth and merit
    Could hardly fail to have a generous heart.
    My lord, a most unfortunate woman comes
    To throw herself at your feet, and since, it seems,
    You know my name and story; be merciful
    To my honor; deign to lend your aid to one
    Who travels far from home in a foreign land.

LISARDA: Nise, Celia, see: evil converts to good,
    And it is hard for me to recognize it!

FLÉRIDA: *[Approaching her]* O beautiful Lisarda! Let me em-
    brace you.
    What gratitude I owe you! You have added
    To your first kindness that of asking now
    Your father to protect me.

LISARDA: *[Aside]*   Preoccupied
    With her own troubles, she helps to cover mine.
    Let's strengthen this deception. *[Aloud]* Do not thank
      me.
    I will do all that's in my power to enforce
    My father to serve you.

GOVERNOR: Do not slight my love
    And tenderness for you; for, as you'll see,
    I will do everything that's in my power
    To serve this lady.

LISARDA: Sir, inform me now
    What I can do for her. Who is this lady?

GOVERNOR: She is a noble lady whom a man
    Has stolen from her home. By her example,
    Lisarda, learn what peril a girl courts
    When she forgets her honor.

LISARDA: *[Aside]*   Another warning!

    [Enter a SERVANT]

SERVANT: A traveler has just arrived, my lord;
    He asks an audience.

GOVERNOR: It is Don Juan
    No doubt. Let him come in!

LISARDA: *[Aside]*   Another blow!

                          [Exit FLÉRIDA.
    Enter DON JUAN in traveling dress, with boots and spurs]

JUAN: I am delighted,
　　My lord, after so many trials, that heaven
　　At last permits me now to kiss your feet.
　　From this time forth, I pardon fickle Fortune
　　The subjects of complaint which she has given me
　　Throughout my life. This single mark of grace
　　Makes me her debtor.
GOVERNOR: Welcome, Don Juan. Already
　　You have been long awaited. You have caused us
　　Considerable anxiety.
JUAN: Since I am still
　　A welcome guest, I count my tardiness
　　A blessing in disguise.
GOVERNOR: Your uniform
　　Becomes you well: your plumes and finery
　　Make a brave show! But have you not a word
　　For your betrothed?
JUAN: I approach her now
　　In trepidation, and seeing her I'm blind
　　With love of her, and dazzled by the rays
　　Of her transcendent beauty. If he who dares
　　To climb so high, deserves so great a favor,
　　Then let me touch your white and lovely hand,
　　Love's veritable quiver, where he keeps
　　His store of arrows: since, being miraculous,
　　A heavenly prodigy of fire and snow,
　　You are their center, where Love burns with ice,
　　Freezes with fire. I had often heard
　　That you possessed a beauty without peer,
　　But this time Fame has not been generous
　　And you might properly complain of her.
　　But, no, señora, it's not the fault of Fame,
　　But yours. Now she acclaims you as unique;
　　She has been overcome by your perfections,
　　Because Reality surpasses far
　　Imagination.[7]
LISARDA: I have often heard
　　That blindfold Love was Mars and Venus's son;
　　I can well believe it now when such a soldier
　　Brings from the war such gracious flatteries.
　　Others say Adonis was his father;
　　And, seeing you, I can believe both true,
　　For now combined in you one may perceive
　　A brave Adonis and a dashing Mars.
GOVERNOR: I must stop there this war of compliments.
　　I want the victory hers.
JUAN: My lord,
　　I want that too: for no one would be so unfair
　　To dispute it with her. How beautiful she is,

       How amiable and charming!
GOVERNOR: You should rest.
    You must be very tired after your journey.
    I offer you a simple hospitality.
    You will be lodged here like a soldier.
    You'll pardon me.
JUAN: But how could it be that,
    Since it's the sphere divine of this bright sun?
                    [Exeunt the GOVERNOR, DON JUAN and NISE]
LISARDA: Celia, now we're alone, what do you say
    Of my adventure?
CELIA: It's a happy end
    To your predicament. To think my lord imagined
    That it was she he had made prisoner.
LISARDA: That is because he found her in the house
    Before I told him that I had received her.
CELIA: I told you, you were foolish to believe
    He recognized you.
LISARDA: It was more surprising
    And more agreeable to see the way,
    Without a prompter she made the right replies.
CELIA: In such matters a woman can rely
    Upon her instinct: for where love's the subject,
    Whatever's said, even if it's said by chance,
    Will suit the case.
LISARDA: I tell you, now
    New problems have arisen.
CELIA: Do not the dangers
    That you have run today, señora, and the arrival
    Of your future husband banish from your thoughts
    This mad caprice?
LISARDA: How little you know, Celia,
    Of love and its peculiarities!
    Cite me a single case where love has been
    Deterred by obstacles, and I will cite
    A thousand in which love has grown and strengthened
    Because of hindrances.
CELIA: What a point of view!
LISARDA: On the one hand, I should not leave in prison
    A man who's sacrificed for me his freedom
    And was prepared to sacrifice his life.
    On the other hand, if this same man's the one
    This lady seeks, I ought not to presume
    To be her rival. I must get away
    From this uncertainty; and therefore, Celia,
    You'll bear a letter to him, in which I'll say
    That if he can leave the castle on parole
    He must come here — since I'll keep up the pretense
    That I'm a prisoner myself.

CELIA: What, madam?
LISARDA: Yes, Celia.
CELIA: But consider...
LISARDA: No.
CELIA: Reflect.
LISARDA: It's not the time.
CELIA: Are you going to let yourself
    Be carried away?
LISARDA: Do you want to have me die?
CELIA: But think, madam...
LISARDA: Stop torturing me.
CELIA: What dangers...
LISARDA: I see them well.
CELIA: And your life?
LISARDA: I do not care.
CELIA: And your honor?
LISARDA: What honor? You're a fool.
CELIA: I seek...
LISARDA: What more?
CELIA: Your happiness; and fear...
LISARDA: What?
CELIA: Your ruin.
LISARDA: Well now, Celia, do you want to be
    The only pilgrim in Jerusalem?
CELIA: Why so,
    Madam?
LISARDA: Because you are the first maid in the world
    Who grieved to see her mistress fall in love.

                                         [Exeunt]

          Scene 2: A Room in the Castle

    [Enter DON CÉSAR and CAMACHO]

CAMACHO: Now we're in a mess, sir.
CÉSAR: I regret nothing
    Since I have seen her face.
CAMACHO: Plague take her face!
    I'd rather she had been a freak — twofaced,
    One of them bearded — even if I'd had
    To look at it, and that you weren't a prisoner,
    Than that you should have seen that spiteful angel,
    However lovely, who's delivered us
    Into the hands of justice.[8]
CÉSAR: Do you think that?
CAMACHO: And why not? There's so much perfidy and treason
    In the world today. Also I'm sure that when she came to
        seek you

The first time, it was simply to spy on you.
For her it was a storybook adventure.
They entered terrified, as if they fled
Some highway robber; and your lady asked you
For aid and succor as from a noble knight,
In telling you I know not what. Stop, sir,
Deceive yourself no more; it is a pity
To tell this tale of an enchanted forest
Where the modest princess spoke so circumspectly
With Esplandián, Belianís, and Beltenebros.[9]

CÉSAR: If it was as you say, why should the Governor
Have her arrested?

CAMACHO: Simply to deceive you.

CÉSAR: No, Camacho; I suspect something else —
That this lady is a woman of high rank,
Whom some mischance obliges to keep hidden,
For Fate has often persecuted Beauty.
And what confirms me in this view, is that
She would not show her face; and since the Governor
Arrested me at the same time, he must have had
Two warnings in a day. Did you not see,
When she was going to tell us who she was,
Her manifest anxiety, and the shame
Which sealed her lips when she prepared to tell us
Of her misfortunes.

CAMACHO: Perhaps you're right, after all.
And so you have forgotten your great love
For Flérida.

CÉSAR: I hope not a first love
Could be effaced so from a heart of man.
Philosophy shows us that it's hard to impress
One form upon another. When a painter
Sketches a form, he traces it with ease
So long as his canvas is still fresh and clean,
But if there's another painting on the canvas,
He must efface it, lest the second's lines
Should be confused with the other's. My heart was once
An empty canvas ready for first love;
But should I wish to introduce another
I must await the erasure of that image,
Celestial and divine, imprinted there.
Although my heart, burning with anger now
Against my first love, seems to be receiving
Upon the canvas a new image, yet
I'm still engaged in trying to efface
The image of the first.[10]

CAMACHO: Efface it? Good. But yet I could reply:
If a cloaked lady had not come to see you.

But it appears that we have not yet finished
With black intrigues and dangerous disguises.

   [Enter CELIA]

CELIA: Hist! Lord Fabio.
CÉSAR: You are welcome, since
   You give back life to one who was half dead.
CELIA: Here is a letter for you from the prisoner
   Who is weighted down with grief.
CÉSAR: For recompense,
   Here is a diamond for you. It flames so brightly
   That one would take it for a star.
         [He reads the letter]
CAMACHO: Let's see it.
   It seems a trifle duller now.
CELIA: Not at all
   It's crystal clear.
         [She motions him away from her]
CAMACHO: Well, I will give you now
   Another diamond, quite as good as that,
   If you will let me see your face.
CELIA: I won't.
CAMACHO: I know the reason why.
CELIA: Because I'm plain?
CAMACHO: Exactly.
CELIA: On the contrary, I'm pretty.
CAMACHO: If that were so, you would not hide your face
   Like a soul in torment.
CELIA: Well, behold and see
   Whether I'm plain or pretty.
CAMACHO: I do not wish
   To see you now.
CELIA: Come. Don't be foolish. Look!
CAMACHO: Now you desire it, I do not.
CELIA: Here, I will give you
   This diamond, if you'll consent to look.
CAMACHO: No, thank you.
CÉSAR: I have read the letter.
   Inform my beauteous captive I'll obey:
   I'll come and see her tonight.
CELIA: Very well, sir.
   May heaven protect you.
                                             [Exit]

CAMACHO: Farewell, damsel. Tell
   Your mistress that she should not be too proud!
   An earlier impression first must be effaced.
   What does the letter say? Another trick?
CÉSAR: That I should go to speak with her tonight

In Lisarda's room, she having bribed her maids.
She adds a thousand and one absurd commands —
As that I should bring no one with me, nor
Confide in anyone.
CAMACHO: And you reply
Coolly that you will go, as if you had
The keys of the castle in your desk?
CÉSAR: Well, then!
Who will prevent me?
CAMACHO: The guards.
CÉSAR: The sound of gold
Is a sweet music which can send to sleep
Even the vigilant...

[Enter DON JUAN]

JUAN: I come to bring you my condolences
And to receive congratulations from you,
One tempered by the other. It is said
That there are certain plants, which part by part
Are deadly poison; taken all together
A nourishing food — so naturalists report.
Thus your misfortunes and my happiness
Are separate poisons which would kill us both,
You by your grief and me by my delight,
So let us mix our qualities and temper
My happiness with your mischance.
CÉSAR: You seem
Extremely happy.
JUAN: Why should I not be
In seeing a happiness within my grasp
Greater than I could dream of? I have been here
In hiding for a day or two: the Lieutenant
Is a close friend of mine; and I have bought
Jewels and trinkets, and been fitted out
With four new suits of clothes — necessities
Before I could properly present myself
To my betrothed. When I was thus accoutred,
I rode up to the palace of the Governor
As if I had just arrived. I say "the palace."
I should have rather said "the enchanted palace,"
For I have seen there as in miniature
All Nature's marvels. For the sky was there
Reduced to a microcosm; Spring to a flower;
The breeze to a faint sigh; dawn to a pearl;
And the Sun into one ray — because Lisarda
Is a light breeze, a microcosm, a flower,
A beauteous pearl, a sunbeam! How happy I am,
My friend, for whom a well-contracted love
Prepares such glory.

CÉSAR: And I, unfortunate
   A thousand times, to whom a baffling love
   Brings but misfortunes! Since my pain must be
   The antidote of your delight, hear me.
   We will not change the subject of our talk:
   I, too, will speak of love. I saw a sun
   Vestured in snow, a pinnacle of flames!
   In a garden
   A statue of jasmine crowned with sweet carnations,
   That gracious May, the King of months, had made
   The Queen of flowers — who had been recognized
   As such by lords and commons of the flowers
   Who had acclaimed her in the midst of bird song
   And fountains' murmuring. Do not ask me
   Her name, for though I wished to tell it you,
   It would be impossible. It is a tale
   Without a parallel. But I can tell you
   That by this letter she engages me
   — If I am able to escape from prison —
   To go this night to see her. I've replied
   That I will go, as though I knew for certain
   That the Lieutenant would permit it.
JUAN: Be sure,
   Since I have come, there'll be no obstacle.
   Camacho.
CAMACHO: Sir?
JUAN: Tell the Lieutenant from me,
   I ask him to come here to speak with me.

                       [Exit CAMACHO]

JUAN: He's the firmest of my friends
   And will agree that you should leave the prison
   So long as I escort you.
CÉSAR: The sun is dying in the western fields,
   And night begins to spread her dusky wings.
   Ask him to let us go at once.
JUAN: I'll do
   As you desire.

   [Enter LIEUTENANT with CAMACHO]

LIEUTENANT: What do you wish, Don Juan?
JUAN: To tell you that I have not left the fortress,
   That I am still your guest, for I have seen
   That Don César is living here.
LIEUTENANT: It is not right
   To insist on obligations, when already
   I've vowed myself your humble servant.
JUAN: He'll come with me tonight, if you believe
   My friendship is deserving such a favor.
LIEUTENANT: I have had strict instructions of all kinds

That he should not leave here: but no command
Can stand against your wish if you promise me
To bring him back again before the dawn.
JUAN: On that you have my solemn word of honor;
    And if some accident should happen, I
    Accept responsibility.
CÉSAR: Before the dawn
    You'll see me back in prison, your slave twice over.
LIEUTENANT: On that condition the gates are open to you.
    May God protect you!

                                                [Exit]

JUAN: Come, César, since you're free,
    Lead me to where your lady waits for you.
    I will keep watch outside.
CÉSAR: It is not fair
    That for my sake you should delay returning
    To your host's house where your betrothed awaits you.
    I won't consent to it. Let us each go
    To see our mistresses.
JUAN: No, if you please.
    It is not right that I should take you out,
    Exposing you to danger, and then leave you.
CÉSAR: But that is what I wish...
JUAN: You can't prevent it;
    I will accompany you.
CÉSAR: *[Aside]*   Cruel dilemma!
    Will it not be a wrongful course to let him
    Keep watch for me and that he should betray,
    Although unknowingly, a host to whom
    He owes so much?
JUAN: What are you thinking of?
CÉSAR: You will believe, perhaps, that I'm ungrateful
    To hide my loves from you. O heavens, Juan!
    Pylades loved not Orestes more
    Nor Euryalus loved Nisus than I you.
    After this firm assurance, let me keep
    The secret of my lady — I can't do otherwise
    And let me visit her alone.
JUAN: So be it.
    Your insistence means I may not press you more.
    [Aside] Foolish distrust! Ridiculous discretion!
    [Aloud] Adieu, César.

                                            [Exit JUAN]

CÉSAR: Camacho!
CAMACHO: Sir?
CÉSAR: Prepare a pistol for me.
CAMACHO: Here's one that I got ready while you chatted.
    But see that it's all right.
CÉSAR: Good. Flint...

Priming... nothing's missing.
CAMACHO: Do I stay here?
CÉSAR: Yes, Camacho.
CAMACHO: *[To the audience]* Let your lordships witness
There was one lackey who did not follow his master.[11]

[Exeunt by different doors]

Scene 3: The Governor's House

[Enter LISARDA and NISE, with a candle]

LISARDA: Nise!
NISE: Madam?
LISARDA: Has my father gone to bed?
NISE: Yes, madam.
LISARDA: And Don Juan?
NISE: Yes.
LISARDA: Our prisoner?
NISE: She, without doubt, is weeping in her bed,
    As is her usual custom.
LISARDA: It is these tears
    Which are increasing my uneasiness.
    And what of Celia?
NISE: She's at the door,
    Awaiting the arrival of this gallant.
LISARDA: When he comes in, remember you're to treat me
    Quite without ceremony. In seeing me here,
    He must be led to think that I'm the woman
    Who was sent to prison; that the Governor
    Arrested me because of him.
NISE: I hear
    A stealthy step in the corridor outside.
LISARDA: It will be he, no doubt.

[Enter CELIA, and behind her, DON CÉSAR]

CÉSAR: *[Aside]* Silence and shades of night, befriend me
       now!
CELIA: Hush! My mistress, Lisarda, is not yet in bed
    And the Governor sleeps in a neighboring room.
CÉSAR: *[Aside]*   May love
    Lend me his wings.
LISARDA: You are welcome, sir.
CÉSAR: May your eyes be a light unto my path.
LISARDA: Dear Celia, will you kindly go and stand
    At that door there which leads to your master's room.
    And please be vigilant.
CELIA: Have no fear.
       [She goes to the door]

LISARDA: [*To NISE*] And you, my friend, go to your mis-
    tress's chamber,
  And wait outside the door.
NISE: I am afraid.
LISARDA: What of?
NISE: To think Lisarda is within
  Makes my heart tremble.
LISARDA: You have naught to fear
  In guarding the door.
NISE: Oh yes I have.
  My mistress is a demon. She would rage
  If ever she found out what's going on.
    [*She goes to the door*]
CÉSAR: Oh señora! How my soul has longed
  To speak with you. I'm in a labyrinth
  In which my mind has wandered endlessly.
  Although I've pondered, I have sought in vain
  Why you were sent to prison.
LISARDA: But you should realize
  They'd seek the woman you had borne away,
  And apprehended me in place of her.
CÉSAR: A woman, you say?
LISARDA: Yes.
CÉSAR: However witty
  You are, señora, this you have invented
  To dissipate my doubts is quite absurd.
  What! would I be a man so vile, unworthy
  Of love, that I should not inspire some jealousy?
  And if I'd a lady with me, as you suggest,
  Would she, without complaint, have allowed me
  To speak with you in private. But you, señora,
  Have you not given me to understand
  That it was desperately important to you
  That you should not be recognized. Your terror
  Must have had some reason.
  There was some reason, then, for your arrest;
  Therefore you were not taken for another;
  Therefore if you are still held prisoner now
  When you could undeceive them, I suppose
  That it is probably some jealous lover
  Who's taking his revenge.
LISARDA: Shall I retort —
  Would I have had a lover so despicable
  That he could revenge an injury so basely?
  Yet I'm not one so little worthy of love
  That I should be unable to inspire
  A lover's jealousy. Believe me, sir,
  That I'm a lady of distinguished rank
  And that has been a cause of the misfortune

Of which you have been witness.
CESAR: I believe you,
   Madam; but would like to know who you are.
LISARDA: Sit there then.
     [As DON CÉSAR goes to sit down, the pistol at his
     belt goes off]
CESAR: Heaven preserve me!
LISARDA: Woe is me!
NISE: I'm dying.
CELIA: I'm ruined.
CESAR: Cursed be the pistol
   Which goes off on its own.
LISARDA: Alas!
CELIA: Ah! Señora!
NISE: Señora!
GOVERNOR: *[Within]* What is that? Who's there?
LISARDA: Make some
     answer.
   I'm too frightened.
NISE: So am I.
CELIA: And I.
CESAR: Who can resist calamity that comes
   By accident.
CELIA: By the feeble light in the next room,
   I think I see the Governor standing there.
   And getting dressed.
LISARDA: Alas! my life is finished!
CESAR: What should I do, señora?
LISARDA: Jump from this window.
   It opens on the court, and the court leads
   Into the porch, from which you can escape.
   My fate is such that I have more to fear
   Than you imagine. But you will know it later.
   I promise that as soon as possible
   I'll tell you who I am.
CESAR: For you, señora,
   I risk my life.

                [Exit through window]

   [Enter the GOVERNOR, in his doublet, with drawn sword
   and shield]

GOVERNOR: Who went out just now?
LISARDA: No one, my lord.
GOVERNOR: What is the matter? Why are you upset?
LISARDA: I heard a pistol shot.
     [Noise outside]   What is this noise?
GOVERNOR:
LISARDA: I do not know, my lord.
GOVERNOR: Let me take this torch —

Although if I have lost my honor now,
I do not hope this torch will help me find it.

                                            [Exit]

          Scene 4: The Courtyard of the Governor's House

     [Enter DON CÉSAR, groping his way]

CÉSAR: I cannot find the door. The night is dark;
     My mind is full of trouble and confusion;
     And in this double darkness, I don't know
     Where I am going. To think that such a thing
     Should happen to me — and in the Governor's house!
     What's to be done? I cannot find this door.
     But I'm beneath the portico. What's this? A sedan-
          chair,
     If I am not mistaken. Usually
     They're put beneath the portico. Someone's coming.
     I'll have to hide. In such a plight as this,
     One has to trust to luck.
          [Hides in sedan-chair]

     *[Enter the GOVERNOR from one side, DON JUAN from the
     other, with drawn swords. The GOVERNOR carries a torch
     in his left hand]*

GOVERNOR: It was on this side that I heard the noise,
     Guard the door, so that he cannot escape.
JUAN: As soon as I heard your voice, my lord, I left
     My chamber.
GOVERNOR: *[Aside]* To add to my embarrassment.
JUAN: What was it?
GOVERNOR: It was nothing. I was mistaken.
     [Aside] My honor! I must pretend. *[Aloud]* I thought
          I heard
     Steps in my chamber. I got up to see.
     But I regret it now. I've searched the house
     Without encountering anyone. This awakened
     My daughter, who had hardly gone to sleep.
     And so, Don Juan...
JUAN: You were not mistaken.
     I'm certain someone entered; for I heard
     Some muffled steps, and then a heavy thud
     As if a man had leapt out of a window.
GOVERNOR: *[Aside]* I seek in vain to cover up my shame.
     It's but too obvious. *[Aloud]* Now that I've searched
     The house, I'm satisfied. But if you are not,
     Take you the light and go through every room.
JUAN: If you will take your stand to block the door,

I'll start my search.
GOVERNOR: There's surely nothing here.
JUAN: Someone might hide within this sedan-chair.
GOVERNOR: You can easily look.
   [JUAN sees CÉSAR, who motions him to keep silence]
JUAN: *[Aside]*   Heaven help me! What do I see?
GOVERNOR: Is there anyone there?
JUAN: No one. *[Aside]* I would
  to God.
GOVERNOR: I've searched the rest.
JUAN: It is apparent, sir,
 That I'm mistaken. Perhaps it was the wind
 Which slammed a door. Go in, my lord.
GOVERNOR: Return
 To bed, Don Juan. No one has come in.
JUAN: Now I'm convinced: it was an illusion which
 I shared with you.

          [Exit GOVERNOR]
      He thinks
He has deceived me, but he is deceived.
We both employ the same ruse to conceal
Our common disaster! May Heaven help me.
What shall I do in such confusion?
Don César hidden here! And I went bail
For him! I've been accomplice in my shame!
How right he was to say he could not tell me
Who was his mistress! For it was Lisarda.
I find outraged here
Trust, Friendship, Honor: well, I will exact
A triple vengeance. Let this dagger strike him
Even to the death where he is hiding now...
But how shall I thereby fulfill my promise
To bring him back to prison? Dreadful dilemma!
Can I kill one entrusted to my word?
O how can I defend him with one hand
And kill him with the other? No, he shall die!
When honor is impugned, no promise binds,
And danger and decorum do not count.
 [Calling] Don César!
CÉSAR: *[Emerging]*   Abashed and overwhelmed at seeing
 you
 I'd throw myself at your feet.
JUAN: Follow me now,
 And leave out such unseasonable remarks.
CÉSAR: Where are you leading me?
JUAN: We'll go alone.
 I only have my sword and cloak. Fear nothing.
CÉSAR: I fear no treachery from you, Don Juan,
 Who come of noble birth. If I address you

     This question, it is but to avert a thing
     You would be sorry for.
JUAN: How so?
CÉSAR: I have
     An excuse.
JUAN: You have?
CÉSAR: Yes.
JUAN: Pray God you have.
CÉSAR: Hear me at once. For if we should leave here
     I'll have to argue only with my sword.
JUAN: What can you say to me who have at once
     Insulted honor, friendship, and my trust...
     My honor since you dared to force your way
     Into this house; my friendship, since you court
     A woman to whom you knew I was betrothed;
     My trust since you have found in her a means
     To prevail against me. Have I not therefore cause
     Of just complaint when you, disloyal, ungrateful
     Betray my honor, trust, and friendship thus?
CÉSAR: If one of us is insulted by the other,
     It is I, Don Juan, whom you now accuse
     Of perfidy and treason — I, who regard
     Friendship a sacred altar upon which
     I sacrifice my soul unto your honor.
     If I have dared to come into this house,
     It was to see a lady living here
     Who was arrested recently with me.
     That was sufficient reason for my coming
     When she had summoned me; and as for friendship,
     Delicacy forbade me to be frank.
     I thought of her to whom you are betrothed,
     And did not wish to tell you that a woman
     To whom I paid attentions lived with her.
     And as for trust, I had so much in you,
     I knew that you would kill me if I wronged
     This house to which you owe such obligations,
     So I said nothing to you. That is why
     You should be satisfied, for it is you
     Who wrong my friendship, honor, and my trust.
JUAN: These explanations
     Do not suffice me. Give me till tomorrow
     Before I give you a reply.
CÉSAR: Agreed.
     You'll find me in my prison.
JUAN: Expect me there.
CÉSAR: Until tomorrow, then. Adieu!
JUAN: Adieu.
     Until tomorrow.

                       [Exeunt]

ᎶᎶ

ACT THREE

Scene 1: The Governor's House

[Enter DON JUAN]

JUAN: Since the cold dawn awakened white and pale,
    Telling the sun the hour was come to rise,
    I have been rooted on the threshold here
    By fierce vexations. I've no better way
    To verify my cruel suspicions.
    Before he sends a warning to this prisoner
    I'll speak with her, catching her unawares.
    I would be satisfied, even at the risk
    Of death itself. If I am dying now
    At the very thought of it, may die indeed
    In knowing it; but desperate diseases
    Need desperate remedies. I'd rather die
    From knowing the truth than die of jealousy.
    Here is Celia.

[Enter CELIA]

    Celia, my dear.
CELIA: You are already here
    So early?
JUAN: Tell me, what is your mistress doing?
CELIA: Thinking of dressing.
JUAN: When she does come out
    She'll bring another morning to the fields.
CELIA: I'm going to assist her. Shall I take a message?
JUAN: Tell her that as I wait outside her door
    I worship her.
                            [Exit CELIA]

JUAN: What tortures do the jealous undergo!
    This woman doubtless will be late today,
    Although I'm waiting for her; but no doubt
    It's a good sign my disillusionment
    Is late in coming! Did it bring fatal news,
    It would have come at once. Would I were undeceived,
    Or would my doubts of her were dissipated!

[Enter the GOVERNOR]

GOVERNOR: Don Juan?
JUAN: My lord?
GOVERNOR: What are you doing here
    So early in the morning? I believe
    The same thought has awakened us.

JUAN: What thought?
GOVERNOR: You doubtless seek me, as I am seeking you?
JUAN: What do you want of me?
GOVERNOR: I have for you
    A warm affection... Therefore I propose
    Not to prolong the impatience of your love...
    And as I know the tedium of delay,
    You shall be, from tonight, the happy husband,
    Of my beloved daughter.
JUAN: *[Aside]*   Another cross!
GOVERNOR: *[Aside]* I can ascertain by this whether or not
    He has suspicions.
JUAN: It was your intention
    To grant this favor in three days or so —
    I'll wait that long.
GOVERNOR: Certain preparations
    Had to be made first, but now all is ready.
JUAN: *[Aside]* What persecution!
GOVERNOR: *[Aside]*   This goes *from bad to worse*.
    He asks now for delay, who was before
    So full of haste. He must have seen something
    During the night. *[Aloud]* Don Juan, if today
    You don't say Yes, tomorrow I'll say No.

                                                      [Exit]

JUAN: How urgent he is! But who approaches now?
    O let me die! For no one can be silent
    When he is jealous.

    [Enter FLÉRIDA]

FLÉRIDA: You're very early, sir.
JUAN: Yes; I desired
    To speak with you, and therefore rose so early.
FLÉRIDA: I'm at your service.
JUAN: Have you trust enough
    To answer frankly?
FLÉRIDA: I trust you absolutely.
JUAN: You're right to do so; for if you are she
    I think you are, you'll have my gratitude —
    So do not fear. Tell me, I pray, señora,
    Are you acquainted with Don César Ursino?
FLÉRIDA: Yes, but would to heaven, I never were!
    It is because of him that I'm exiled,
    That I am suffering in prison here
    And that my reputation is destroyed.
JUAN: *[Aside]* This first reply already brings relief.
    [Aloud] Inform me further: have you ever had
    Occasion to converse with him at night?
FLÉRIDA: Alas! Yes, often — too often, to my grief.
JUAN: *[Aside]* This is good news. One last question, señora.

Were you not both together at one time
In a garden where...
FLÉRIDA: Do not go on, I beg.
Yes, we were in a garden when there happened
My dreadful tragedy. Yes, we were there
The jasmine, silent witnesses of love,
Saw...
JUAN: That is enough, señora. Do not burden
Your heart with such sad memories. You have
Restored my life and soul... *[Aside]* Forgive me,
    friend,
My wrongful thoughts of you. I'm undeceived
For evermore! *[Aloud]*... Pray speak not to Lisarda
About our conversation; and goodbye.
    [He moves away]
FLÉRIDA: One moment, please. Where are you going now
So hurriedly?
JUAN: I know all I need to know.
Señora, you have entirely reassured me,
And therefore I should go and see Don César
Who waits for me in prison.
FLÉRIDA: Stay.
JUAN: I cannot.
                                        [Exit]

FLÉRIDA: He goes to see Don César — so he said!
What does that signify? He questions me
About our love, and afterward declares
He goes to see him! But the riddle is simple.
In questioning me, he wished to be assured
That it was really me. My answers proved it,
Since he displayed such joy; and telling me
He was going to see him was to show me plainly
He came on his behalf. And then he added,
Don César is a prisoner. Well, let's find him.

    [Enter LISARDA and CELIA]

LISARDA: Where are you going?
FLÉRIDA: Señora, give me joy.
As I know well the generous interest
You take in me, and the pleasure you will have
At my happy fortune, you must know, señora,
The man I seek is here a prisoner
And knows I'm living with you. It was truly
A good idea to shelter in your house.
He'll not be able to accuse me of
Imprudent conduct while he was away.
I'm mad with joy. I go to see Don César.
                                        [Exit]

LISARDA: Celia, there is yet another grief.

CELIA: What grief?
LISARDA: It is in jealousy alone
    That the spectator sees less of the game
    Than he who plays. Do you not then observe
    There are fresh cares for me and fresh vexations?
    Have you not noticed that each thing that's happened
    Has always made my situation worse
    Than it was before?
CELIA: In what way?
LISARDA: Listen, Celia,
    Camoens, the Portuguese Virgil, in a sweet song
    Remarked: "I have seen the good convert to evil,
    And evil to still worse." Another writer
    Compared evil to a hydra. He was right:
    For every grief that dies, two griefs are born.
    I know it by experience. I escape
    Out of one crisis only to find that I
    Am landed in another. One day I thought
    I was a prisoner. Luckily I was saved
    Out of that peril, only to be burdened
    With jealousy a lady had aroused.
    So joyful first, then sorrowful, I've seen
    The good convert to ill and ill to worse.
    When this gentleman came out of prison
    To come and see me I interrogated him
    On my suspicions. Whether it was his answers
    Which satisfied me, or not, I do not know,
    But I was satisfied. While we conversed,
    His sword-hilt knocked his arm, his gun went off;
    It was just my luck! My fears were soon dispersed;
    I fancied that he'd reached the outer door
    Without my father seeing him; but when
    I rendered thanks to Love for this success:
    "I've seen the good convert to ill, and ill
    To worse." This prisoner came here in pursuit
    Of one who'd promised marriage to her — before,
    After a quarrel, he had had to flee.
    This man, who stole my freedom, also came,
    Fleeing because of something he had done,
    So he could be the one this lady seeks,
    Since both are here, and both are now in prison.
    So now you know my reasons for distress.
    And tell me, Celia, if the common saying,
    "It's worse than ever" does not fit me now?
    And can I not apply the poet's words,
    And say, like him, to heaven and earth: "I've seen
    The good convert to ill, and ill to worse."[12]
CELIA: You would not be wrong,
    If there were but one killer in the world;

But there are many killers nowadays.
There's even a game of cards where there are three.
If you were made to imagine such a thing
By jealousy, it's an astrologer,
And for that reason should not be believed.[13]

[Enter CAMACHO]

CAMACHO: "Let's come in,
    Because it's raining" as the old song says.[14]
    I wish to God that spell would cease to work!
CELIA: It's Fabio's servant who has just come in.
LISARDA: He doubtless told her his master's a prisoner.
    He hasn't seen my face — without my mantle...
CELIA: How did you enter without being announced?
CAMACHO: I came in on my feet: if that mislikes you,
    I'll dance right out again. I am still
    A bit of a dancer, so, as I came in
    On the left foot, I'll go out on my right.[15]
LISARDA: Tell me, soldier, who are you?
CAMACHO: If I knew
    Myself, it would be little news to you.
    But I can't tell you, since I do not know.
    Heaven has given me a master who
    Holds me under a spell; and the one thing
    I know about myself at the present time
    Is that I am a wandering squire who travels
    Through the forests of love, still following a sun
    That always shows a muffled face. To speak
    The vulgar tongue I have been searching here
    For the worst deceiver and the biggest trickster
    In Europe. If one of you two is by chance
    A lady who is prisoner in this palace,
    In God's name, let her speak; for I have come
    In pilgrimage to see her. My head is split
    By praises of her beauty, and I wish
    To see her, so that my master in the future
    Will let me be at peace.
CELIA: *[Aside to LISARDA]*   Well, señora,
    Has the astrologer lied?
LISARDA: *[Aside to CELIA]*   He seeks the prisoner,
    And he does not believe that she is one.
CELIA: That's very subtle.
LISARDA: While jealousy tells lies,
    Let love reveal the truth. *[To CAMACHO]* Your master,
        sirrah,
    Praises her much?
CAMACHO: Yes, señora.
LISARDA: What?
    Her beauty, or her wit?

CAMACHO: Both, señora.
   She holds a doctorate in each.
LISARDA: He sings
   Her praises?
CAMACHO: Yes.
LISARDA: He loves her?
CAMACHO: Not in the least,
   Another lady occupies his thoughts.
   He does not paint this lady of today,
   But to efface.
LISARDA: Efface what?
CAMACHO: I don't know,
   But it appears to me this word *efface*
   Has piqued you. If you are this lady then,
   Please tell me.
LISARDA: *[Aside]*   I am dying. *[Aloud]* No, insolent,
   Villain, traitor, I am not that lady.
   I am the daughter of the Governor,
   And here one does not deal in love affairs.
   If this woman should be in my house,
   Do not attempt to speak with her. This house
   Is Honor's sacred refuge. If you return,
   By heaven, I'll have you thrown out of the window
   By four of my servants.
CAMACHO: I should be very sorry.
   Four, señora? Three would be enough,
   Three, did I say? Two would suffice. Two, did I say?
   One would do — not even one, a half,
   A quarter, an arm, a hand, a finger, a nail
   Is quite enough. And that is why I'm going
   Before they throw me. Farewell.

                                                   [Exit]

LISARDA: My misfortune
   Is such that in the least important things
   Good converts to ill.
CELIA: There is no need
   To take on so.
LISARDA: Well, Celia, I must find out where I stand.
   I thought of a plan this morning. I have written
   A letter telling him that if he can
   By any means escape from prison today,
   I'll meet him where he likes. I have pretended
   That I myself have bribed my jailers.
CELIA: Well!
LISARDA: I'll take this lady to the rendezvous,
   And if my fate decrees that he is hers,
   May cruel Love avert such misery!
   I will renounce my passion; and if he's not,
   My love will conquer every obstacle.

CELIA: If he be the abductor of her honor,
    And if you should insist on going to see him,
    You are bound to come away dissatisfied.
LISARDA: There will be wit enough to cope with matters.

   [Enter FLÉRIDA with her mantle]

                         Where are you going, Laura?
FLÉRIDA: With your permission, señora, I am going
    To visit a prison where my soul is housed.
LISARDA: *[Aside]* To kill me would be nearer to the truth.
    I can't permit that she should go and see him
    When I'm not sure of his identity.
    [Aloud] What! In a house like ours, is it enough
    To take your mantilla and say "I'm going out
    Whenever I like"?
FLÉRIDA: I'm so preoccupied
    With my own troubles, that they leave no time
    For proper thought; nor can it be surprising
    That one who came from Naples to be a captive
    Should go from here to prison.
LISARDA: But there are people
    Responsible for your honor. What would my father say
    If he returned and did not find you here?
FLÉRIDA: I will return before. It is not late.
LISARDA: You must accompany me this afternoon
    Upon a visit.
FLÉRIDA: You wish to teach me patience!
LISARDA: You must come with me.
FLÉRIDA: I will soon be back.
    I only wish to see him.
LISARDA: I'll not consent.
FLÉRIDA: I will return as soon as possible.
LISARDA: No, it is useless for you to insist.
    You shall not go.
FLÉRIDA: There's no need to insist;
    If that's how it is, I can't do otherwise.

   [Enter the GOVERNOR]

GOVERNOR: You're quarreling? What's the matter?
LISARDA: *[To FLÉRIDA]* You'll do what I say.
GOVERNOR: Well?
LISARDA: The señora wished to leave the house
   Without consulting you.
FLÉRIDA: Yes sir, I wish to go.
GOVERNOR: Is it enough to say "I wish to go"?
FLÉRIDA: I must confess I should have asked your leave;
    But since you know the reason why I'm here,
    You'll understand that I desire to go
    To see my betrothed.

GOVERNOR: Yes, I understand.
   But it is to prevent that that you're our prisoner.
FLÉRIDA: Your prisoner?
GOVERNOR: Your memory is short.
   Have you forgot what happened in the garden?
FLÉRIDA: No, sir, I remember it too well.
GOVERNOR: Were you not brought thence as a prisoner?
LISARDA: *[Aside]* I fear that all will be discovered.
FLÉRIDA: No, sir;
   I came into your house of my own free will.
GOVERNOR: Did I not find you?
FLÉRIDA: Did I not come alone?
GOVERNOR: Did I not send you prisoner?
FLÉRIDA: *[To LISARDA]*   Explain
   This mystery.
LISARDA: Did you not come a prisoner?
   You said they found you hidden in a house.
   How should I know it if you had not told me?
FLÉRIDA: I do not understand what's happening to me.
GOVERNOR: She still denies it. I leave you with her. God
   Restore her wits. My own are all confused.
                                  [Exit]
FLÉRIDA: Tell me, señora, was I brought here a prisoner?
LISARDA: No, my friend.
FLÉRIDA: Why did you say I was?
LISARDA: Forgive me, Laura; I was forced to do it.
   I had to think of myself. You shall come with me
   This afternoon, and you'll learn all about it.
FLÉRIDA: Patience, my heart. Till then I'll be your shadow.
                                  [Exeunt]

Scene 2: A Room in the Castle

JUAN: Don César, I approach you with some shame
   That I misjudged your friendship. My excuse
   Must be that Love is always painted blind
   And that he always lets himself be led
   By jealousy. Yes, I compare suspicions
   To ragamuffin lads who lead the blind,
   Make them obey and credit every lie.[16]
   But leaving that, I wish to tell you now
   That I have no more fear and no more doubt
   And that I humbly beg you to accept
   A full apology. If you're not satisfied
   I offer you my breast. Avenge yourself!
   Punish me!
CÉSAR: I would have the right, Don Juan,

But will not use it, for I would not be
A true friend, as I claim myself to be,
If I did not condone a friend's first fault.
I must admit, things being as they were,
It was a generous act for you to spare me.
But yet from another I would not have borne it,
If he'd refused to hear my explanations.
How were you disabused?
JUAN: For both our sakes
    Allow me now to set the seal of silence
    On what can only painfully remind us
    That I have injured you. Your prisoner
    Is beautiful.
CÉSAR: Is she not very beautiful?
JUAN: Oh yes, she is, she is! But it is true
    That she, compared with Lisarda, is as darkness
    To daylight, or a gray cloud in the sun.
    Lisarda is a sea of beauty, drinking
    Her rivals up like tributary seas.
CÉSAR: Even if she's as lovely as you say
    I doubt if she's as witty as the captive.
    I'd like to read a letter I've received
    From my masked love-sick lady — it would not be
    An indiscretion since we hold in common
    Our blessings and our ills.
JUAN: I shall be delighted.
CÉSAR: I praised it so much, I don't dare to read it.

    [Enter CAMACHO]

CAMACHO: Have I actually managed to escape from that hor-
    rible situation? I thank God for it, for I was so
    frightened, my legs would hardly carry me.
JUAN: What do you mean?
CÉSAR: Why were you afraid?
CAMACHO: It seems to me I have servants and balconies at my
    heels. I wanted to go and see your prisoner to check
    whether she was what you say she is; and I found in her
    place the Governor's daughter who, furious on learning
    why I was there, said to me: "This is not a house to
    which one brings secret messages, and if you dare again
    to put your foot over the threshold, I will order four
    servants to throw you out of the window."
JUAN: That's just like her: she is as circumspect as she is
    beautiful. But let us read the letter and see the wit
    you say is marvelous.
CÉSAR: "If you can win over your guards, as I have won over
    mine, I will go to see you this evening, but on three
    conditions. First, that you have a sedan-chair in
    readiness at the door of the Parish Church; second, that

you will have a house at my disposal where we can talk;
and third, that you will leave your pistol at home."
JUAN: She certainly writes well; but it seems to me that she
has conceived a project which is both rash and difficult
of execution.
CAMACHO: Listen to a tale.
One day a peasant started out with a rope, a stake, a
hen, an onion, a pot, and a goat. On the way he met a
roguish wench. She called him and said to him: "Come
here, Gil, and have a chat in this meadow." "I can't,"
said he, "with all this gear: I should lose everything."
"How so?" said she. "What a fool you are! You don't
know how to manage things! What are you carrying?
Let's see." "Look: an onion, a pot, a goat, a hen, a
rope, and a stake." "What a thing to make a fuss about!
Stick the stake in the ground, then fasten one foot of
the goat with the rope; then in a jiffy, to make things
more secure, put the hen in the pot and let the onion
serve as a lid for the pot. So you'll have naught to
fear, and you'll be sure of recovering the onion, the
hen and the pot, the stake, the rope, and the goat."
When a woman wishes for a thing, nothing will deter her:
she is capable of the impossible.
JUAN: And what do you intend to do?
CÉSAR: I should have gone to see her with great pleasure if
she had said at night, or if the Lieutenant would give
me permission. I would have to find a convenient place
in which to meet her.
CAMACHO: By my faith, you're as encumbered as my peasant
was — more so, in fact.
JUAN: I'll guarantee to obtain the permission of the Lieutenant and I offer you the use of my apartment. You
won't run any risk because the door opens on another
street. You'll leave here in a carriage and arrange
everything as the lady desires.
CAMACHO: Splendid! You fix up everything so efficiently
that one might say you had learned my wench's lesson.
JUAN: Go, Camacho, hire a chair. There's the key of my
apartment. Get everything in readiness. Be off with
you — don't delay.
CAMACHO: I shall be prompt only in this, for the go-between
is very like a cook — for a cook prepares tasty morsels
for other people, and though he doesn't get a bit himself he still enjoys his work, if it gives satisfaction.
                                                    [Exit]
CÉSAR: You're showing me precious marks of friendship.
JUAN: Because I'm rejoicing at being undeceived.
CÉSAR: You are indeed offering me leave, house, and coach?
JUAN: The favor I do for you is not so very great. I'm more

than willing to arrange for you to visit her by day, be-
cause that means you won't visit the house by night.
But here is the Governor.
CÉSAR: It's unusual for him to come to the prison.

[Enter the GOVERNOR]

GOVERNOR: You are here, Don Juan?
JUAN: Yes, my lord:
I too am a prisoner.
GOVERNOR: You? But how is that?
JUAN: Since my friend, Don César, is a prisoner
I can say truly I am also one.
GOVERNOR: We are all prisoners by such reasoning
Since all of us desire to serve Don César.
CÉSAR: I am silent, sir; and in this way, I think,
I best can show my gratitude; for words
Are powerless to express what's in my heart.
So I'll content myself with saying to you:
May God prolong your days!
GOVERNOR: Would you, Don Juan,
Now leave me with Don César? We have much
To say together.
JUAN: I hasten to obey.
CÉSAR: *[Aside]* Alas! I lose the chance of seeing her!
It will be long before I have another.
[To JUAN] You see what's happened. If by any chance
The lady is already with my servant
At your apartment, go there (for I know
Her face will be concealed) and without showing
That you know who she is, inform her that
It is impossible for me to see her,
And that I'm dying of despair and grief.
JUAN: Rely on me.
CÉSAR: Though you know who she is,
Don't let her guess you know it.
JUAN: Be content.
                                              [Exit]

GOVERNOR: Sit down, Don César.
CÉSAR: I obey you, sir,
As is my duty.
      [They sit]
GOVERNOR: You should know, Don César,
That in my youth I was the closest friend
Of Don Alonso Colona. I therefore come
To speak with you, not as your judge but simply
Out of my interest in his life and honor.
He has himself asked me to intervene
In this affair. My friend, a prudent man,
Who makes a virtue of necessity,

An obligation out of an offense,
Solicited for your pardon. He obtained it,
And sends it in this letter. He assumes
That in return for this you will consent
To restore his honor. Lastly, he assures you,
Provided you come back his daughter's husband,
You can return to him without a care:
He will receive you as a loving father
With open arms.

CÉSAR: You act, sir, like yourself,
And make me everlastingly your debtor.
Jealousy was the cause of my mad rage,
But now I am convinced that it was baseless:
I belong heart and soul to Flérida,
And I am ready to give her my hand.

GOVERNOR: Then that will be no later than this night.

CÉSAR: Have you a license for us to wed by proxy?

GOVERNOR: What need of that when you will both be there?

CÉSAR: What! Flérida here! Explain, I do beseech you.

GOVERNOR: You do not know it? Have you forgotten, then,
That she is in my house?

CÉSAR: I did not know.

GOVERNOR: Come, Don César, did I not find her with you
The day you were arrested?

CÉSAR: What a strange mistake!
You are mistaken in thinking that this lady
Is Flérida! It is not she, I swear.

GOVERNOR: One of her servants saw her — would he lie?
Why would she say the same?

CÉSAR: You have, for sure,
Another prisoner.

GOVERNOR: No, I've only the lady
Who was in the garden with you.

CÉSAR: Well, you're wrong.
She is not Flérida.

GOVERNOR: My patience
Is at an end! If she herself admits —
And bitterly regrets — the incidents
Of her affair with you, though she denies
She is my prisoner, how can I be mistaken?

CÉSAR: But the same facts,
The self-same indications, might well fit
Another woman.

GOVERNOR: That's impossible.
Besides, a servant who had followed her
Saw her, I say, saw her with his own eyes.

CÉSAR: He must have lied.

GOVERNOR: You'll make me lose my temper.

CÉSAR: Lead me to her, and if she still asserts

    That she is Flérida, I'll marry her
    Without delay.
GOVERNOR: So be it. Come.
CÉSAR: *[Aside]*   O heavens!
    Deliver me from this inexplicable web
    Of intrigue.
GOVERNOR: *[Aside]* O God, enlighten me, beset
    By manifold vexations.
CÉSAR: You still insist
    That Flérida was hidden in the garden?
GOVERNOR: Yes, yes a hundred times.
CÉSAR: It was not she.
GOVERNOR: Well, things are going now *from bad to worse*.
                                        [Exeunt]

    Scene 3: Don Juan's Room in the Governor's House

    [Enter LISARDA and FLÉRIDA, with their faces covered,
    accompanied by CAMACHO]

CAMACHO: Here is the house, señora. We have been
    All round the town, so that we shouldn't be followed.
    I'll wager that you don't know where you are.
LISARDA: It's quite impossible for us to know it,
    Since we came with muffled faces in a chair
    With curtains drawn, and from which we descended
    Only inside the house.
CAMACHO: My orders were to close
    The door from outside when you entered here.
    Stay here. This hospitable room belongs
    To a young man, and you can pass the time
    In looking at it. Farewell, señoras.
                                        [Exit]
FLÉRIDA: *[Aside]* I have not said a word for fear of being
    Recognized by Camacho. I do not doubt
    That César's here, because his servants are,
    Why does Lisarda stay all muffled up?
    Why with myself as witness does César act
    In this mysterious way? May heaven grant
    A happy ending!
LISARDA: Laura, we can breathe
    A little, since no one sees us.
        [She removes her mantle and recognizes the room]
                            Heaven protect me!
FLÉRIDA: Why are you so surprised?
LISARDA: I do not know...
    I'm dying.
FLÉRIDA: What's the matter?

LISARDA: The matter is...
  I'm in my own house, when I hoped to hide
  For an interview which I must have — as you'll
  Discover — with a man. This room you see
  Is Juan's. You've been here a little while;
  You've not been in this room and would not know it.
  I recognize it well. It has a door
  Which opens on another street. I came here,
  Not seeing where we went. I've been a night bird —
  I'm taken in a snare. Alas! I'm lost,
  And can't complain since I'm alone to blame.
  Let us make sure it's not a vain illusion,
  That it is true. How could there be a mistake?
  The evil that's befallen us is only
  Too real!... These chairs, these pictures, and that
      desk,
  That mirror and that tapestry... they are ours!
  It is our house! O heavens! How could this be?
  But nevertheless I'll not submit to fortune
  If there's a remedy for everything
  There must be one for this. There is a door
  Opening on my apartment. If someone were there
  To unlock the door, we could escape from here.
  That is the first essential — afterward
  It will be easy to excuse ourselves
  For having failed the rendezvous. And if
  We cannot, once I'm out of here, I care not
  If we have no excuse. Look through the keyhole,
  Laura, I beg you.
FLÉRIDA: Celia's there, señora,
  Sewing before the window which overlooks
  The garden.
LISARDA: Stand aside a moment while I call her.
  Tst! Tst! Celia!... Tst! Tst! Celia! She does not
      see us,
  And as she doesn't know who is calling her,
  She gazes wildly round the room. Through here,
  Celia, through here!
CELIA: Who's calling me? Who is it?
LISARDA: It's I. I'll tell you all about it afterward.
  Open this door as quickly as you can.
CELIA: My master has the key — it's on his desk.
  I'll go and find it.
LISARDA: Quick! May she come
  In time!
FLÉRIDA: Too late!
LISARDA: Why?
FLÉRIDA: The key is turning
  In the other door. It is a man!

LISARDA: It is Don Juan, heaven help me! Laura,
    Take off this mantle; cover up your face,
    While he is locking up the door again,
    And let us turn the tables on him now!

    [Enter DON JUAN]

JUAN: *[Aside]* She's not in the outer room. She will have
        wished
    To look at the apartment. *[Seeing LISARDA]* It is you!
LISARDA: Yes, Don Juan, it is I. For since this lady
    Awaited you, I bore her company
    Till you arrived. I used the other door
    From my own room. You are, upon my word,
    A rare gallant. You wed one lady, sir,
    And court another.
JUAN: Señora...
LISARDA: Hold your tongue.
    Don't try to excuse yourself.
JUAN: But...
LISARDA: You are not merely
    Lacking in courtesy, but a faithless lover.
JUAN: You know this lady?
LISARDA: Sir, I have no need
    To know her, who has not offended me,
    I'm not so inconsiderate as you are.
JUAN: Please listen to me...
LISARDA: I am not so in love with you, Don Juan,
    That I want satisfaction. It's not jealousy
    That animates me, but a sentiment
    Of wounded pride. You receive in my house,
    Under my very eyes, a veiled woman!
    She comes in a sedan-chair to see you
    — With curtains drawn — followed by a footman.
    The door outside is guarded by a watchdog —
    A servant whom my people do not know,
    And who no doubt has often served you thus
    In your intrigues with women. I know all.
JUAN: But...
LISARDA: Say no more.
JUAN: Please listen.
LISARDA: That's enough.
JUAN: A friend...
LISARDA: A stale excuse. You'd have me think
    That it's a friend who's borrowed your apartment
    To speak to a woman — an ordinary service
    That young men do each other. A fine excuse!
JUAN: Señora, listen to me, for God's sake!
LISARDA: When a woman listens to excuses,
    She wishes to be satisfied. I do not.

Give me the key.
JUAN: This lady shall not leave
   Till you know first...
LISARDA: There's nothing to be known,
   Step aside. *[To FLÉRIDA]* Come, señora, depart;
   Think yourself lucky that I am who I am,
   And he is who he is. *[Aside]* Forgive me, Laura.
   I'm forced to do this.
JUAN: *[Aside]*   O cruel law of friendship!
   [To LISARDA] This lady shall not leave here till you've
       heard
   From her own mouth my full exoneration.
LISARDA: Since I've no wish to hear, why do you press me
   To listen to it?
JUAN: *[To FLÉRIDA]*   Then you, señora, tell her
   Whether you know me, tell her your love's name,
   Or else I swear I'll tell her who you are.
LISARDA: Your cause is bad, if you must lose your temper!

   *[Enter CELIA, by the door at which the women had been
   knocking]*

CELIA: *[Whispering]* Señora.
LISARDA: *[Whispering]*   What do you want?
CELIA: *[Whispering]*   I've opened it.
LISARDA: *[Whispering]* A little late, but never mind.
CELIA: *[Whispering]*   What's
       happening?
LISARDA: *[Whispering]* A piece of trickery in which I've had
   To involve this lady. *[Aloud]* You see the door was
       open.
JUAN: I don't deny it. Alas! Someone is coming.
   It is your father. All that I request
   Is that you will not ruin me with him.
LISARDA: *[Aside]* I must look after myself. If I have found
   A good excuse for breaking our engagement.
   And freeing myself, why should I lose the chance?

   [Enter the GOVERNOR, DON CÉSAR and CAMACHO]

GOVERNOR: What's going on?
   I heard your voices as I entered, so
   I came to see. You here, my child?
LISARDA: I came here...
GOVERNOR: Why?
LISARDA: To call upon a lady.
GOVERNOR: A lady here?
   Who is she?
LISARDA: Don Juan can inform you
   Better than I.
GOVERNOR: Don Juan, you must be mad

To behave in such a manner in my house —
To bring a woman here.
JUAN: Since you accuse me —
You too — I will tell all. The law of friendship
Does not require a man to sacrifice
His honor for his friend; and as the truth
Will not be compromising to this lady —
For you'll soon see she is Don César's bride —
Know that she is the lady whom you keep
As prisoner, and that she came this afternoon
To speak with him. Then if I have committed
A fault in doing a kindness to a friend,
I ask your pardon humbly.
FLÉRIDA: *[Aside]*   Did I ask
To see Don César?
CÉSAR: *[Aside]*   If the one whose face
I see now, is the one to whom I spoke,
Who can this woman be?
GOVERNOR: Señora, you can lift your mantle now;
You are known here; and there is no great harm
In going out to speak with your own husband.
So I will prove what he will not believe.
That you are Flérida.
FLÉRIDA: Yes, sir, I am;
I am that luckless woman.
          [She uncovers]
CÉSAR: Heavens! What do I see?
GOVERNOR: Well now, Don César,
Is this Flérida? Is it really she?
Are you at last convinced?
CÉSAR: Yes sir, but yet...
GOVERNOR: It was not right, Don César, to maintain
It was impossible it should be she,
When you were coming to rejoin her here.
LISARDA: *[Aside]* I'm now somewhat consoled — since I have
          been
So disillusioned, things cannot be worse.
Since love must be renounced, let me at least
Preserve my honor. *[Aloud]* If you wish me now
To explain the riddle, you should know that I
Brought Flérida here, both to restore her honor
And to teach Don Juan
Never to lend his wife's house to his friends.
FLÉRIDA: *[Aside to LISARDA]* What is the use of searching
          out the Hows,
The Whys, and Wherefores, since I have regained
The honor I had lost. *[To CÉSAR]* César, I'm yours.
CÉSAR: *[Aside to LISARDA]* Since you desire it,
I will not contradict you.

LISARDA: *[Aside to CÉSAR]* Yes, I do wish it.
    I hope the consciousness of doing right
    Will assuage my sorrow.
GOVERNOR: Since love invites you, Juan and Lisarda,
    Do what is right and let me join your hands.
JUAN: My faith is yours for life.
CAMACHO: *[To the audience]* Now is the time, since they are
      being wed,
    To apply the saying "From bad to worse." And so,
    Be off, the comedy is over.
CÉSAR: *[To the audience]* And, ladies and gentlemen,
    Be kind enough to overlook the faults
    Of the poet who kneels to you for pardon now.

ᘐᘐᘐᘐᘐᘐᘐᘐᘐ

THE END

ᘐᘐᘐᘐᘐᘐᘐᘐᘐ

El
secreto
a voces

Calderón finished writing *El secreto a voces* on 28 February 1642, the date beside his signature on the autograph manuscript, preserved in the Biblioteca Nacional, Madrid. The manuscript contains a note from the censor, Juan Navarro de Espinosa. He insisted, on religious grounds, on the deletion of certain of the *gracioso*'s jokes, and of one of his anecdotes, but allowed the play to be performed in Madrid in June 1642.[1] Almost thirty years later, in 1671, the play was performed at the Viennese court by the servants of the Spanish ambassador, for the entertainment of the Emperor Leopold and his Spanish wife, Margarita Teresa. It seems reasonable to assume that the work was performed regularly in Spain during the intervening years, though no further documentary evidence has so far come to light.

In 1938 José M. de Osma published an edition of the autographed version, the only edition to include, in italics, passages that Calderón himself had marked for deletion. And rightly so: for the passages in question add nothing to the quality of the play; rather they hinder the smooth progress of the dramatic action. Consequently, these passages were ignored for the purposes of this translation.

"Secreto a voces" is a well-known phrase in Spanish, the equivalent of our "open secret." But Calderón contrives to give it a new meaning in his comedy. For the love affair between Federico and Laura is a very well-kept secret indeed, shared only with the audience until the last scene of the final act. Yet this secret is in a special sense truly a "secreto a voces," since, thanks to a special word-code devised by Federico, the couple are able to speak aloud in public about their love, without any of the other characters realizing the real significance of what they say. Not even the *gracioso* is in his master's confidence in this play. The secret lovers use the code in three different scenes, and not only to express their love, but to communicate precise information, to arrange meetings, to warn each other of dangers to their love, and so on. As a result, the word-code assumes a vital function in the development of the plot. It also presents a translator, especially a translator who has chosen Calderón's own medium of verse, with an extremely exacting task. Somehow, like Calderón himself, he must construct passages of verse which convey one meaning when they are read or heard in their entirety, but which carry a different, concealed message, made up of the first words of each verse-line. *El secreto a voces* must surely be one of Calderón's most difficult plays to translate.

Various critics have suggested Tirso's *Amar por arte mayor* as a possible source for Calderón's comedy, on the grounds that there too a cypher is used to further a love affair. But Tirso's cypher is a very different one, in the form of a letter, and fulfills none of the intricate dramatic functions accomplished by Calderón's code. Nor do the two plays have anything else in common. A play much more likely to have influenced Calderón's *Secreto a voces* is Lope's *El perro del hortelano (Dog in a Manger)*. The Duchess Flérida in Calderón is in the same situation as the Countess Diana, the "dog in a manger" of Lope's title. Both women are in love with men who are socially inferior: their secretaries. And both women interfere jealously and ruthlessly in their secretaries' courtship of another woman. Of course, the dramatic emphasis and the development are different. Diana is the heroine of Lope's play. Also, her secretary, Teodoro, has political ambitions and is therefore willing to give up his love for Marcela. So in the end Diana marries her secretary. In Calderón's play the heroine is not the Duchess, but her lady-in-waiting, Laura. And Federico, despite the Duchess's interest in him is entirely unambitious, and devoted only to Laura. With the help of the secret code, mainly conceived for that very purpose, they outwit the jealous vigilance of Flérida, and the comedy ends with their marriage.

El secreto a voces belongs to the category or subcategory of Golden Age comedies known as *comedias palaciegas,* much of its action taking place in Flérida's palace or in the palace gardens. Therefore the play would lend itself to a rich display of color in costume and scenes. Furthermore, the palace setting contributes an additional hint of politics to the play's significance. Flérida is not simply a jealous woman; she is a jealous ruler. She continually misuses her authority as ruler to interfere in Federico's private life, and love. Perhaps her greatest misuse of power occurs in the scene toward the end of act 2, in which she goes so far as to make false charges of treachery against Federico, purely as an excuse to make him surrender evidence that would identify the woman he secretly loves. Federico and Laura are so greatly persecuted by their jealous ruler that they decide upon the drastic step of flight from their own land of Parma and a life of exile under a friendlier ruler, the sympathetic Duke of Mantua. This play then is hardly an apology for the feminine ruler; though admittedly, Flérida does control herself in the end and agree to the marriage of Federico and Laura. Ironically, it is here where Flérida behaves at last as a ruler should, where her authority is most seriously threatened. Both Arnesto, Laura's father, and Lisardo, Laura's betrothed, refuse to obey Flérida and accept Federico as Laura's husband. They reach for their swords; and to restore her authority Flérida is forced to seek support from the Duke of Mantua, whose hand after all she accepts in marriage.

Laura, one cannot help feeling, would have made a much better ruler than Flérida. She is a remarkably resolute and resourceful woman. It is she, not Federico, who conceives the bold plan of fleeing together into exile. At the crucial moment in act 2 when Federico is greatly perturbed, and Flérida is firmly determined to see the portrait that he carries with him, it is Laura who steps in, and thwarts Flérida's jealous purpose (to learn the identity of Federico's mistress) by cleverly changing her own portrait for one of Federico himself. Also, unlike Flérida, Laura is an extremely perceptive woman with admirable insight both into other people's motives and into her own nature. Her self-perception is nowhere more evident than in the "debate" scene in act 1. The question being debated is "What is the greatest pain in love"; and her answer is a profoundly accurate analysis of her own emotional state, though nobody understands this particular "secret spoken aloud," least of all Flérida, who dismisses Laura's comments as mere "sofisterías."

Calderón has an extraordinary talent for the skillful and subtle use of dramatic irony; a talent particularly well exercised in the cypher scenes of *El secreto a voces*, but perhaps most notably in the scene between Federico and Arnesto in act 3. Federico is about to leave his house to visit Laura, with whom he plans to elope that night, when Laura's father arrives. He has been sent by Flérida with express instructions to keep Federico under his supervision until the morning. Arnesto does not know the real reason for these instructions; he has been led to believe that it is to prevent Federico's fighting a duel with another nobleman. Calderón creates an excellent dramatic contrast between Federico's edgy eagerness to be rid of Arnesto, and the old man's phlegmatic refusal to leave. Moreover, Federico's guilty conscience disposes him to imagine that Arnesto has discovered the secret of his affair with Laura, and he misinterprets nearly every move made by Laura's father. So when Arnesto looks round for a chair, Federico displays unease as if afraid that Arnesto might be trying to familiarize himself with the room prior to challenging him to a duel. Federico also misinterprets almost every word spoken by Arnesto. When the old man refers to his honor, for example, Federico wrongly believes that he alludes to the dishonor that he feels because of Federico's attentions to Laura. The two men talk increasingly at cross-purposes, the dramatic irony reaching its height where Federico, for the briefest of happy moments, mistakenly supposes that Arnesto has agreed that Laura may give him her hand in marriage. What Arnesto has agreed upon, as the audience knows full well, is that Federico should accept in friendship the hand of the man who, Arnesto thinks quite wrongly, is waiting to fight a duel with Federico.

Fabio, the *gracioso* of *El secreto a voces,* must be one of Calderón's most original lackeys and as such deserves special comment. He represents a deliberate, sustained endeavor by the playwright to break with the traditional type. Fabio differs from most *graciosos,* first, because he is not in his master's confidence. He has no idea who his master's lady is. He makes prodigious efforts to find out, for example, by hiding under the desk or buffet in act 3. But he fails to discover Laura's identity until the end, when, in a last bid to save face, he insists that he really knew the secret all the time. The fact that Fabio goes disloyally to Flérida with any information he can discover about his master's affairs is not in itself untraditional behavior; but Fabio's main reason for such disloyalty is decidedly unconventional. He is mercenary, like most *graciosos,* so he accepts the chain that the Duchess offers him. Like most *graciosos,* he is a natural gossip, therefore he enjoys telling Flérida what he knows. His main motive, however, for betraying his master's interests is resentment. Fabio resents very much Federico's refusal to confide in him. He feels affronted in his peculiar way and tells tales to Flérida by way of revenge. His disloyalty to Federico almost costs him his life. For Federico discovers it and attacks Fabio with a dagger; only the timely intervention of Enrique saves Fabio's life. This fact too gives Fabio individuality. Of all the lackeys in Golden Age comedies none comes closer than he to dying a violent death at the hands of his master, and before the startled eyes of the audience.[2]

Notes

1. Compare notes 2 and 16, pp. 282 and 284.
2. For notes to the text of *The Secret Spoken Aloud* see pp. 282-84.

The Secret Spoken Aloud

ꙭꙭ

DRAMATIS PERSONAE

Flérida, Duchess of Parma   Lisardo
Laura   Enrique, Duke of Mantua
Flora   Arnesto, old man, Laura's father
Livia   Fabio, Federico's servant
Federico   Musicians

The scene is laid in Parma

ꙭꙭ

ACT ONE

Scene 1: A Park adjoining the Palace

[Enter the MUSICIANS, then the LADIES who carry hats and sticks, then the DUCHESS, giving her hand to ARNESTO; then, some time afterwards, ENRIQUE, FEDERICO, FABIO]

MUSICIANS: *[Singing]* Yes, heart, you have the right
    To sigh that plaintive strain;
    But yet, it is in vain —
    It cannot ease your plight.
    You loved in Reason's spite,
    Why hope for love again?
FLORA: *[Singing]* So many years have passed,
    Beholding but disdain,
    Feeling Denial's pain —
    Are you not tired at last?
    Forget, forget the past:
    Your music is in vain.
MUSICIANS: *[Singing]* You loved in Reason's spite;
    Why hope for love again?[1]
        [The DUCHESS, ARNESTO, the LADIES and the MUSICIANS cross the stage and move away. FABIO eavesdrops on FEDERICO]
FEDERICO: Since you have trusted me to bring you here

        To see the lovely Flérida in secret,
        Stay now in this secluded spot and watch...
ENRIQUE: Ah! Federico! What do I not owe
     To your assistance?
FEDERICO: I owe you still more
     For the confidence with which you've honored me.
ENRIQUE: It's true I would not show it to another.
FEDERICO: Don't speak of that. This servant does not know
     Your true identity.
FABIO: *[Aside]* I've not been able to discover who this mys-
     terious guest is.... I'm quite baffled.[2]
FEDERICO: How do you like this park?
ENRIQUE: I'm not afraid
     To say that in romances I have read
     In leisure hours, when I indulged my fancy,
     I've not imagined anything more beauteous,
     So brilliant and so noble as this park
     Which now is spread before me. It's better than
     Diana's groves or lovely Venus's gardens.
FEDERICO: Now Flérida is plunged in melancholy —
     The punishment of heaven for her perfection —
     So that she searches, and we also search,
     For new distractions. With this aim in view,
     On this May morning, she came to this fair place
     To hear a concert.
ENRIQUE: I must wonder greatly
     That at her age, with loveliness and wit,
     She has allowed this sadness to hold sway
     Over her spirits; and that, being born
     Duchess of Parma, and endowed by heaven
     With qualities so rare, she's not been spared
     The harshest blows of Fortune. Can it be
     That no one knows the cause.
FEDERICO: No, no one.
FABIO: How! No one? I know it.
FEDERICO: You?
FABIO: Certainly.
FEDERICO: Speak then... Why are you waiting?
ENRIQUE: Hurry up.
FABIO: You'll keep the secret?
ENRIQUE: ⎫
FEDERICO: ⎭ Yes.
FABIO: Well, know then the cause of her illness...
FEDERICO: Don't hesitate.
ENRIQUE: Finish!
FABIO: Yes, the cause is that she has fallen in love with
     me; she's afraid of my indifference, and doesn't dare to
     confess her feelings.
FEDERICO: Idiot! Be off.

ENRIQUE: Leave us, you fool!
FABIO: Well, on my word, if it's not that, it must be some-
     thing else.
ENRIQUE: The company is returning.
FEDERICO: Then please retire. I want to mingle with the
     crowd so that my absence remains unnoticed. Besides, I
     wouldn't for my life lose the opportunity of speaking to
     one of these ladies.
ENRIQUE: I've no intention of inconveniencing you — far from
     it. I'll leave and speak with her later. After seeing
     her miraculous beauty, I'm curious to enjoy her wit.
     The stratagem we thought of last night, which consists
     of having written this letter, acting as my own secre-
     tary, will be a means to speak with her. And now that
     I'm near her, I'd like to know if it is really true that
     fortune favors the brave.
                                                      [Exit]

FEDERICO: *[Aside]* I'm in a strange embarrassment: If I
        reveal
     Who is the Duke, then I betray his secret.
     If I am silent, I betray the faith
     I owe the Duchess, of whom I am the servant,
     The vassal, and the kinsman. What shall I do?
     Why hesitate? Was not my duty fixed
     Before the trust which he reposed on me?
     And yet, if I should lose the Duke's protection
     I lose all hope of finding in his house
     The refuge of my love, as soon as Laura...
     What do I say? May that last word return
     Into my bosom, to be buried there;
     I seem to offend her even by uttering
     Her very name.
FABIO: Señor, who then is this guest who arrived last night
     in disguise and who now avoids showing himself, and even
     goes into hiding?
FEDERICO: It is one of my friends to whom I have all kinds
     of obligations.
FABIO: Were they intimate ones? But, after all, why should
     I meddle with it. Whatever happens, he will be welcome.
     At the very least, we shall dine better during his vis-
     it. For if it is boring to stand on ceremony at bed,
     it's a mark of good taste to do it at board.
FEDERICO: They're coming back, Fabio. Be silent!

     [Reenter DUCHESS and her retinue]

FLORA: *[Singing]* If you adore the fair,
     Despite unworthiness,
     Never your pain express,
     But, silent, learn to bear.

> Accuse your hostile star
> And not her waywardness.
> Do not commit that treason,
> Nor think you've lost your reason.

FLÉRIDA: Whose are the words?
FEDERICO: They are mine, señora.
FLÉRIDA: I've noticed that in all these songs of yours,
> You still complain of love.
FEDERICO: It is because
> I have no fortune.
FLÉRIDA: What does fortune matter
> In things of love.
FEDERICO: It matters for desert:
> And so you see that I bewail my lot,
> Not in my love, but since I lack desert.
FLÉRIDA: What! Federico, do you love a lady
> So little worthy that she lets herself
> Be guided by self-interest?
FEDERICO: It is not she
> Who pays attention to my poverty.
FLÉRIDA: Who does, then?
FEDERICO: I.
FLÉRIDA: But why?
FEDERICO: Because it stops me
> From telling of my love, not so much to her,
> Nor to her parents, nor her family,
> But to her servants, for I know too well
> That when a lover comes without a gift
> He cannot ask for anything himself.
FLÉRIDA: A lover who has not obtained, can yet
> Reveal the object of his love; for if
> He admits his ill success, he does not fail
> In the respect he owes her. So I wonder,
> That loving, Federico, unrewarded,
> You do not yet confide in anyone
> The object of your love.
FEDERICO: It seems to me,
> That I should guard the secret in this way,
> Since I've resolved a thousand times, señora,
> To say no more about it, lest my feelings
> Should thus escape me; and my love appears
> So sacred to me, that I watch the air
> And hardly let it enter in my breast;
> For even the air is suspect, and I'm unwilling
> That it should come to know whose is the image
> I bear with so much mystery in my heart.
FLÉRIDA: Enough, enough; all that is foolishness
> And affectation. How, in speaking to me,
> Do you talk thus of your love? Do you forget

Who I am?
FEDERICO: Whose fault is it, señora?
  You asked me, and I answered.
FLÉRIDA: You replied
  To things I had not asked. Arnesto!
ARNESTO: Señora.
FLÉRIDA: See that Federico's brought at once...
FEDERICO: *[Aside]*   I'm lost!
FLÉRIDA: Two thousand ducats, so that he can win
  The favor of his lady's retinue
  I do not wish that, through his lack of courage,
  He speaks again to me as he has done,
  So timorous with her, so bold with me.
FLORA: *[Aside to LIVIA]* Her melancholy humor carries her
  From one extreme to the other.
LIVIA: *[Aside to LAURA]*   I've never seen her
  In such a humor.
LAURA: *[Aside]*   Unhappily for me,
  I've hit upon the cause that none else knows.
FEDERICO: A thousand times I humbly kiss the earth
  On which you tread, and where your charming feet
  Have made to spring more flowers than April can.
FABIO: As for me, señora, I would not dare to kiss the earth
  on which you tread, for that is not the earth but heaven
  itself. I will content myself by kissing the ground on
  which you are about to tread. Which way do you intend
  to go? I'll go before you to kiss the road.

  [Enter LISARDO]

LISARDO: Señora,
  A gallant gentleman who calls himself
  A kinsman of the Duke of Mantua,
  Asks for permission to deliver to you
  A letter from the Duke.
FLÉRIDA: Ah! How the Duke
  Wearies me with his messages!
ARNESTO: And why, señora,
  Since by his rank the Duke is the one man
  You could accept?
FLÉRIDA: For the simple reason, sir,
  Marriage is hateful to me. Let him approach,
  Lisardo.
FEDERICO: *[Aside]* I'll not betray him. It is important
  For me to keep his friendship.

  [Enter ENRIQUE]

ENRIQUE: Distressed, señora,
  I throw myself at your feet, where my misfortunes
  Would like to find a refuge.

FLÉRIDA: Rise.
ENRIQUE: The Duke,
     My lord, has sent me to you with this letter.
FLÉRIDA: How is His Highness?
ENRIQUE: I would answer, señora,
     That he is dead of love, but hope revives him.
FLÉRIDA: Do not stay kneeling while I read the letter.
ENRIQUE: *[Rising, aside]* The painter who has tried to make
          her likeness
     Was far from flattering her. She's much more lovely
     Even than her portrait.
LISARDO: *[Aside to ARNESTO]* Señor, my father's sent
     The marriage settlement.
ARNESTO: *[Aside]*   I'm glad it's come.
FLORA: Laura, how smart the gentleman is
     Who's brought the letter.
LAURA: I didn't notice him.
FLORA: I'm not surprised at it — your cousin's here.
     You know how he adores you, and that Arnesto
     Treats of your marriage with him, and you'd show
     Little esteem if you should pay attention
     To another man.
LAURA: And yet it's not my cousin
     Who now distracts me and disquiets me.
FEDERICO: *[Aside]* While the Duchess reads her letter, and
          Arnesto
     Talks with Lisardo, may Love give me boldness!
     [To LAURA] What of the letter?
LAURA: *[To FEDERICO]*   I've just written it.
FEDERICO: How can you give it me?
LAURA: Haven't you a glove?
FEDERICO: Yes.
LAURA: Well, by that means you could...
FEDERICO: I understand.
ARNESTO: *[To LISARDO]* That's very good.
LISARDO: Laura, my love, my hope,
     Each moment we're unwed will seem a year.
FLÉRIDA: *[To ENRIQUE]* The Duke informs me in this letter,
          señor,
     That you're his nearest kinsman, and that he wishes
     That you should stay away from Mantua,
     Until he's solved a problem which concerns you,
     About a duel which Love cast upon you.
ENRIQUE: It's true that Love has caused my only crime
     And brought me here.
FLÉRIDA: Both for your own sake, señor,
     And for the Duke's, I offer my protection,
     And so you can remain here at my court.
     I shall reply immediately to the Duke,

And send my letter to him.
ENRIQUE: Heaven preserve you
   For ever and ever, and may the noble vassals
   Of the Duke of Mantua soon rejoice at...
FLÉRIDA: Do not say more, and let me warn you now,
   During the time I have you as my guest
   You must not speak to me upon this subject
   Unless I ask you.
ENRIQUE: You shall be obeyed.
FLÉRIDA: And so that in your letters you can tell
   The Duke what are my pastimes — for no doubt
   You are instructed so — sit down, my ladies,
   While that the sun half hidden by thick clouds
   Seems now to spy on us, and you, my lords
   Stand on this side; and you, Arnesto, now
   Suggest a subject for debate.
      [The ladies sit on one side, the gentlemen stand on
      the other]
ARNESTO: Señora,
   My white hairs could excuse my taking part
   In such a game; but never mind, I'm glad
   To contribute to your pleasures. This is the question:
   "What is the greatest pain in love."
FLÉRIDA: *[To ENRIQUE]*   You, señor,
   Shall answer first.
ENRIQUE: I, señora?
FLÉRIDA: Yes,
   Because you are a guest here.
ENRIQUE: By that title
   I have an advantage: and to seek to show
   I'm not unworthy of it, I haste to answer
   And say the greatest pain — the one I suffer —
   Is not to be beloved.
FLORA: And I say rather
   That it is not to love.
LISARDO: It's jealousy.
LIVIA: It's absence.
FEDERICO: It is hopeless love.
FLÉRIDA: And I —
   To love and bear one's suffering in silence,
   Unable to explain.
LAURA: And I: To love
   In being loved.
FLÉRIDA: That's a new thesis, Laura,
   That it is bad to have one's love returned.
LAURA: I hope to demonstrate it in a moment.
ARNESTO: Now each one prove his thesis.
ENRIQUE: Since I spoke first,
   In speaking of the pain of him who's scorned,

I will begin.

FABIO: *[Aside]*   Now listen! It is here
That even the wittiest utter foolishness.

ENRIQUE: Love is a star, whose influence gives to us
Happiness or misfortune. Then it follows
Love's greatest pain is loving in despite
Of its decree. The man who lives disdained
By a proud beauty, loves against his star;
So that must be the greatest grief of all
For he who is disdained loves in despite
Of the will of heaven.

FLORA: When a lover's scorned,
That will become for him a future merit,
For suffering for his love. But he who scorns,
And does not love, suffers without deserving
That this should be counted unto him as merit.
Then he who's scorned is not so much to be pitied,
As he who scorns.

LISARDO: The one who's been disdained,
And one who's scorned at least they bear a harm
Which came from heaven, but not the one who suffers
From jealousy, since this is born of envy
Of one more happy. Therefore his grief is greater,
For the same difference as between man and heaven
Exists between those two and he who's jealous.

LIVIA: It has been seen a thousand times that love
Is brought by jealousy to its fruition
But not by absence. Absence has been called
The death of love. So it's the strongest pain.
Because if jealousy revives the flame,
And absence quenches it, the first is life,
The second, death.

FEDERICO: One who loves though scorned,
One who is loved and scorns, one who suffers
From jealousy, and one who weeps for absence,
All these can bear their sorrow in the hope
Their state will change. And therefore all this proves
That the worst torment is that of the man
Who loves without a hope.

FLÉRIDA: The man who loves
Without a hope can say at least he has none,
And from that gains relief; but he who's bound
To hold his tongue and keep his love in secret,
Must suffer so much more of grief and pain,
Who cannot even say he has no hope.

LAURA: The one who loves and finds his love returned
Lives in continual unquietness,
For sometimes in his happiness he fears
A future moment when he'll be unhappy;

And, thinking himself deprived of what he loves,
Begins to hate it. And therefore he who is loved
Suffers as much as he who is disdained,
And the same anger as the one who scorns.
And as for jealousy, I call heaven to witness
That he's not free of it, though self-begotten,
For if he's separated for a moment
From his beloved, it seems a hundred years.
So even the happiest experience both
The pangs of jealousy, the grief of absence.
Has he not hope? His very happiness
Will answer No — for how should he have hope
When he has nothing more for which to hope?
At the same time he suffers from his silence,
Since he cannot express the wondrous joy
Which he can feel; and so the one who's loved
Endures the sadness of a lack of hope,
And also the sorrow of enforced silence.
But could one say that he is not unhappy
Because he is aware of being loved?
No, no, he feels continually the threat
Of being loved no longer. That is why
He suffers in himself as many pains
As one who's scorned and one who gives the scorn
And one who's separated from his love,
As one who has no hope, as one who's jealous,
And as the one who may not tell his love.[3]
    [All the ladies rise]
FLÉRIDA: All these are merely paradoxes, Laura,
    In which you wanted to display your wit;
    But yet, when all is said, they're not convincing.
LAURA: But how could they be otherwise. The aim
    Of love is to be loved...
    [She drops her glove]
FLÉRIDA: Your glove.
FEDERICO: Let me.
ARNESTO: Stop, señor.
LISARDO: It is for me to pick it up.
FEDERICO: If I'd intended to walk off with it,
    I'd do it still — but that was not my plan,
    Señor Lisardo, so we need not quarrel.
    There is no merit in arriving first,
    It's only luck. See, I restore her glove
    To Laura. *[Gives Laura a glove like the one she has*
        dropped] Here, señora. I'm already
    Rewarded for my promptness, for I serve you
    Without offending you.
LISARDO: Your wit has saved me
    From an awkward situation.[4]

FLÉRIDA: As for me,
   I'm equally displeased with both of you.
   It is audacious, in my very presence
   To pick up the most trivial thing that's dropped
   By one of my ladies. You should give me thanks
   That I refrain from showing further anger,
   And that, for this time, I content myself
   With this expression of my discontent.
   [Aside] O heaven, protect me! I am the first woman
   Whom ever silence killed.
      [Exit FLÉRIDA, followed by all her ladies except LAURA]
ARNESTO: Her royal highness
   Has left in a bad humor — and certainly
   She had no reason. Do not follow her
   To her apartments, Laura: come back to ours.
   I know her character, and so foresaw
   The trials which would follow when I took
   The post of chancellor and a palace lodging;
   And I would not have had you in her service,
   Save it's our duty.
LAURA: I must obey you, señor,
   In everything. *[Aside]* This outburst of the Duchess
   Is most revealing. May it be love's will
   That it is not what I suspect.
        *[As ARNESTO and LAURA retire, all the gentlemen
        follow]*
ARNESTO: Where are you going,
   Gentlemen?
FEDERICO: We are prepared to serve you.
ARNESTO: Go no further. *[To LISARDO]* You, nephew, set the
      example.
LISARDO: Regretfully, I obey.
ENRIQUE: *[Aside]*   And I, with all my heart —
   For like the heliotrope I turn my face
   Toward the brightest sunshine.
                        [Exeunt ARNESTO and LAURA]
                        Federico,
   I will return at once.
                  [Exit, in the same direction as FLÉRIDA]
LISARDO: Since I perceive
   Only that light which emanates from you,
   I cannot leave you, Laura; for your beauty
   Is my thought's polar star.
                  [Exit, in the same direction as LAURA]
FEDERICO: How I rejoice
   To be alone at last! I shall be able
   To read this letter.
FABIO: If I don't lose my wits now, it's because I've none
      to lose.

FEDERICO: Why are you surprised?
FABIO: At your coolness. For you've had this letter since
   last night, and yet you haven't opened it.
FEDERICO: Do you know which this letter is?
FABIO: What you will — it is nonetheless certain that you've
   kept it since yesterday without opening it.
FEDERICO: I've only just received it.
FABIO: You'll make me mad. Don't I know that since this
   morning, no one has visited you? Has the wind brought
   it to you?
FEDERICO: What brought it to me was the fire — the fire in
   which I burn.
FABIO: The fire?
FEDERICO: Yes.
FABIO: I begin to believe now that it's true...
FEDERICO: What is true?
FABIO: That you are mad, and that, gallant ghost, you have
   created a spectral lady who dwells in your mind, and
   whom you love mentally.[5] So I'd beg you to grant me one
   favor.
FEDERICO: What favor?
FABIO: That since it's a lady who lives in your imagination,
   without having more soul or body than you've wished to
   give her, that at least her letters should be full of
   love and tenderness; for it would be too annoying if she
   could treat you with kindness, yet treats you with
   scorn.
FEDERICO: Move away.
FABIO: Come, the writing's not important.
FEDERICO: That's true, if the handwriting is disguised — but
   yet, move off.
FABIO: I'm truly a valet of purgatory, for I live in a place
   between paradise and hell.
FEDERICO: *[Reading]* "My dear señor, my misfortune over-
   whelms me. My father forces my consent. Despite my
   wishes, he is treating of my marriage, and he will sign
   the settlement tomorrow." *[Aside]* Ah! unhappy that I
   am, I've only a little while to live — from now until
   tomorrow. Fabio!
FABIO: What is it?
FEDERICO: I'm going to die soon.
FABIO: You would be making a mistake, if you can avoid it,
   for, I assure you, it's a tasteless thing to do.[6]
FEDERICO: How avoid it, when this letter is my sentence of
   death?
FABIO: Very easily. Since the letter is in your hand,
   you've only to add a little P.S. which is a bit more
   humane.
FEDERICO: *[Aside]* Although deprived of life and soul, let

me continue. *[Reading]* "And so, although I should expose by it the secret of our unlucky love, it is very
necessary that I should talk with you tonight about what
is to be done. Consequently the window facing the garden will be opened, and rather than lose you, I will
lose my life. For that commitment all I ask is that you
give me a fair exchange for that portrait I gave you the
other day." *[Aside]* Was ever man more happy? Fabio!
Fabio!

FABIO: What is it now? Not dying then?

FEDERICO: On the contrary, I'm alive and full of joy.

FABIO: There you are! Didn't I give you good advice?
There's nothing like loving oneself.

FEDERICO: Proud and joyful, I can speak tonight
With the beauty whom I love. O radiant sun,
Who like the brilliant conqueror of heaven
Moves slowly in your proud triumphal march,
Deign to cut short this day your normal course,
On hearing how your light brings misery
To one poor mortal! And you potent stars,
Who wield so great an influence over love,
Rise now against the sun's usurping sway,
Establish new republics in the sky,
Because the sun has misconceived his rights,
And seized a power which is yours alone.[7]

[Exit]

FABIO: He is as foolish as all the fools put together. But
what amazes me most is not so much seeing him foolish,
as seeing myself so idiotic that I cannot...

[Enter FLORA]

FLORA: Fabio?

FABIO: What would you, señora?

FLORA: Follow me.

FABIO: If it's for a duel, give me a moment while I go and
find four or five of my friends.

FLORA: Follow me.

FABIO: Why? Tell me first, are you the lady who gives me
jealousy, or am I the gallant who gives you nothing?[8]

FLORA: It is Her Highness who wishes to speak with you.
Just now she was busy writing, and she instructed me to
come and find you.

FABIO: Her Highness wishes to speak to *me!* By heaven, what
if she were to risk declaring her love for me?

Scene 2: A Room in the Palace

[Enter FLÉRIDA, holding a letter]

FLÉRIDA: Flora, have you summoned the valet?
FLORA: Here he is, señora.
FLÉRIDA: Well, wait for me without.

[Exit FLORA]

We are alone now.
FABIO: Yes, señora, and you won't find me ungrateful. I
   would like to know in what way I can serve you, and you
   can speak without fear, for I am the most serviceable
   man in the world. You won't have any great difficulty
   in obtaining from me what you desire.[9]
FLÉRIDA: It is necessary, Fabio, that you should tell me
   something I ought to know. It belongs to my authority
   as Duchess to be enlightened on it.
FABIO: If I can, there will be no difficulty; for if you
   have a desire to know it, I have a still greater desire
   to tell you.
FLÉRIDA: Take this chain.
FABIO: With great pleasure... It is valuable in my eyes because it comes from you...and also because it is made of
   gold. Question me, señora. I'm longing to speak.
FLÉRIDA: Which is the lady Federico loves?
FABIO: I'm a very unlucky gossip, señora. I'm ignorant of
   the one thing you ask me.
FLÉRIDA: How disturbing! [Aloud] How is it possible that
   you should not know it, since you never leave your master?
FABIO: How do you expect me to know it, when he doesn't know
   it himself?
FLÉRIDA: His passion cannot be so secret.
FABIO: Well, in that case, señora, tell me what it is, and
   I'll give you your chain. In fact, he doesn't confide
   in anyone: he laughs alone and weeps alone. If he gets
   a letter, one doesn't see who gives it him; and if he
   answers it, one doesn't know to whom he writes. It was
   today that I learned most about his love; for after
   reading a letter that Barabbas must have brought him in
   person, he said that a divine beauty was awaiting him
   tonight to speak with him.
FLÉRIDA: What! He is to talk with his lady tonight?
FABIO: Yes, unless they have a lovers' tiff before.
FLÉRIDA: [Aside] What torture! I'm in agony. [Aloud] You
   should at least know the house or the street where this
   lady lives?
FABIO: Yes, I know that. She lives at the palace.
FLÉRIDA: How do you know that?

FABIO: By deduction. He loves without inconstancy; he
   adores without hope; he woos without desire; he re-
   joices without a reason; and, lastly, he scribbles night
   and day in an immense portfolio. Now aren't all these
   the follies one sees only at the palace?[10]

FLÉRIDA: Well, listen to my instructions. You will do your
   best to discover who the lady is; from today you will
   observe his behavior as well as you can; and, if you notice anything new in it, come and find me. From this
   moment I authorize you to present yourself before me
   whenever you like.

FABIO: Thanks to this favor, I become what is called, if I'm
   not mistaken, a gentleman of the chamber.

FLÉRIDA: And lest you should ever forget what will bring you
   profit or loss, expect from me all profit, Fabio, if you
   serve me well, and equally all loss, if you ever decide
   to reveal this conversation to anyone.

FABIO: Believe me, señora, that I shall be the dumbest of
   the curious, if there are any curious who are also dumb.

FLÉRIDA: Leave me.

FABIO: Farewell, señora.

                                                   [Exit]

FLÉRIDA: O foolish thought! What a tyrannic rule
   You exercise, since you can take away
   Freedom of will. Well, do I so lack
   Faith in myself that I will yield the fight
   At the least fear? No, I'll conduct myself
   In a manner worthy of a valiant heart
   And of myself. But alas! I cannot hide
   My jealousy, and think that I do well
   That I can hide my love. What uncertainty!
   What torments! For this very night, I'll suffer
   A thousand tortures, while they are given up
   To joy and happiness! No, that shall not be...
   I acquiesce that they shall see each other
   Unknown to me; but now that I am warned
   About their meeting, it would be a blunder
   If I did not prevent them. Pity, pity
   Kind heaven! For, alas, I cannot hide
   My jealousy, and think that I do well
   That I can hide my love. But with this letter,
   Which I have written for another purpose...
   He's coming. I must hide my suffering.

[Enter FEDERICO, carrying writing materials]

FEDERICO: Your Highness,
   I bring the letters for your signature.

FLÉRIDA: *[Aside]* Courage, intelligence, greatness of soul —
   Now all are needful to me. *[Aloud]* Put those letters

On one side, Federico. I will sign them later.
First, you must serve me in another thing
Which is of great importance to me now.
FEDERICO: What is it, señora?
FLÉRIDA: I desire you
This very night to make a little journey.
FEDERICO: Tonight?
FLÉRIDA: Yes.
FEDERICO: *[Aside]*   What a disaster!
FLÉRIDA: There is the letter I want you to deliver.
FEDERICO: You know, señora, with what eagerness
And zeal I'm always ready to employ me
Upon your service. Therefore, I believe
That for today the fact that I'm not well
Allows me for this once to make excuse,
And that...
FLÉRIDA: I admit no excuse. You'll not be absent long.
You will return tomorrow. Understand,
I beg you, that I am entrusting to you
The care of my very honor. Say no more.
Take now this letter and prepare to leave
Immediately. I tell you once again
It is essential that this letter should
Be carried by yourself. The address will tell you
To whom it must be taken. You will bring me
The answer. Adieu.

[Exit]

FEDERICO: O Heaven! In that same night
When beauteous Laura has permitted me
To speak with her, O will there not be found
But one auspicious star? What's to be done?
How reconcile my love and loyalty?

[Enter FABIO]

FABIO: Señor, doesn't it seem to you that the day is very
    long?
FEDERICO: It was the devil brought you here. Go at once,
    Fabio, and saddle two horses.
FABIO: Has another letter come, brought either by the fire
    or the air?
FEDERICO: Yes, another letter has come.
FABIO: Well, you have only to make a small correction and
    you'll be as delighted as you were this morning. Read
    it again, and you'll cease to complain.
FEDERICO: I've not yet read even the address.
FABIO: Read it, to see if it differs with what you first
    suspected.
FEDERICO: I shall see only where I'm being sent. *[Reads]*
    "To the Duke of Mantua." Here's another problem.

Doubtless she has recognized the Duke, and she wishes to
inform me in this way that she knows that I've been
guilty of a kind of treachery by receiving him as a
guest. Indeed, didn't she tell me sharply that her hon-
or was involved? O foolish thought! I escape from one
danger only to fall into another.
FABIO: Have you emended it?
FEDERICO: The more I think of it, the less I understand.
FABIO: Is it in cipher?
FEDERICO: What a puzzle!
FABIO: Is she, perhaps, like the man in the story?
FEDERICO: How do I know?
FABIO: Well, if you don't know it, this is the story. Once
upon a time, an inhabitant of Tremecén, a glazier by
trade, was paying court to a lady. He had a close
friend who lived at Tetuán. Now one day the lady begged
her suitor to write to his friend to send him a monkey;
and as a lover is always ready to comply with the desires of his lady, this one asked for three or four so
that she could choose one to her taste. Now you must
know that the silly fellow wrote three or four in figures; and as in Spanish the "O" is equivalent to "or" as
well as zero, our friend in Tetuán read thus: "My dear
friend, so that I can give pleasure to a person who is
dear to me, send me without delay 304 monkeys." The man
of Tetuán at first found it difficult to find what he
was asked; but the glazier was in a still greater fix
when at the end of some days he saw arrive with a great
hullabaloo before his fragile shop three hundred monkeys, plus three hundred thousand monkey-tricks. If the
same thing happens to you, read without the naught; for
it's plain, after this story, that one monkey in writing
can mean 100 monkeys in figures.
FEDERICO: To give me the letter at this moment! She must
have found me out.
FABIO: Can't you have fewer monkeys?
FEDERICO: Was ever a man in such uncertainty?

[Enter ENRIQUE]

ENRIQUE: What have you there?
FEDERICO: *[Aside]*   I know not what to do.
    [Aloud] May I have a word with you in private?
FABIO: *[Aside]* I can't stand that! To distrust me! Has
one ever seen a guest whispering like that?
FEDERICO: What course shall we pursue?
ENRIQUE: Go to your house;
We can talk there, and the letter itself will tell us
What we must do. If we see that she knows,
Of my disguise, well, my reply will be

To throw it off. If, on the contrary,
She seems without suspicion, I'll reply
This evening to her letter, and tomorrow
You'll take her my reply.
FEDERICO: You have said well:
And if my only gain from this arrangement
Is not to be obliged to leave tonight,
It's worth the pains it's cost me. Acting thus,
I shall not fail in loyalty. Since the letter
Is meant for you, it is enough for me
To give it you, no matter where you are.
ENRIQUE: We shall see clearly when we read the letter
The Duchess's intention. Let us go.
          [ENRIQUE and FEDERICO move off]
FABIO: Must I keep the horses ready, señor?
FEDERICO: Yes, Fabio; for, even if I don't depart, it's im-
portant for people to believe that I have gone.
FABIO: Why, in fact, are you so joyful?
FEDERICO: Love is more discreet than you would wish.
FABIO: You seem happy now.
FEDERICO: Does that surprise you?
FABIO: Not at all, for I know why.
FEDERICO: Why is it?
FABIO: Simply that you have understood the cipher, and that
you've not been asked for so many monkeys after all.
                                        [Exeunt]

Scene 3: A Room in the Palace, and the Terrace Outside

    [Enter LAURA]

LAURA: Ah! how the day before a longed-for hour
    Is slow to disappear. But now at last
    Day yields to night, which like a great black bird
    Deploys his wings above us bringing darkness.
    Ah! Federico, if our hour of meeting
    Were come already, how my deadly grief
    Would find both consolation and relief!
    But what can mean the Duchess's strange behavior
    By which she sought to hide some secret trouble?
    I'm going to show myself in her apartments
    Before I keep my rendezvous outside,
    To which I'm summoned both by grief and love.
    This will have two advantages — the first
    Is that she will not think to look for me;
    The second, that I will distract my thoughts.
    If company does not cut short the hours,
    At least it sometimes makes them seem less long.

[Enter FLÉRIDA and FLORA. FLORA carries lights]

FLÉRIDA: Laura, my cousin, why throughout the day
  Have I not seen you? Surely my friendship for you
  Did not deserve such usage?
LAURA: I thank you, señora,
  For being pleased to notice I was absent.
  A trifling accident kept me at home;
  And though I'm still not feeling very well,
  I did not wish, señora, to retire
  Without kissing your hand; and I came, too,
  To find out how you were.
FLÉRIDA: I'm very sorry
  It was your health which caused you to be absent,
  But I rejoice that you have come to see me,
  Although a little late. I've need of you,
  And I am keeping you with me for tonight.
LAURA: But yet consider, señora...
FLÉRIDA: What do you wish
  I should consider? Have you not out of friendship
  Stayed with me for a thousand times or more?
  Stay once to oblige me. It concerns a secret
  I can entrust to you alone.
LAURA: *[Aside]*   How vexing!
  If I object, it will arouse suspicion.
  O heaven, help me!
FLÉRIDA: What do you say?
LAURA: That I am yours, and ever at your service.
FLÉRIDA: *[To FLORA]* Leave us alone.
          [Exit FLORA]
      Now, Laura, listen to me.
  I have discovered — I don't know how to tell you —
  Discovered that a gentleman of the court
  Has just received a letter from a lady
  Giving a rendezvous for this very night.
LAURA: *[Aside]* What do I hear?
FLÉRIDA: I know the gentleman,
  But not the lady yet.
LAURA: *[Aside]*   So much the better!
FLÉRIDA: Now I am anxious, Laura, to discover
  Which of my ladies will presume to speak,
  From one of the terrace windows, with a man,
  Thus failing in her duty both to me
  And to the Court.
LAURA: You will do well, señora.
  Such conduct is audacious!
FLÉRIDA: It would not be
  Seemly or proper that I myself should go
  To keep watch on the terrace. And so, my dear,
  As, when I think of all my ladies, you

Are the only one of whom I've never had
A breath of suspicion, it is you alone
That I will trust.
LAURA: What do you ask?
FLÉRIDA: I wish
That every hour this night, nay, every moment,
You go down to the garden, like a sentry
Watching over my honor; that you try
To recognize the lady who betrays it.
And do not think my only motive, Laura,
Is to maintain propriety — I wish
Also — I wish above all — to know which lady
It is, who favors Federico... *[Aside]* Ah!
Imprudent as I am, I've named him now!
But no matter!
That, cousin, is the service I expect.
LAURA: Your orders are enough. With the desire
I have to comply with you in everything,
And to do anything I can to please you,
It will not be enough for me to go
A thousand times, at intervals, to the garden.
I'll stay there all the night, and I'll be happy
In saying it's for you.
FLÉRIDA: You are my cousin,
And my friend too. As you're intelligent
And prudent, I entrust to you my honor
And my heart's secrets. Do as you wish,
And I will lend approval.

                                                [Exit]

LAURA: God protect me now!
How many things are crowding in my mind!
So mingled that I don't know which of them
I first should think on. But why need I worry?
It will be better not to think at all
But wait till I can talk with Federico.
I shall soon gather by his voice and words
If he's devoted to me, or betrays me.

    Scene 4: The Palace Garden. To one side an expanse
        of wall with a window, shuttered and barred

LAURA: Delicious garden, April's fertile realm,
    Which recognizes only him as god
    And king of springtime, I was used to come
    To your fresh-smelling lawns, and I entrusted
    Unto your fountains and your fragrant flowers
    The secret of my love. Now I'm reluctant

And overwhelmed with sadness to discover
Which is the traitress who has touched my heart
With venomous jealousy.
            [A noise is heard outside the grille]
                              Someone has given
The signal in the street. O how I tremble!
But why am I afraid, since jealousy
Is my companion? Who is there?
            [She opens the shutters]
            [FEDERICO appears at the grille]
FEDERICO: What need to ask,
    Beloved Laura? Do you wish that doubt
    Should banish trust? Who could it be but me?
LAURA: Don't be astonished, and do not complain
    That I've not recognized you, since you are
    So different from the one I had imagined.
FEDERICO: How so?
LAURA: The Duchess has commanded me
    To stand close to this window to observe
    With whom you come to speak; and I concluded
    That you had lacked discretion and that she
    Suspects our love.
FEDERICO: In heaven's name, dear Laura,
    Do not suspect me so. May heaven destroy me,
    May thunder blast me if I have allowed
    The slightest word to escape me which could show
    My secret to a soul! Is it not enough
    To undeceive you, to think it was to you
    The Duchess gave this mission? How indeed
    Could she have meant you to stay there to meet me
    When she believed me absent?
LAURA: On one point,
    Federico, you are justified;
    But what will you say, I wonder, when you learn
    That Flérida is anxious to discover
    Who is the lady that you love?
FEDERICO: Suppose
    She has such an anxiety — a thing
    I hardly credit — that would be because
    Of her feelings for me, not for royal pique.
    And then what follows? That the victory
    Which you have won is yet more glorious —
    Although there is no real victory
    When there has been no enemy to vanquish.
    But my complaints have more substantial cause.
    Here there is not appearance, but the truth;
    For, after all, you're marrying.
LAURA: It's not I,
    But my misfortune.

FEDERICO: Who loves well, 'tis said,
  Can overcome all obstacles.
LAURA: 'Tis true.
  But also, who loves well has all to fear.
FEDERICO: Why did you write, then, that you'd rather die
  Than lose me, asking me to bring my portrait
  In exchange for yours.
LAURA: There was not then, Federico,
  The problem of Flérida.
FEDERICO: What a reason
  To give me! Ah! But if your resolution
  Is taken already, why do you waste your time
  And words with me. There is my portrait, Laura,
  Which I have brought, no doubt, to be the witness
  Of the sitter's jealousy. As for the setting,
  It is the same as of the one you sent me,
  When Fortune smiled on me. I could not give you
  An equal treasure, but I wished at least
  That it should have an equal setting. Take it.
  I charge you only, if you marry him,
  Beware of it, for painting as it is,
  It will not stand to be affronted by you.
LAURA: Me,
  Federico?... But look! I hear the sound
  Of people in the street.
FEDERICO: Ah! Laura, you
  Were probably going to tell me something pleasant,
  For you've been interrupted.
LAURA: I was about to tell you
  That I was yours forever...and I say it.
FEDERICO: Then come who will! But no, they've turned the
        corner.
LAURA: Yet, Federico, I must shut the window;
  And I'll content myself with warning you
  That we are spied upon.
FEDERICO: It should be easy
  To hoodwink this surveillance.
LAURA: By what means?
FEDERICO: Tomorrow I will bring a letter to you
  By means of which we can converse aloud
  Before them all — and no one will suspect.
LAURA: That will be, then, a *secret spoken aloud*.
FEDERICO: Only make certain that you are alone
  When you read the letter.
LAURA: Very well. God keep you!
FEDERICO: May heaven prolong your life, beloved Laura!
LAURA: O Love, how dear the price I have to pay!
FEDERICO: Laura, do not forget the love you owe me!
                                        [Exeunt]

ꐠꐠꐠ

ACT TWO

Scene 1: A Room in the Palace

*[Enter FEDERICO and FABIO in traveling clothes
and ENRIQUE]*

ENRIQUE: Believe me, Federico,
 Flérida's letter had no hidden purpose;
 It merely answers mine: and if she told you
 To bring it me in person, that would give it
 Greater authority. As I brought the other —
 I who am thought to be the Duke's own kinsman —
 She will have deemed it proper to entrust you
 With the answer to it. So there is no reason
 To fear she knows me; and, in my opinion,
 The wisest plan is the one you've formed already —
 Seem to return from Mantua and hand her
 This letter of mine; and when she sees my seal
 And writing, by these means she will not doubt
 That you have made the journey.
FEDERICO: I realize,
 Perfectly, señor, the rightness of your words;
 And, in addition, this letter reassures me.
 She does not know your true identity,
 Yet as the Duchess wished me far away,
 To break my rendezvous, and as my lady
 Informed me that Her Highness was aware
 Of feelings which might be an obstacle
 To her own chances, I am bound to feel
 A certain sadness.
ENRIQUE: We will talk of that
 At a more convenient time. But for the moment
 Here is the letter. We must dissipate
 The first suspicions. We'll have time for the rest.
 Take it, Federico, and farewell.
FEDERICO: Will you return soon to the palace, señor?
ENRIQUE: Of course if it contains — as it does indeed —
 The realm, the sphere, the center of my soul,
 Living outside is life on sufferance.
               [Exit]
FABIO: *[Grumbling]* How can an honorable man put up with it?
FEDERICO: What are you complaining of, Fabio?
FABIO: I complain of nothing. But reckon up, señor, the
 amount owed for the time I have served you; for even if
 you were to give me by the hour what you do not give me
 by the year, I swear before God that I would refuse to
 serve you an hour longer.

FEDERICO: Why?
FABIO: Because my head is so full of reflections that it's
    bursting; and there's not enough money in the world to
    pay a valet who reflects — above all, on so many affairs
    so diverse as yours.
FEDERICO: What do you mean?
FABIO: This. "Fabio, I'm dying. Fabio, my hope has but an
    hour to live." "Well, señor, I go to organize your fu-
    neral." "Stay, I'll not die. I'm reborn; and this dark
    night smiles on me like the brightest day." "Congratu-
    lations, señor." "Fabio." "Señor." "I must leave at
    once. Saddle two horses without delay." "The horses
    are ready." "Now I'm not leaving after all, but bring
    the horses and mount one." "There I am in the saddle."
    "How far have we ridden?" "A league." "Well, let's re-
    turn." "So be it." "Good." And then: "Go back to the
    house; don't follow me." And so many annoying things,
    little mysteries and little secrets, that the devil him-
    self would lose himself in them. As for me, I don't
    wish to serve any longer a master who, without being
    Pope, has so many reserved judgments.
FEDERICO: Hold your tongue. There's Her Highness. And re-
    member, once again, that no one must ever know that I
    have not left Parma this night.
FABIO: Certainly. *[Aside]* I'm bursting to speak, and I
    will speak for three reasons. First, to regale this
    tongue of mine; second, to avenge me on my master; and
    third, to render service to the Duchess.
        [FEDERICO and FABIO retire to one side]

    [Enter FLÉRIDA and LAURA]

FLÉRIDA: So, Laura, you assure me no one came
    Last night into the garden?
LAURA: How many times
    Must I repeat it?
FLÉRIDA: Only once again.
LAURA: Oh, well, señora, I repeat once more
    That I remained there till the dawn appeared,
    Covering the flowers with mocking pearls of dew,
    And I saw no one; so you can suspect
    No one in all the world, excepting me.
FLÉRIDA: I've other suspicions, Laura.
LAURA: What are those?
FLÉRIDA: That the lady was informed of the departure
    Of Federico, and in consequence
    Did not go down into the garden — but,
    No matter. I have still the consolation
    That last night I prevented them from meeting
    And talking with each other.

LAURA: That is true.
   [Aside] Ah! If she knew that in her jealousy
She was a go-between for these same lovers,
And brought about their meeting.
    [FEDERICO and FABIO come forward]
FEDERICO: Allow me, señora,
   To kiss your hand.
FLÉRIDA: What! Federico, back already?
FEDERICO: One travels fast, señora, when one has
   Due zeal and due devotion.
FABIO: Besides which,
   As it is but a league from here to Mantua...
FEDERICO: What did you say?
FABIO: Pardon — I am wrong.
   I meant to say that there are only a dozen.
FLÉRIDA: Do you bring a letter from the Duke?
FEDERICO: Indeed.
   I would not, surely, have returned without it.
FABIO: *[Aside]* I've never heard anyone lie with such casual
   impudence.
FEDERICO: There is the letter, señora.
FLÉRIDA: *[Aside]*   It is his writing:
   My plan succeeded.
FABIO: *[To FEDERICO]* Whose is this letter, señor?
FEDERICO: The Duke's.
FABIO: You want to fib to me as well?
FLÉRIDA: How did you fare last night?
FEDERICO: But... Oh! Señora,
   The loyal devotion which I feel for you
   Is so delighted to be thus employed
   Upon your service — this I do assure you —
   That I have never passed a better night.
FABIO: *[Aside]* I well believe it. Though he tries to dis-
   semble
   He cannot hide the truth.
LAURA: *[Aside]*   I see from his face
   The true sense of his words.
FLÉRIDA: *[Reading]* "Señora, I am very grateful to the kind-
   ness you have shown to Enrique, and not less for the
   honor you have done me in replying to me, and sending
   this reply by your secretary. It will be impossible for
   me to acquit myself of both the debts I have thus con-
   tracted, especially as my soul is already enslaved to
   you." The rest is off the point.
   Thank you, Federico, for the diligence
   With which you've managed to serve me.
FEDERICO: I am proud,
   And happy, señora, that I have been successful
   In doing so.

FLÉRIDA: No doubt you are fatigued.
   Go now and rest. Later, you shall return
   And I will sign those letters.
FEDERICO: Before I go,
   Permit me to deliver now to Laura
   This letter in your presence. I esteem
   A person in your service far too highly
   To give a message to her at a time
   Which might offend you.
FLÉRIDA: Whom is the letter from?
FEDERICO: I do not know. At the moment when we left,
   From the apartments of the Dowager
   A lady came out to entrust me with it.
   The lady must be one of her relations
   Or else one of her friends.
FABIO: *[Aside]*   The more I hear
   The more I'm stupefied.
LAURA: I recognize
   The handwriting, señora. It is Celia's,
   And, if you'll allow me, I'll retire to read it.
   [Aside] Till I've completely vanished from her sight
   I'll be more dead than alive.
FEDERICO: *[Aside to LAURA]*   Read it quickly.
LAURA: *[Aside to FEDERICO]* Never fear.
                                         [Exit]
FLÉRIDA: God be with you!
FEDERICO: Long live your royal Highness: may your days
   Be brilliant as the sun.
                                      [Exit]
FLÉRIDA: How glad I am
   To have deprived him of the opportunity
   For which his love had hoped! I have to fear
   New rendezvous, it's true, but being forewarned
   I'll work to prevent them.
FABIO: *[Aside]* If she goes on like this, she'll never get
   anywhere.
FLÉRIDA: Fabio?
FABIO: I was waiting to speak with you, señora, and while he
   was here I pretended to look at these pictures.
FLÉRIDA: Tell me, did your master show much grief during the
   journey at his absence from Parma?
FABIO: What absence?
FLÉRIDA: Last night's.
FABIO: What! Señora, you think he traveled last night?
FLÉRIDA: How could he not, since he brought me the Duke's
   answer, not merely sealed with his seal, but entirely in
   his own hand.
FABIO: Really? He left with me, but at the end of a league,
   or thereabouts, he returned with me.

FLÉRIDA: What are you saying?

FABIO: The truest truth in the world. He left me at home,
    ordered me, as he usually does, not to go out, and went
    out to amuse himself.

FLÉRIDA: It's not possible.

FABIO: If not to amuse himself, to be bored.

FLÉRIDA: Continue.

FABIO: In the morning he returned, and so joyful, so satis-
    fied,
    That one saw that he'd had what he wished.

FLÉRIDA: You're lying, you impudent fellow!

FABIO: He who lies, lies — as one says in duels.

FLÉRIDA: Who did he send in his place?

FABIO: No one.

FLÉRIDA: Then how did he get those letters?

FABIO: That wasn't so difficult! A man who has a demon who
    brings him messages and takes them back can also ask him
    to come and go with letters. My master must have a fa-
    miliar spirit, and in supposing this, I do not lie.

FLÉRIDA: I can't help believing that you are lying.

FABIO: You are hard to convince! Well, I swear to God that
    he didn't go, and that he spent all last night with his
    lady.

FLÉRIDA: Hold your tongue and go. Here is Laura; and to
    clear my mind of doubt, I would like to know about the
    letter he brought her.

FABIO: *[Aside]* Poor Duchess! God help her in the midst of
    the worries she suffers in trying to find out with which
    lady my master is in love!... As for him, he's a fool
    not to see what she wants. I wish that she had a pas-
    sion for me like that.

                                                    [Exit]

    [Enter LAURA]

LAURA: *[Aside]* Now that I've got the cipher, I'll return
    To Flérida, lest she should be suspicious.

FLÉRIDA: What has Celia written?

LAURA: A thousand follies.
    Here is the letter if you wish to see it.
    [Aside] I'll give the one which was enclosed.

FLÉRIDA: No, Laura.
    I have no wish to see it. There are things
    Nearer my heart of which I now would talk.
    I told you yesterday that I had learned,
    By certain means, that a lady had requested
    That Federico should come and speak with her
    During the night.

LAURA: Yes, señora.

FLÉRIDA: This

At first concerned me for decorum's sake;
And then I was a little curious;
And then, more so... You know that to discover
The lady's name, I asked you to keep watch.
Well, Laura, now I have to let you know
That one I keep to spy on him has found
That Federico did not go away,
But that he spent the whole night here in Parma,
Conversing with his lady.
LAURA: What audacity!
And has he told you who the lady is?
FLÉRIDA: No.
LAURA: Then, señora, don't believe his story:
For even if Federico could deceive you
With the Duke's letter, what would be the point
Of his deceiving me with the other letter?
FLÉRIDA: You're sure it's from your cousin?
LAURA: Absolutely.
FLÉRIDA: Then he'll have sent another messenger
Who will have brought both letters, and of him
My spy knows nothing.
LAURA: That must be it, señora.
FLÉRIDA: Another thought occurs to me. Last night
You were in the garden, yet you did not see
Another lady there; and yet my spy
Told me that Federico spent the night
Conversing with his lady. I conclude
She does not live here in the palace.
LAURA: No —
She must live in the town.
FLÉRIDA: Well, I will try
All kinds of ways until I know the lady.
LAURA: Why so, señora?
FLÉRIDA: Need you ask me, Laura?
When I've confided in you and admitted
Even to myself the feeling which inspires me,
It matters little whether he knows or not.
My heart's so full of pride, I cannot pardon
The injury that's done in ignorance.

                                              [Exit]

LAURA: I must warn Federico he is spied on...
Alas! to warn him to beware would be
To tell him of the Duchess's jealousy;
And to make known to even the most loyal lover
That another woman loves him is not wise.
For even a modest man becomes so vain
That all that one accords him afterward
Seems to him but his due. But nevertheless,
O heaven, it still is better that he know

That spies encircle him and dangers threaten.
To warn him, I will read this note again,
That I may get it clear. *[Takes paper from her bosom]*
"Whenever you have anything to tell me, I beg you first
to make me a sign with your handkerchief, so that I
shall pay attention. Then, on whatever subject you
speak, the first words in each line will be for me, and
the rest for everyone; in this way I can join all your
initial words together and understand your message. It
will be the same when I make the signal to you."
This code is easy and ingenious;
But yet it will be difficult to use it
In such a way as to make proper sense
To all the people present. I'll reread it
To understand it better.

[Enter LISARDO]

LISARDO: *[Aside]*   Laura's so busy
    Reading this paper, that if the suspicions
    Of jealousy can hardly touch her, yet
    My curiosity is keenly roused,
    And I am very anxious to discover
    What so absorbs her. Oh! If I could read it
    Without her seeing me.
LAURA: Who's there?
LISARDO: I, Laura.
LAURA: *[Aside]* Good God!
LISARDO: What does this fear and agitation mean?
LAURA: I am not agitated or afraid.
LISARDO: This paper which you hide, this sudden blush
    Would make me think it.
LAURA: You are mistaken, señor.
    If I have hidden this paper, and if a blush
    Has mounted on my cheeks, dismay or shame
    Were not the cause, but rather it was scorn
    At your insulting lack of trust. You came
    To spy on me. *[Aside]* When one is in the wrong,
    It's best to claim that one is in the right.
LISARDO: No, Laura, I have absolute faith in you,
    And lest you doubt the true security
    With which your nobleness inspires my love,
    I ask now, confident that you will tell me,
    What you were reading.
LAURA: *[Tearing up the letter]* It is a paper, señor,
    Whose pieces I will cast upon the wind,
    For to your foolish words, as light as wind,
    The wind alone should answer.
LISARDO: If you do
    I shall recover it.

LAURA: You shall not, señor.
    Not that I fear you will collect the pieces,
    Fix them together, so that you can read them;
    But it's a point of honor not to yield
    To vile suspicions that you entertain.
LISARDO: It is a point of honor for me too
    That I should know the contents.
LAURA: There I give
    The pieces to the wind: you're not my husband,
    And so I hope the matter will rest there.
LISARDO: Though I am not your husband, I'm your cousin,
    And your betrothed. I wish to join together
    The writhing coils of this serpent, full of venom.
LAURA: Take care, señor! This serpent, as you call it,
    I'll trample underfoot.
LISARDO: Whatever happens,
    I'll risk its venom, pick the pieces up,
    And fit...
LAURA: I will stop you.
LISARDO: Leave me alone!
LAURA: Stop it, you jealous creature!¹¹

    [Enter from one side ARNESTO, and from the other
    FLÉRIDA, and a little afterwards FEDERICO and FABIO]

ARNESTO: What is this noise,
    Lisardo?
FLÉRIDA: Why these cries, Laura?
LISARDO: It is nothing.
LAURA: On the contrary, it is much. *[Aside]* Love's wiles,
    assist me!
ARNESTO: *[To LISARDO]* To act like this...
FLÉRIDA: *[To LAURA]*   You're quarreling in this way...
ARNESTO: To your cousin?
FLÉRIDA: With your future husband?
ARNESTO: What's happened?
FLÉRIDA: What has passed between you?
LISARDO: Nothing
    That I know.
LAURA: On the contrary, I have much
    To complain of. Did you not leave me here,
    Not long ago, señora, with a letter
    From Celia?
FLÉRIDA: True.
LAURA: Well, I appeal to you
    Against the insolence of this man, who showed
    Odious suspicions of me. *[She shakes her handkerchief]*
    And so that you shall know the whole affair,
    Please pay attention. You, señora, and you, too,
    Father, and all the people who are present;

> For I am anxious now to speak out loud
> The secret of my heart.[12]

FEDERICO: What's happened, Fabio?
FABIO: I do not know. *[Aside]* So long as it's not caused
     By what I told the Duchess, let it be
     Whatever it likes.
FEDERICO: *[Aside]*   She has made the signal.
     I must pay attention to the initial words.
ARNESTO: Why are you waiting, Laura?
FLÉRIDA: Tell us all.
LAURA: *Flérida,* with her insight and intelligence
     Knows how entirely I'm devoted to her;
     Already I have given proof of it.
FLÉRIDA: It's true, but why do you refer to it?
FEDERICO: The message runs: "Flérida knows already."
LAURA: *You* were present when the letter came,
     Were you not, señora? And so you are
     Not able to credit such unjust aspersions. *[She weeps]*
     [To LISARDO] Away! Your conduct is intolerable.
ARNESTO: You've said enough, my child. Why do you weep?
FEDERICO: The Duchess knows that "you were not away."
LAURA: *Flérida,* who must share my views about it
     Knows that it is a treachery to love;
     You, assuming I belonged to you,
     Spoke words no woman could or should forgive.
LISARDO: You failed in duty to our mutual love.
FLÉRIDA: Be silent. Go on, Laura.
FEDERICO: "Flérida knows
     You spoke" — last night, to a lady, she implies.
LAURA: *Suddenly* taken by an angry fit
     Horrible to witness, in a tempest of
     Jealousy, he has insulted me.
LISARDO: When I asked to see the letter she was reading,
     She tore it up.
ARNESTO: She was quite justified.
FEDERICO: "Suddenly horrible jealousy" — of the Duchess.
LAURA: *Do not* presume, Lisardo, to discuss me.
     Speak to him, father; if he were the last
     Of living men, he should not marry me,
     Me! When he treats me thus before we're wed!
ARNESTO: Your conduct is deplorable indeed.
LISARDO: I swear to you, señor...
ARNESTO: Go, hold your tongue.
FEDERICO: She means to tell me: "Do not speak of me."
LAURA: *Distrust* a man that's so uncouth and rude.
     Men who forget themselves in such a way,
     Near to their wedding day, will be much worse,
     You may be sure, after the knot is tied.
LISARDO: I was wrong, Laura, I confess it now;

But may love serve as an excuse.
ARNESTO: Love makes you
   Surely more guilty still.
FEDERICO: "Distrust men near you."
LAURA: *Come,* señor, you will find no comfort here,
   Speak no more sophistries in your defense.
   Again I tell you, all is over between us.[13]

                                             [Exit]

ARNESTO: I share my daughter's righteous indignation.

                                             [Exit]

FEDERICO: "Come speak again."
FLÉRIDA: Lisardo, you have failed
   Sadly in the respect you owe to Laura;
   But I shall see she pardons you this crime.
   I know what jealousy is. *[Aside]* Though unlike yours
   My jealousy perforce may not be spoken.

                                             [Exit]

FABIO: *[Aside]* Thank God, the Duchess has left without
   speaking to me, and I've not got to fear that my master
   will guess that I've sneaked on him.
LISARDO: Heaven help me! Señor Federico,
   Do you regard it as a dreadful crime,
   That I should wish to know the letter's contents?
   Should it have vexed both Laura and her father
   So strongly, and distressed the Duchess too?
   You've understood, I think, the trifling cause
   Of this ado?
FEDERICO: Surely it's clear enough.
   Laura's affronted by your lack of trust.
LISARDO: Unhappy that I am! My hope is dead,
   And I'm a fool indeed.

                                             [Exit]

FEDERICO: *[Aside]* My hope is scarcely better.
FABIO: *[Aside]* Decidedly I have no more to fear.
FEDERICO: *[Aside]* Now I must put together all she's said,
   If I can still remember it. I'll ask
   Her portrait. It will seem to be herself
   Who speaks to me. *[Takes out a portrait]* Beautiful,
      sweet image,
   What did you say to me?
FABIO: *[Aside]*   Ah! Is that a portrait?
   It is indeed! I'm very glad to know it.
   It's a new thing to tell.
FEDERICO: *[Aside]*   "The Duchess knows
   Already that you were not away; she knows
   You spoke to a lady; she is horribly jealous;
   Don't speak of me; distrust men near you; come
   Speak with me again." *[Aloud]* By heaven, traitor,
   You were the one who sold me! It was you

Who said I was not absent. *[Beats him]*
FABIO: Señor, what anger
    Has seized you all at once? And why do you treat me so?
FEDERICO: I know why, traitor.
FABIO: But, señor, weren't you pleased with me when we en-
    tered this room? What kind of accusation or evidence
    have you found here against me? No one having spoken to
    you, who can have spoken ill of me?
FEDERICO: Yes, rogue, since I came in I have learned that
    you have revealed that I was not absent last night and
    that I went to see my lady.
FABIO: You've learned that since you came in?
FEDERICO: Yes.
FABIO: But, señor...
FEDERICO: I'll punish you as you deserve.
FABIO: But, señor, who told you that?
FEDERICO: Recollect to whom you told it... It is this person
    who has informed me.
FABIO: I've told no one. *[Aside]* I'll die, if need be, but
    I'll not confess.
FEDERICO: *[Drawing his dagger]* Good God! You're going to
        die this instant at my hands.

    [Enter ENRIQUE]

ENRIQUE: What is happening?
FEDERICO: I wish to kill a scoundrel.
FABIO: Calm yourself, señor.
ENRIQUE: Remember, Federico, you are in the palace.
FEDERICO: Let me shed his vile blood.
ENRIQUE: Flee!
FABIO: I ask nothing better, and I'll disappear in a twink-
    ling, as I've often had to do before. *[Aside]* So Her
    Highness has sneaked on me then?
                                                    [Exit]
ENRIQUE: Why are you so beside yourself, Federico?
    What is the cause?
FEDERICO: That I have been betrayed.
    Flérida knows I did not go away.
ENRIQUE: Who told her?
FEDERICO: There were only three who knew:
    You, myself, and Fabio.
ENRIQUE: Did she tell you?
FEDERICO: No, she is too discreet, and she pretends
    Not to know it.
ENRIQUE: Could the one who told you
    Have made it up herself?
FEDERICO: No — she is the one
    Most interested.
ENRIQUE: Could she be mistaken?

FEDERICO: Impossible.   I see no other course
   But to confess the truth.
ENRIQUE: I shall appear
   The guiltier, and draw her wrath upon me;
   But yet — so much I wish for your repose —
   I'll not dissuade you from your course, unless
   I thought there were a better plan to follow.
FEDERICO: Give me your counsel then.   What would you do?
ENRIQUE: I would say nothing and await events.
   I'd see her first, and act accordingly.
   Either she knows, or does not know, what's passed.
   If she does know, and modesty prevents her
   From saying anything, would you not act
   Against yourself to speak to her of something
   She chooses to ignore?   And if she knows nothing,
   Would it not work against us both to tell her
   What no one else could tell.   So, in your place,
   I would treat Fabio very well indeed,
   So that if he has not told the Duchess yet,
   He will not later; and, if he has spoken,
   He'll not complain to her, and so compel her
   To come into the open.
FEDERICO: That is far
   From my opinion, but I'll follow yours,
   So that no one can say that I was ruined
   By my own willfulness.   I will recall
   My valet, and when next I see the Duchess
   I will not speak of this unless she does.

                                     [Exit]

ENRIQUE: I have inherited the uncertainty
   In which he was.   He goes and leaves me bewildered.
   I came to Parma only for the purpose
   Of seeing the lovely Flérida, and I stay
   Here at her court under a borrowed name.
   Have I not cause to fear at any moment
   I shall be recognized, and this adventure
   Will not advance me in her eyes?   My aim
   In coming here was but to further my suit.
   What am I waiting for?   Or why delay
   To realize my plan?

                                     [Exit]

Scene 2: The Garden

[Enter FLÉRIDA on one side, ENRIQUE on the other]

FLÉRIDA: *[Aside]*   Blind, tyrannous passion,
   Why do you lead me to this place again?

[Aloud] What are you doing, señor?

ENRIQUE: Noble lady,
   I murmur to these flowers and these fountains
   To which you are the dawn, the plaints of love.

FLÉRIDA: Why so?

ENRIQUE: Because, O lovely goddess, seeing you
   Slay everything around you with your rays
   Which equal those of the sun, and with your arrows
   Which are as dangerous as those of love,
   I wished to say that, to enslave the world,
   You would not need to bring up all your powers:
   One of your rays, one arrow, would suffice.

FLÉRIDA: I am astonished doubly at this language,
   Señor Enrique: first, because you dare
   To offer it to me; and then because I listen.
   Retire you from my presence. If the Duke
   Dispatched you to my court, he little thought
   That you would fail both him and me.

ENRIQUE: Señora,
   I do not think to fail you. As for the Duke,
   I'm sure I've not failed him, for he agrees
   With all the sentiments that I expressed.

FLÉRIDA: Though people often marry, they do not woo,
   By proxy; and although I were to admit
   The excuse you speak for him, did I not warn you
   Never to speak to me upon this subject
   Unless I spoke of it myself.

ENRIQUE: 'Tis true,
   Señora, but you never laid it down
   That you would never speak of it; and thus
   Ensure that I should always hold my peace.

FLÉRIDA: Well, if it's absolutely necessary
   That I should speak to you, Señor Enrique,
   Today will serve; and therefore I must tell you,
   Since you have just compared me to the sun,
   That the Duke of Mantua would be imprudent
   To go too near the sun with waxen wings;
   And I request you, once again, to go.
   Before my anger in another fashion
   Answers the Duke and you.

ENRIQUE: I obey, señora,
   Fearing a greater punishment; if anything
   Is worse than separation from your beauty.
   [Aside] Alas! I'm in despair.

                                      [Exit]

FLÉRIDA: This strange audacity gives me much to think of.
   Love, leave me tranquil for a little while,
   So that I can reflect. But who comes here?

[Enter FABIO]

FABIO: It's me, your Highness, who comes in anger to complain
about all sorts of things. Yes, I'm furious at myself
for being such a gossip, but nowadays it seems that's no
disgrace, seeing your Highness is a gossip too.
FLÉRIDA: What do you mean to say?
FABIO: And you, señora, what have you said?
FLÉRIDA: I understand still less.
FABIO: Were you afraid, señora, that what I told you about
my master would turn to vinegar if you kept it an hour
longer in your breast?
FLÉRIDA: In whom, then, am I supposed to have confided?
FABIO: To no one, doubtless, except to him; for as soon as
you left, he fell upon me in a fury, and if he hadn't
been restrained he would certainly have killed me.
FLÉRIDA: Why?
FABIO: Oh heavens! Because your Highness has blabbed.
FLÉRIDA: But how could I have told him, since I haven't
spoken with him?
FABIO: Well, if it wasn't you, it must have been the devil —
that's certain. I would have had more news to tell you
— but I daren't risk it.
FLÉRIDA: Tell me what happened.
FABIO: I know nothing.
FLÉRIDA: Did he receive a letter?
FABIO: I know nothing.
FLÉRIDA: Where is he gone?
FABIO: I know nothing.
FLÉRIDA: Has someone come to talk with him in secret?
FABIO: I know nothing.
FLÉRIDA: You will almost make me think that you repent serv-
ing me, and that you are more devoted to Federico than
to me.
FABIO: It's not that.
FLÉRIDA: What is it, then?
FABIO: It's simply that your Highness has blabbed; and, if
my master came again to suspect anything, he would kill
me.
FLÉRIDA: I notice that he hasn't killed you up till now.
FABIO: True. But apropos, here's a little story: —
A gallant was in conversation with his lady; and, prof-
iting from the opportunity, a louse said to itself: "It
is not the moment when he scratches and I can, without
fear, regale myself at leisure." Yet, in the end, tired
by this repast, the gallant brought his fingers to the
place where the louse was dining and succeeded in im-
prisoning it. But, at the same instant the lady turned
and saw her gallant holding his hand like a man who is
going to take snuff; and lest there should be anyone to
overhear them, she asked him with a serious air: "Well,

have you killed the gentleman?" The gallant was struck
dumb at first; but soon recovering, and holding his
hand as I've said: "No, señora," said he, "I've not yet
killed him, but I press him hard." And I, your Highness, will say the same thing now. I'm not yet killed,
it's true, but I'm pressed hard. So, after your treachery, I won't tell you that today I saw my master holding
a portrait which could let you discover who is the beautiful lady with whom he's in love, if you could somehow
get hold of it. That, señora, is what I would tell you,
and other things besides, if I didn't fear your tattling
tongue. But don't count on my ever telling you that or
anything else; especially when I consider that Señor
Federico is my master, and that your Highness blabs.

                                                    [Exit]

FLÉRIDA: He has a portrait! It is here I need
    Wit and resource to make him show it me
    But in a way that's seemly! But not here —
    We should be too exposed to people's eyes.

    [Enter FEDERICO]

FEDERICO: *[Aside]* The best plan, after all, is not to speak
    But wait for her to speak of it. *[Aloud]* Señora,
    Since your Highness sent for me, do you wish
    To sign the dispatches?
FLÉRIDA: Yes, but the garden perhaps
    Is hardly suitable, especially now
    When the sun is setting in his brilliant tomb.
    Bring the dispatches, then, without delay
    To my apartments; and, before you come,
    Do not forget that you have much to write
    During the night. So if your lady waits you,
    You can inform her that you cannot see her,
    For even though tonight you have no journey,
    This time you will not be less absent, señor,
    I do assure you.
FEDERICO: *[Aside]*   Heavens! What do I hear?

    [Enter LAURA]

LAURA: *[Aside]* Flérida here with Federico! Well,
    She takes away my opportunities —
    I'll do the same for her. *[Aloud]* I see, señora,
    That you have made a contract with the Spring,
    Its profits without losses.
FLÉRIDA: What do you mean?
LAURA: Your Highness now assists Spring in this garden
    From which you never go; and you have added
    To the rose redness, whiteness to the jasmine.
FLÉRIDA: It's time for me to leave. Laura, let's go.

[_To FEDERICO_] Do not delay to come with the dispatches,
And as you go to fetch them, why not pass on
What I have said to you.
FEDERICO: I'm not so happy
As you presume, señora; [_waves handkerchief_] yet even now
I could pass on a message.
LAURA: [_Aside_]   He's given the signal.
FEDERICO: _I'm_ tossed from one vexation to another.
Unhappy that I am, my life's a burden.
LAURA: [_Aside_] He says "I am unhappy."
FEDERICO: _Today,_ when you spoke with me, I could but feel
_I_ had forfeited your former kindness, and
Cannot recover it, whatever I do.
Speak what I can, you take offense at it.
With harsh reproaches or worse raillery
You make me know that I have lost your favor.
LAURA: He says: "Today I cannot speak with you."
FLÉRIDA: Enough. Let us leave this.
LAURA: [_Aside_]   Let me put
The words together. "I am unhappy — today
I cannot speak with you."
FLÉRIDA: Follow me, Laura.
[_To FEDERICO_] And you, señor, do not delay to come.
FEDERICO: [_Aside_] Is there a love unluckier than ours
FLÉRIDA: [_Aside_] Is there a more unworthy sentiment?
LAURA: [_Aside_] Is there a jealousy more visible?
                              [_Exeunt FLÉRIDA and LAURA_]

[_Enter FABIO_]

FABIO: Which way could I get out of here without risking a
    meeting with my master. But it's no use talking, here
    he is!
FEDERICO: Fabio.
FABIO: Don't start on me again. [_Moving away_]
FEDERICO: Why are you fleeing from me? [_Aside_] I'm forced
    to pretend with this rogue.
FABIO: Because I'm afraid of that cursed demon, who whispers
    in your ear, and may have been telling more lies about
    me.[14]
FEDERICO: I know the truth now. I know that you're loyal to
    me.
FABIO: I should hope so. Would to God certain people in
    Madrid had been like me![15]
FEDERICO: I wish to give you a coat in compensation.
FABIO: A coat? To me?
FEDERICO: Yes, to you.
FABIO: In that case, may you in the next world have a soul
    attired in a dressing gown of scarlet, breeches of crys-
    tal, and a doublet of ambergris.

FEDERICO: But you must tell me something.
FABIO: Anything you like.
FEDERICO: Quick, then — I'm obliged to go.
FABIO: May the Lord bridle my tongue!
FEDERICO: Has the Duchess interrogated you about my love?
FABIO: Certainly not; but from what she said to me I've
    deduced that if you don't understand what she wants,
    you're not very bright.
FEDERICO: Has she said anything?
FABIO: Undoubtedly — and a very great deal, be it said.
FEDERICO: You lie, you rogue. Do you hope to make me be-
    lieve that such a noble beauty, like the sun's proud
    neighbor, the heron, would stoop so low as to confide
    in a dastardly buzzard like you?
FABIO: Well, señor, pretend to love her for a few days and
    you will see...
FEDERICO: Even if your malicious suspicions had any founda-
    tion, I would not attempt to check them; for a love,
    just as ill-fated, but to which I am less unfitted,
    wholly occupies my heart.
FABIO: As for that, have you never loved two women at once?
FEDERICO: No.
FABIO: Then do not believe...
FEDERICO: Go on.
FABIO: That you have experienced true happiness.
FEDERICO: That's not loving, but deceiving.
FABIO: For that reason there's more pleasure in it.
FEDERICO: How can one love on two sides at once?
FABIO: This is how. *[FEDERICO paces back and forth in dis-
    tracted fashion, while FABIO tells his tale]* Near Rat-
    isbon there are two villages of great renown, of which
    one is called Agere and the other Macarandon. Now a
    single priest served the two parishes, and on feast days
    said mass at the two places. Now an inhabitant of Maca-
    randon, having gone to Agere, and having heard the pref-
    ace chanted, noticed that on that day the priest had
    pronounced in a loud voice *gratias agere,* and that he
    had not given thanks also to Macarandon. Very discon-
    tented with this, he said: "The priest gives thanks to
    Agere as if we had not paid our tithes." In hearing an
    observation so grave, the noble Macarandonians withheld
    their offerings. Now, the priest seeing that, asked the
    sacristan what was the reason for it. The latter told
    him why; and from that day, each time he intoned the
    preface, so that he would get his dues, the priest never
    failed to chant in a clear and powerful voice: "Nos tibi
    semper, et ubique gratias ad Macarandon." And there-
    fore, señor, you serve two parishes of Love — that blind
    god — pay your duties on both sides, and you will see

that in a short time you and I will have a quantity of
offerings and of feasts so long as you sing the praises
of "Macarandon" — I mean Flérida.[16]
FEDERICO: Do you think I'm listening to you?
FABIO: Why not?
FEDERICO: I'm thinking only of my own troubles.
FABIO: Since for Agere you disdain Macarandon, I greatly
fear that you'll be deprived of the blessed bread of
love.

                                              [Exeunt]

Scene 3: A Room in the Palace

*[Enter FLÉRIDA, LAURA, LIVIA, and FLORA, who carries
lights]*

FLÉRIDA: Leave the torches, and then all depart;
   I do not wish for company: I'm weary
   Even of my own.
LIVIA: *[To FLORA]*   What strange melancholy!
FLORA: It's more than melancholy, it is frenzy.
FLÉRIDA: You, Laura, stay.
                        [Exeunt LIVIA and FLORA]
LAURA: How can I be of service?
FLÉRIDA: I hope of your friendship something I can ask
   Of you alone.
LAURA: What do you ask?
FLÉRIDA: I want,
   When Federico comes, that you should stay
   There at the door, and see that no one listens
   To what I say to him.
LAURA: I'll do my best —
   But is there something new?
FLÉRIDA: I wish to know
   Who is his lady.
LAURA: Who is his lady?
FLÉRIDA: Yes.
LAURA: That will be difficult. *[Aside]* Oh, if I could find
   The means she will employ! I then could warn him
   When he arrives.
FLÉRIDA: I ought to tell you, Laura...
LAURA: I'm listening.
FLÉRIDA: I've learned that Federico
   Has always on him...but he's coming now,
   And he will hear me. Listen, and you'll see
   What I have devised. Go now.
LAURA: Yes, señora.
   [Aside] Who cares that she has given me permission

To listen; I should have done it all the same.
> [*LAURA hides; and FEDERICO enters with writing
> materials*]

FEDERICO: Here are the letters, señora.
FLÉRIDA: Put them there;
  For it is terrible that I should leave them
  In your hands, señor, and that I should accord you
  My absolute trust, when you have so betrayed
  My interests, and failed in your sworn duty.
FEDERICO: What have you to reproach me with, señora?
  What crime have I committed that provokes
  Such a reward for all my services?
FLÉRIDA: Do not presume to question me, when I
  Have numerous proofs as evidence against you.
FEDERICO: Of what am I accused?
LAURA: *[Aside]*   How will this lead her
  To find the lady's name.
FEDERICO: I have the right
  To justify myself.
FLÉRIDA: Well, I'll explain.
  I've learned that you are in communication
  With my greatest enemy.
FEDERICO: Believe me, señora,
  Although I hid the Duke of Mantua,
  It was only for the night he came disguised.
FLÉRIDA: What's this? The Duke! *[Aside]* O heavens! I
        feigned my wrath.
  And did I have a real cause for complaint?
FEDERICO: He now is in the palace.
FLÉRIDA: What! Is the Duke
  This gentleman whom I received as guest?
FEDERICO: Yes, señora.
FLÉRIDA: *[Aside]*   How many times a lie
  Brings out the truth!
LAURA: *[Aside]*   I cannot yet perceive
  What her intention is.
FLÉRIDA: Why have you hidden this?
FEDERICO: As the Duke wished to marry you, señora,
  I thought that you would easily forgive
  A fault which love inspired.
FLÉRIDA: I realize now
  That it was easy, without leaving Parma,
  To bring his letter to me.
FEDERICO: Yes, señora,
  I was about to leave when he arrived,
  And I gave it him.
FLÉRIDA: By this you are acquitted
  With him, but not with me. What of the letter
  You gave to Laura?

FEDERICO: That letter...it was brought
  By the Duke himself.
LAURA: *[Aside]*   That was a narrow shave!
  But what's she trying to do? How will she thus
  Find who the lady is?
FLÉRIDA: You think, perhaps,
  This is the sole proof of your treachery?
  It is not so. Give me at once the letter
  That you have just received from the Duke of Florence,
  Concerning old pretensions which he has
  Upon my lands.
FEDERICO: I humbly beg, señora,
  That you would but remember who I am;
  And if I have committed a small fault
  In serving in his love one who aspires
  To win your hand, do not on that account
  Suspect me of an act that's so unworthy
  Both of my birth and of my manliness.
FLÉRIDA: The man who could deceive me on one point
  Need not have many scruples on the other.
  Give me the letter.
FEDERICO: I have no such letter!
  Well take, take all the papers that I've brought,
  And if that's not enough, here, take this key
  By means of which you will have all my papers,
  And if you find a single line to accuse me,
  Strike off my head.
      [He takes out of his pockets a handkerchief, keys,
      and lastly a box which he tries to hide]
FLÉRIDA: What are you hiding there?
FEDERICO: It is a box.
FLÉRIDA: I wish to see that too.
FEDERICO: *[Aside]*   I see her purpose.
  [Aloud] That, señora, cannot be a proof
  Of treachery, and therefore, I beseech you
  Do not demand it.
LAURA: *[Aside]*   That must be my portrait.
FLÉRIDA: I wish to know the contents of that box.
LAURA: *[Aside]* We're lost.
FEDERICO: It is a portrait; and if that
  Was what you wished to know, you know it now.
FLÉRIDA: Till I have seen it, I will not believe you.
  Show it me.
FEDERICO: If it's that, señora...
LAURA: *[Aside]*   Alas!
FEDERICO: Which is the cause...
LAURA: *[Aside]*   What peril!
FEDERICO: that you have called me traitor...
LAURA: *[Aside]* How terrible!

FEDERICO: You're right, señora...
LAURA: *[Aside]*   Alas!
FEDERICO: For know that rather than hand over this...
LAURA: *[Aside]* What torture!
FEDERICO: I'm ready to be slain a thousand times.
          [LAURA comes forward, takes the portrait from FEDER-
          ICO's hands, changes it for another, and gives this
          to FLÉRIDA]
LAURA: You shan't resist us, traitor!
FEDERICO: What are you doing?
LAURA: I've seen and heard what's passed, and hastened here.
     Was it not sufficient for you that Her Highness
     Desired to see this portrait, for you to give it
     Immediately, you ill-bred gentleman.
     Take it, señora.
FLÉRIDA: You have never rendered me
     A greater service.
FEDERICO: *[Aside]*   Laura must have wished
     To reveal all at once.
FLÉRIDA: Give me a light.
          [LAURA brings a torch]
     Let's see this prodigy, this miracle
     Of love. *[Aside]* At least I'll know who causes now
     My jealousy.
FEDERICO: *[Aside]* When she beholds the portrait
     Of Laura, what will she say?
FLÉRIDA: What do I see?
LAURA: In truth, it's his own portrait!
FLÉRIDA: Is it that
     You've hidden so carefully?
FEDERICO: Don't be surprised,
     Señora; it is what I love the most
     In all the world.
FLÉRIDA: Since you love it indeed
     As much as you love yourself. What does this mean,
     Laura?
LAURA: What you see. I know no more.
FLÉRIDA: *[Aside]* I hardly can contain the wrath I feel;
     And not to make a scene, I will retire.
     [Aloud] Give back his portrait to this new Narcissus,
     And tell him... But, no matter, tell him nothing.
     [Aside] I have a thousand serpents in my breast,
     A fire within my heart.
                                             [Exit]
FEDERICO: Why did the Duchess,
     When she had seen your portrait, not display
     More anger against you, and against me?
LAURA: I changed the portraits: I kept mine and gave her
     Yours.

FEDERICO: You alone could've got us out of this.
LAURA: For the moment; but the danger still remains.
FEDERICO: We must avert it.
LAURA: Tomorrow I will tell you
   What I suggest. *[Gives box]* Take this, and so adieu.
FEDERICO: Which is this portrait?
LAURA: It is yours, in case
   She asks for it again.
FEDERICO: You are right. Adieu.
                                          [Exit LAURA]
   I've never been in a crueler situation, and...

   [Enter FABIO]

FABIO: Señor, which of these two coats can I take?
FEDERICO: Infamous scoundrel! Wretch!
FABIO: Now he's on another tack!
FEDERICO: It's only through you that I'm ruined.
FABIO: It's only through you that I haven't a coat for my
   back!
FEDERICO: You thought that this portrait was of a lady?
   Well, it's mine!
FABIO: I always knew you loved yourself.
FEDERICO: By the living God, you're going to die at my
   hands!
FABIO: Jesus Christ!
FEDERICO: *[Aside]* But no, I'm wrong! Since I'm out of dan-
   ger, it's better not to make a fuss. *[Aloud]* Fabio.
FABIO: Señor?
FEDERICO: Come with me and choose the best of the two coats.
   I know that I've nothing to reproach you with, and that
   you have a proven loyalty.
FABIO: Has anyone ever seen such caprices. By God, he must
   have lost his wits if he ever had any.
                                          [Exeunt]

   ꩜꩜

                         ACT THREE

             Scene 1: A Room in Federico's House

   [Enter FABIO]

FABIO: Who by chance has found the good sense of a poor
   valet, which he has lost, because his master has lost
   his — though it would seem he never had much anyway?
   Please tell me where it is — because there it's of little use, but here one would give something for it...

It's a waste of time to ask — nobody answers. But, indeed, what good sense, once lost, is ever recovered?
Come, memory, let's run over the whole affair, and let's
think about it, if you don't mind. What is there new?
I don't know... How does it happen that at the moment
when I thought myself on the best of terms with my master, it was just then that he fell on me and belabored
me with blows? Because he's mad... And when, being
guilty, I avoided him, how does it come about that just
then he gives me a coat, and loads me with caresses?
Because he's drunk... There are two admirable conclu-
sions. And I don't proceed to the third because I see
Don Enrique and my master coming here and whispering together; and if in coming into this room they intend not
to be seen by me, I'm going to forestall them so as not
to be seen by them. In this way it's possible that I
shall hear their confidences; and besides, as my master
is sometimes furious and sometimes affable with me, and
it's now fury's turn, I'll gain by letting it expend itself in a void... But to succeed in this, I must hide as
fast as possible. I don't see any other hiding place
than underneath this buffet. Quick! It won't be the
first time that I've been buffeted! *[He hides]*

[Enter FEDERICO and ENRIQUE]

ENRIQUE: What are you waiting for?
FEDERICO: I am afraid
    That we are overheard.
ENRIQUE: But all the valets
    Are still outside.
FABIO: *[Aside]*   Except me; I'm within.
FEDERICO: It's not without a motive that I've led you
    To the back of the house. I wish to speak with you
    Without a witness.
FABIO: *[Aside]*   I'm a false witness, so I can't be
        real.
ENRIQUE: Speak.
FEDERICO: First let me close this door.
    Now that we are alone, I beg your Highness
    To listen well. It's time to tell you all.
FABIO: *[Aside]* Highness! That's good.
ENRIQUE: What motive makes you treat me in this fashion?
FEDERICO: There are two motives, both of them important.
    One concerns you, and the other me.
    The one concerning you — and here I hope
    You will not form a bad opinion of me
    If to the Duchess I appear disloyal
    Necessity compels me — is that you
    Are known to Flérida now, and it is useless

To affect a mystery between us, which
Is known to everyone. The other motive,
The one concerning me...
ENRIQUE: Before proceeding,
First tell me this — how Flérida found out.
FEDERICO: I do not know.
FABIO: *[Aside]* Fancy! My master's pimping for a prince!
FEDERICO: It was she herself that told me.
ENRIQUE: Pass now to what concerns you — for the other
We'd lose ourselves in suppositions.
I will continue still in this disguise,
Until we know what her intentions are.
FEDERICO: Before I speak of that which touches me,
Promise that you will bury in your heart
What I confide in you.
ENRIQUE: I give my word.
And think that if you write your words on wax,
They'll be preserved in marble.
FEDERICO: You know already,
Illustrious Enrique de Gonzaga,
Duke of Mantua, that I love a lady
Here in this court. This human miracle,
This divine prodigy, has given me,
In spite of many frightening obstacles,
Today, the highest proof of constancy
And tenderness. This letter that you see
Was carried by the wind into my hands,
For it descended from the height of heaven
Into the dark abyss of my despair —
This letter tells me of my liberty —
But no — it tells me of my slavery;
For, from the moment that I read it first
I wish to live eternally the slave
Of Love who has imposed on me those chains
Which Time itself can never break nor loose.
This letter tells me...but I'd better read it.
You will appreciate better the true love
She bears me, and the love that I return.
[Reads] "My comfort, my lord, my master — Fortune de-
clares itself more and more against us. Let us fore-
stall these fatal blows. Please have ready two horses
for tonight, beside the bridge, between the park and the
palace. I will come out at your signal, and we will
flee from the jealousy which persecutes us, if one can
ever escape from jealousy. Adieu! May Heaven ever have
you in his keeping."
That's what was written me, my noble lord,
And I rely upon your kindness now.
You came to me to aid you in your love —

And now I ask for yours. I wish to beg you
To give me a letter now for Mantua,
And take up my defense until the lady
Is placed in safety.
ENRIQUE: I am very glad
That heaven has furnished me with the occasion
To recognize what you have done for me;
Not only will I give you what you ask,
But also I'll accompany you myself
Till we have reached the frontier of my realm;
And I shall count myself as glorious
In having you as subject.
FEDERICO: No, I prefer
To go alone; and to be frank, your Highness
Will do me greater service here in Parma;
So I will be assured of your protection
In Parma as in Mantua.
ENRIQUE: Well, I will do
All that you wish.
FEDERICO: Then will you kindly write
A letter, while I go as usual
To the palace, so that no one shall suspect.
I must find Fabio too, whom I've not seen
Throughout the day.
FABIO: *[Aside]*   That's not my fault —
I'm not so far away.
FEDERICO: He must know nothing.
FABIO: *[Aside]*   No; of course not.
FEDERICO: But he must get the horses ready.
ENRIQUE: Yes —
And while you are away perhaps I'll see
What a stern destiny ordains for me.
FEDERICO: I will return to seek you.
ENRIQUE: While I wait,
I'll write the letter in the neighboring room.
FEDERICO: *[Aside]* O Love, give aid to an unfortunate!
ENRIQUE: *[Aside]* O Love, take pity on my heartfelt prayer!
                          [Exeunt FEDERICO and ENRIQUE]
FABIO: *[Emerging]* Listeners hear ill, the proverb says.
But sometimes the proverb lies — for I have
Listened, and have heard nothing but good.
Indeed, I've gained four advantages — namely:
The first, that I know who our guest is;
The second, I have learned the state of my master's
      love;
The third, that I can relate all this to the Duchess;
And the fourth is that by this means I shall
Obtain from her a nice reward.
                                        [Exit]

Scene 2: A Room in the Palace

[Enter ARNESTO and LAURA]

ARNESTO: No, my dear Laura, for Lisardo's fault
 Is not so grave that you should not forget it
 When he beseeches pardon. The fits of temper
 Which love inspires have never been considered
 An injury. I therefore urge you now,
 Speak gently to him, since the dispensation
 May come at any time.
LAURA: I would obey you:
 I much prefer to obey you than to vex you.
 So I agree to accept without a murmur
 The place that Fate reserves for me, and I
 Consent to wed the man who is most eager
 To be my husband now. [17]
ARNESTO: I knew that you would readily obey.
 [Calling] Come, Lisardo. Wait here, Laura.

[Enter LISARDO]

LISARDO: I hasten,
 Señora, to lay my life now at your feet
 In return for the pardon which I here solicit.
LAURA: Ask permission from my father, señor;
 It's he who guides my conduct; it is he
 Dispenses my poor hand: and if I obey...
LISARDO: Señora, it's enough for me to obtain
 This precious hand; so long as I obtain it
 I'll not consider how I have obtained it.
 How should the source of happiness concern me,
 If I am happy? O lazy, tardy sun,
 Hasten, abridge your course, that at long last
 I may behold the hour for which I wait!

[Enter FLÉRIDA]

FLÉRIDA: Laura? Arnesto?
ARNESTO: Your Highness, we were coming
 To your apartments.
FLÉRIDA: My congratulations,
 Lisardo, that you have obtained forgiveness.
LISARDO: My hope has been reanimated by your favor.
ARNESTO: Oh! Laura is obedient and tractable...
LAURA: How is your Highness now?
FLÉRIDA: As sad as ever.
LAURA: Try to distract yourself.
FLÉRIDA: Every distraction
 Is an additional burden: it's an evil
 The remedy increases. But to prevent

The accusation that I'm given up
To melancholy *[To ARNESTO and LISARDO]*   both of you
    invite
All the nobility of Parma to
A great feast for tomorrow. *[Aside]*   And perhaps
By this means I'll discover the dread rival
Who's killing me.
ARNESTO: I hasten to obey.
LISARDO: My life is yours.
                              [Exeunt ARNESTO and LISARDO]
FLÉRIDA: You are happy, my dear Laura; you
    Are going to wed the man you love.
LAURA: I am,
    Señora, I confess it, for I hope
    To wed the man I love.
FLÉRIDA: Woe to the woman
    Who gives her heart to an insensate passion:
    What can she do but die? But no, my will
    Will triumph over my unfriendly star.
LAURA: That will be best. But what is to be done?
FLÉRIDA: There is a means to cure this frightful fever.
LAURA: Which is?
FLÉRIDA: To declare it.
LAURA: That will not defeat it.
FLÉRIDA: Yes it will.
LAURA: *[Aside]*   This will kill me.
FLÉRIDA: To submit
    To fate would bring a kind of triumph;
    And, Laura, would I be the first to make
    An unequal marriage?
LAURA: *[Aside]*   I cannot endure it.
FLÉRIDA: Federico is a gentleman
    Of noble birth.
LAURA: That cannot be denied.
FLÉRIDA: And while we're talking of him, tell me, Laura,
    Did it not seem peculiar to you
    That he should carry his own portrait on him?
    What do you think of that?
LAURA: Nothing, señora;
    As it was no concern of mine, I paid it
    Little attention. *[Aside]* I'm mad with jealousy.
FLÉRIDA: Why should he keep his portrait with such care?
LAURA: I do not know, señora; but if I'd been you,
    I would not have returned it quite so soon!
    For I suspect the portrait of his lady
    Was also in the box.
FLÉRIDA: Perhaps you are right.
    But love, and even jealousy, alas,
    Don't think of everything.

LAURA: I do not doubt
   His lady's was there too.

   [Enter FEDERICO and FABIO]

FEDERICO: I found you, Fabio, only with great difficulty.
FABIO: I could say the same thing to you, for I've been
   searching for you since this morning.
FEDERICO: *[Aside]* The Duchess! Don't go away. I shall
   have need of you.
FABIO: As for me, I don't believe that I shall have any need
   of you.
FEDERICO: Coming to speak with her, I fear her anger.
FABIO: Why?
FEDERICO: For a certain episode.
FABIO: Remember my little story, and you'll see that you'll
   be all right.
FEDERICO: How?
FABIO: Just remember to give thanks to Macarandon.
LAURA: Consider, señora...
FLÉRIDA: No, I wish to declare
   Everything.
LAURA: *[Aside]* And I must bear it?
FLÉRIDA: Federico!
FEDERICO: Your Highness?
FLÉRIDA: How is it you have not appeared
   Throughout the day, and only show yourself
   This evening at the palace?
FEDERICO: In seeing you,
   One always sees the bright and glorious sun,
   And so I did not think it was so late;
   It seems, when I behold you, that the sun
   Has just arisen.
FLÉRIDA: Do you flatter me?
FEDERICO: Those are not flatteries.
FLÉRIDA: What are they then?
FABIO: *[Aside]* A fashion of Macarandon.
FLÉRIDA: *[To LAURA]* Ah! My dear Laura, do you see? Already
   He understands me.
LAURA: *[Aside]*   He does well.
FEDERICO: I have
   Another excuse to give you.
FLÉRIDA: What is that?
FEDERICO: As I believed you were annoyed with me
   I have put off appearing in your presence.
FLÉRIDA: Annoyed? At what?
FEDERICO: I should be ill advised
   To tell you, if you did not know.
FLÉRIDA: It is not
   That I do not know it.

FEDERICO: What is it then?
FLÉRIDA: That I
    Don't wish to know it.
FEDERICO: My happiness
    Is by so much the greater that you've been
    More generous; for when one has complaints
    It's generous to keep them to oneself.
FLÉRIDA: I do not follow.
LAURA: *[Waving her handkerchief]* If you will allow me,
    I think I can explain.
FLÉRIDA: Speak, I permit you.
    [Aside] Explain so that he understands my feelings.
LAURA: *I* think myself that it is generous to
    Suffer in silence, rather than reveal
    Anguish and jealousy that love has caused.
FEDERICO: *[Aside]* She means to say, "I suffer anguish" now.
    I must reply. *[Aloud]* Permit me, your Highness.
    [Waving handkerchief] You're partly right, but notwith-
        standing this
    Wrong, for the context gives a different meaning.
LAURA: He says: "You're wrong." I pray that that is true.
FLÉRIDA: And yet it seems to me that Laura said
    The same as you.
LAURA: I meant he was a miser
    Who spread his plaints abroad, and generous
    Who keeps them in.
FEDERICO: Yes, you have understood me,
    And have explained my meaning to perfection.
LAURA: It was not difficult to understand.
FABIO: *[Aside]* I think, indeed, they both understand ex-
        tremely well.
FLÉRIDA: From all you have both said, I understand
    Only that generosity to you
    Consists in not revealing what one suffers.
FEDERICO: ⎫
LAURA: ⎭ Exactly.
FLÉRIDA: Well, Federico, although I say
    I do not know in what you have offended,
    And yet you know I know it, come and see me
    In a short while, and you may be assured
    I'll not complain, and that you've naught to fear.
    That should suffice you. Come, Laura, follow me.
                                          [Exit]

LAURA: Federico.
FEDERICO: Laura?
LAURA: What I said still stands.
                                          [Exit]
FEDERICO: Well, Fabio, what do you say? Is it not strange
    That at the moment when I expect to find

The Duchess vexed with me, I find instead
That she is friendlier than ever?
FABIO: It's just like me, who find you angry when I expect
to find you contented. But as for her, I know the rea-
son for it.
FEDERICO: Tell me.
FABIO: It's the Macarandon in which you compared her with
the sun.
FEDERICO: Stop your bad jests and get two horses ready at
once.
FABIO: I might have known. As you've sung mass in Macaran-
don
You'll sing it next in Agere.
FEDERICO: Hold your tongue, and don't forget this evening to
wait with the horses at the entrance to the park.
[Aside] Beautiful Flérida, may your pride forgive me.
A woman runs this risk when she makes a declaration to a
man whom she knows is in love with another.
                                                  [Exit]
FABIO: What! Today when I would have more to speak than
ever, I'll speak less than usual? No, no, that would be
pitiable, that would be frightful to allow a secret to
rot in my heart so that it will be useless to anyone;
but as says the Cordovan a secret to which no one is
privy, becomes like a privy indeed, smells so foul, it
makes one ill.[18] I'll go and find the Duchess — but
here she comes.

[Enter FLÉRIDA]

FLÉRIDA: *[Aside]* Though I have every confidence in Laura,
I've left her in another room, to follow
Alone this victory of a cruel love.
[Aloud] What! Federico is no longer here?
FABIO: You want to know, señora, why he's no longer here?
FLÉRIDA: Yes.
FABIO: Because he is gone.
FLÉRIDA: Where to?
FABIO: To Agere, I presume.
FLÉRIDA: I do not understand you.
FABIO: I will speak plainly here in Macarandon, provided
that you reward me for it.
FLÉRIDA: I wish to know nothing. It is enough to have seen
that I have a new cause of grief.
FABIO: How now!...and what was the use of my spying all day,
crouched on all fours.
FLÉRIDA: Leave me, I say.
FABIO: Well, I ask nothing from you... I'll tell it to you
free, gratis, and for nothing.
FLÉRIDA: I do not care to hear you.

FABIO: But consider that if I keep my secret I shall burst.
   I'm going to look for someone to tell that my master is
   going to escape tonight.
FLÉRIDA: Stop! What did you say?
FABIO: Nothing, señora.
FLÉRIDA: Wait and tell me.
FABIO: I don't want to.
FLÉRIDA: Take this diamond and speak.
FABIO: O God! A plague on ceremonies! I'm a valet, you're
   a woman; I'm dying to speak, you're dying to hear.
   Well! You must know that my master and his lady propose
   this very night...
FLÉRIDA: Go on.
FABIO: To flit.
FLÉRIDA: What?
FABIO: To depart. But not on foot. On the contrary, I have
   orders to have ready two horses beside the bridge.
FLÉRIDA: At the bridge in the park?
FABIO: Yes, señora.
FLÉRIDA: I return to my former belief, that it is a lady of
   the court. He hasn't told you?
FABIO: No, señora; but our guest, who is the Duke of Mantua,
   is giving them asylum in his territories. And now, come
   what may, I have spoken, and I feel better for my inter-
   ests come first; let my master look to his own.

                                               [Exit]

FLÉRIDA: May heaven protect me! What have I heard?
   What a horrible situation!

   [Enter ARNESTO]

ARNESTO: I've just invited, on your behalf, señora,
   The most distinguished gentlemen and ladies
   Of our nobility.
FLÉRIDA: Enough, and welcome,
   Arnesto: I have need of you this night.
ARNESTO: I'm at your service. What do you require?
FLÉRIDA: Federico has had a violent quarrel.
ARNESTO: With whom?
FLÉRIDA: I do not know. But I was told
   That it was due to rivalry in love
   And that his adversary has summoned him
   By letter to a place where he awaits him.
   You know how I esteem him?
ARNESTO: Yes, señora,
   And I know also how much he deserves it.
FLÉRIDA: I do not wish to seem to know what's passed:
   For that would be to make the insult public.
ARNESTO: That's just. What do you order?
FLÉRIDA: Go and find him,

And without telling him you're sent by me,
Don't let him, for an instant, from your sight.
Wherever he goes, go with him. If, by chance,
He tries to escape you, then arrest him straight,
And therefore take the necessary guards
So that you keep him in a place of safety
All night until the morning.
ARNESTO: I will go
At once to find him, and I'll answer for it,
I will not leave him.

                                                [Exit]

FLÉRIDA: Ingrate, you will learn
To what extremes a jealous woman goes.

              Scene 3: A Room in Federico's House

[Enter ENRIQUE and FEDERICO and a VALET who retires
after bringing torches]

FEDERICO: You've finished writing.
ENRIQUE: Yes, there is the letter;
And I am hoping you'll be satisfied
With my protection, as I have been, Federico,
With your assistance.
FEDERICO: You're a sovereign prince,
And I entrust my interests, life, and honor
Unto your care. Farewell. The night is come,
And I would rather wait than lose my chance.
ENRIQUE: Very well — but you will surely let me
Come with you to the outskirts of the town.
FEDERICO: Excuse me if I don't accept this honor;
But yet, I am afraid of everything,
Even of my own shadow; and though I hide
From you, believe me, were it possible
I would hide from myself.
ENRIQUE: And so you wish
To go alone?
FEDERICO: Yes. Once again, farewell.
ENRIQUE: Since I may not go with you, as I'd wish,
Farewell.
        [Knock at the door]
FEDERICO: Was that a knock?
ENRIQUE: Yes.
FEDERICO: [Opening]   Who is it?

        [Enter ARNESTO]

ARNESTO: It is I.
FEDERICO: What! Señor, out at this hour?

ARNESTO: Yes,
    I came to seek you.
FEDERICO: Me? What do you wish?
    [Aside] I tremble!
ARNESTO: I hear that when you came back to your house,
    Señor, you were a little indisposed.
    That troubled me, for as you are aware,
    I have a high regard for you; and so,
    Before I went to bed I wished to see you,
    And find out how you were.
FEDERICO: May heaven bless you
    For being so solicitous for me!
    But they were wrong to tell you I was ill:
    Never have I felt better.
ARNESTO: I am delighted
    They were mistaken. What are you doing now?
FEDERICO: Passing the time with Señor Enrique, talking
    Of this and that.
ARNESTO: Indeed, the conversation
    Of a wise and witty friend is better worth
    Than all the books in the world. It is instructive
    As well as amusing.
FEDERICO: *[Aside]*   He's terribly long-winded.
ENRIQUE: *[Aside]* I will cut short this interview by going,
    Then he'll have less to say. *[To ARNESTO]* Will you
        permit me
    To take my leave.
ARNESTO: What! When I come, you go?
ENRIQUE: Yes and no — no, since I wished to go
    Before I saw you; yes, since Federico
    Will not perceive my absence now you're here.
ARNESTO: Adieu, then.

                                            [Exit ENRIQUE]
FEDERICO: Señor, now that we're alone,
    Have you some orders for me? Why do you look
    On every side?
ARNESTO: I'm looking for a chair
    On which to sit. I'm dropping with fatigue.
    Come, let's sit down.
        [They sit]
FEDERICO: *[Aside]* I'm in a state. I'm in such a hurry, and
    he comes here so complacently.
ARNESTO: What have been your distractions during these past
    evenings?
FEDERICO: *[Aside]* I'm having a nice evening now! *[Aloud,*
    rising] I'm in the habit of going to the palace. If
    you wish, let us go. I shall have the honor of escort-
    ing you to your home.
ARNESTO: Later, later... It's still early.

[Makes him sit]
FEDERICO: What! Is it early? *[Aside]* Ah! Laura, shall I
   lose you then today?
ARNESTO: Do you play piquet?
FEDERICO: *[Aside]* What coolness! And I'm in despair.
   [Aloud] No, señor.
ARNESTO: As I had much ado to go out, and as I'm comfortable
   here, I don't want to return so soon.
FEDERICO: *[Aside]* Does he call this "soon"? *[Aloud]* I
   wish to go because the Duchess gave me today some dis-
   patches which will occupy me at the palace all night.
      [He begins to rise; ARNESTO stops him]
ARNESTO: Well, we'll go together and I'll assist you. I
   have a superb handwriting.
FEDERICO: I would not dream of giving you such trouble.
ARNESTO: It would not be a trouble, but a pleasure.
FEDERICO: It would not be proper for me to accept. And then
   I want to take you home because I have to see one of my
   friends.
ARNESTO: I'll go with you. Surely I should not be a hin-
   drance to you? If I must wait, I'll wait till tomorrow
   if need be, and if by chance it's an affair you're hav-
   ing, I'll give you my word to keep watch in the street.
   Fear nothing — count on me.
FEDERICO: I know that I can rely on your courage. *[Rises,*
   and ARNESTO does likewise] But I must go alone. God be
   with you.
ARNESTO: Be assured that you will not go — or that I will
   accompany you.
FEDERICO: But, señor, what compels you?
ARNESTO: You have only to ask yourself, and your uneasiness
   will give you your answer.
FEDERICO: I don't know what you're talking about: I'm not
   uneasy.
ARNESTO: I know well that you are, and that you will not go
   out except accompanied by me.
FEDERICO: *[Aside]* What a strange and awkward situation!
ARNESTO: You seem astonished?
FEDERICO: Yes, and more than astonished.
ARNESTO: Well, Federico, let us stop beating about the bush.
   I know that someone has given you a rendezvous by a
   letter.
FEDERICO: *[Aside]* Heavens! He knows everything! What a
   disaster!
ARNESTO: As I am the Governor of Parma,
   My duty and my honor both require
   I should prevent this meeting. You yourself
   Will realize that if I let you go,
   I should at once be failing in my duties

To the office I hold, and in the obligation
To my personal honor. So, I repeat,
I am compelled either to keep you here,
Or else to go with you. I can't allow you
To bring your enterprise to a conclusion.
FEDERICO: *[Aside]* He could not be more plain. *[Aloud]* I
    understand you
  Señor; but will you be good enough to believe
  Your honor does not run the slightest risk?
ARNESTO: How could that be?
FEDERICO: Will you allow me, señor,
  To speak with equal frankness.
ARNESTO: Yes, of course.
FEDERICO: You know I am a gentleman.
ARNESTO: I know
  That your nobility is pure as day.
FEDERICO: On this reply. I hope you will arrange matters
  So that the person who has written to me
  Will accept my hand.
ARNESTO: I will arrange for that
  With the greatest pleasure; and I hope, Federico,
  It will be soon as possible.
FEDERICO: A thousand thanks!
ARNESTO: Tell me only who this person is.
FEDERICO: *[Aside]* Was I then wrong to think that I was
    happy?
ARNESTO: For I will go to where the person waits you.
FEDERICO: You don't know who it is?
ARNESTO: No — all I know
  Is that you've had a quarrel and been challenged.
FEDERICO: You know no more?
ARNESTO: No.
FEDERICO: Well, now...
ARNESTO: Now?
FEDERICO: I will not ask you more. It would not be
  Proper for me to tell you what the name is
  When you are ignorant of it, and I'll know
  Without your counsel what I ought to do.
ARNESTO: And do you think that I shall not know too
  What is my duty?
FEDERICO: I don't deny it, señor;
  But the person who awaits me will not wait
  Much longer.
ARNESTO: I will stop you meeting him.
FEDERICO: How?
ARNESTO: You will see. *[Calling]* Hola!

  [Enter GUARDS]

GUARDS: Señor?

ARNESTO: Guard all the doors.
  [To FEDERICO]   Surrender — or see to what you are ex-
      posed.
FEDERICO: *[Aside]* O Heavens! My happiness is over now.
  And my misfortune starts! I might have known.
  [Aloud] You have no need, señor, of so many guards.
ARNESTO: Possibly. But I warn you, as I go,
  Not to attempt to flee. You would be slain.
                                [Exeunt ARNESTO and GUARDS]
FEDERICO: It is not fear of death which stops me now;
  The thing I fear, what I dread more than death,
  Is to cause a scandal, which will compromise
  Her whom I love. But, on the other hand,
  It is impossible for me to stay
  In ignorance of what has happened to her.
  I know a way by which I can escape
  Into the neighboring house. Wait for me, Laura,
  I'll see you soon, despite your father's soldiers,
  Despite the Duchess's rage.
                                                    [Exit]

      Scene 4: The Palace Garden. Night. At one side
      an expanse of wall, with a shuttered window

  [Enter LAURA]

LAURA: O shades of night, which are at once the cradle
  And tomb of light! If the misdeeds of love
  Are written on your scroll of ebony,
  Holding as many tales as there are stars,
  Pray let my destiny be traced on you
  Until it vanish at the break of day;
  And do not wonder that unlucky love
  Parades his jealousy here; for, by my honor,
  If that's a fault, I have some large excuses;
  My father tyrannizes over me;
  The man to whom I am betrothed constrains me;
  My rival persecutes me. Federico
  Delays his coming and the time is passing.
  What can have happened to him? I ought not
  To fear that he would change, though Flérida
  Declared her heart to him: he is too faithful,
  Too constant... Doubtless, then, some accident
  Keeps him at home; but in my situation
  One always assumes the worst. I don't know why.
  That love has this effect — it always does.

  [Enter FLÉRIDA]

FLÉRIDA: *[Aside]*   Fabio informed me
   His master ordered him to wait for him
   Upon the bridge, and I've deduced from that,
   That Federico's lady must inhabit
   The palace... Laura went to bed so early
   I could not ask her to keep watch again;
   And as I cannot trust another lady,
   I've come myself: thus both I and Arnesto
   Are working to prevent this rendezvous.
   But what do I see? If the uncertain starlight
   Which plays upon those dark clouds does not cheat me
   I see a moving body — and my hope
   Is realized. *[Aloud]* Who goes there?
LAURA: *[Aside]*   O heavens!
   It is the Duchess! May my wits defend me!
   [Aloud] It's someone who is waiting here because
   Flérida ordered her to come and see
   Who in the night outrages and insults her.
FLÉRIDA: Don't speak so loudly, Laura.
LAURA: Who is it?
FLÉRIDA: I.
LAURA: You, señora, alone in the garden here?
   At this hour.
FLÉRIDA: Yes, it's I.
LAURA: *[Aside]*   I am upset.
FLÉRIDA: As I forgot this morning to request you
   To watch again tonight, I've come myself.
LAURA: You wronged me, señora; for there is no need
   To repeat each day what has been told me once,
   Besides, another thing compelled me to come down.
FLÉRIDA: What has happened?
LAURA: *[Aside]*   Love, let my fault itself
   Now serve as my excuse. *[Aloud]* As I was standing
   Just now, at the window opening on the park,
   I heard some horses passing. I suspected
   Something was up — to reassure myself
   I have come down.
FLÉRIDA: The thing you have described
   Exactly fits what I've already heard:
   I thank you for your zeal. What have you seen
   Since you came down?
LAURA: I have seen nothing, señora,
   Which links up with the sound which made me come,
   But you can now retire: it is enough
   That I am here.
FLÉRIDA: Stay, then.
LAURA: Yes, señora. *[A knock]*
FLÉRIDA: Listen,
   Was that a knock?

LAURA: The wind often deceives. *[Another knock]*
FLÉRIDA: This time it's not the wind. Open and answer.
LAURA: I?
FLÉRIDA: Yes, I will come behind you, and we'll try
   To find out who it is, and whom he seeks.
LAURA: My voice is too well known.
FLÉRIDA: Disguise it, then.
   Go on.
LAURA: *[Aside]* I am afraid. It's hard to play
   A double role in this nocturnal comedy
   In which our figures can be good for nothing.[19]
     [Another knock]
FLÉRIDA: What do you fear?
LAURA: That I shall be recognized
   As soon as I speak.
FLÉRIDA: How odd you are! Go on.
LAURA: *[Opening]* Who's there?
FEDERICO: *[Appearing]*   A man who's dying, beauteous
     Laura.
LAURA: *[To FLÉRIDA]* You see! I have been recognized al-
   ready.
   It was enough to utter but one word.
FLÉRIDA: I too have recognized you all at once.
LAURA: Señor, since you know me, you must know
   I am not her you seek. Be off. Be glad
   That my insulted honor is contented
   For all my vengeance now, to slam the shutter
   Upon your face. *[She shuts]*
FEDERICO: *[Within]* Laura! My lady! My life!
   It's not my fault that I have come so late.
   Listen to me, and kill me — otherwise
   I'll kill myself at once.
LAURA: *[To FLÉRIDA]*   I was quite right
   To say he'd recognize me!
FLÉRIDA: Hold your tongue!
LAURA: Ah! If my father or Lisardo knew!
FLÉRIDA: Do not shout! Don't shout!
LAURA: What misery!
FEDERICO: Listen to me and kill me. For pity, Laura,
   Open.
FLÉRIDA: *[Opening and disguising her voice]* What would you
     say to me?
FEDERICO: It was Flérida in her jealous rage
   Who sent your father to prevent my coming.
   He kept me in the house and I could not
   Escape till now. Why do you delay?
   The horses now are waiting in the park
   And I've a letter from the Duke of Mantua
   Which gives to us asylum and protection

In his dominions. Come now, let us go.
The dawn is breaking — but that matters little
Once we have left the town.
LAURA: *[Aside]*   If he had more
To tell me, he would have told it by this time.
FLÉRIDA: Federico, it is too late now.
It's best for you to go back to your prison,
And then tomorrow we can make new plans.
FEDERICO: My life and soul belong to you, and so
I must obey you. But are you still annoyed?
FLÉRIDA: Yes, with my star, but not with you. Adieu!
       [Shuts window]
FEDERICO: Adieu!
FLÉRIDA: Well, Laura? Say nothing to me
Since I ask nothing. *[Aside]* I die of jealousy.
LAURA: Notice, señora...
FLÉRIDA: Go in. You cannot stay here the whole night.
LAURA: *[Aside]* I greatly fear her vengeance.
FLÉRIDA: *[Aside]* The world shall learn that I am who I am.
Come, Laura.
LAURA: *[Aside]* Unlucky that I am, I've lost all hope.
FLÉRIDA: But who is opening the postern gate?
LAURA: As far as I can judge, by these first streaks
Of dawn, it is my father.
FLÉRIDA: Yes, it is he.
Wait for me there — I wish to know the reason
He opens at this hour the garden gate.
LAURA: *[Aside]* O heaven, protect me! Let me not lose at
      once
Both life and honor. *[They retire]*

[Enter ARNESTO, FABIO, and GUARDS]

ARNESTO: Come, Fabio, I charge you,
Tell me at once the reason why you waited
With horses at the entrance to the park?
FABIO: Believe me, señor, that never in my life have I done
anything for a reason, for I never meddle with reasons.
ARNESTO: Why were you there?
FABIO: As for me, señor, I have to sit at table with my mas-
ter, and therefore I do what he wishes.
ARNESTO: Tell me with whom Federico had a quarrel yesterday?
FABIO: That must have been with his mistress, because he
didn't know how to get rid of her.
ARNESTO: I'll make you tell the truth. You shan't escape
me.
FABIO: A doctor was out hunting and one of his friends said
to him: "There's a hare couching. Lend me your arquebus, which I'll fire before he rises." The doctor replied: "Don't be afraid that he'll rise: for since a

doctor has seen him in his bed, he'll never get up."
ARNESTO: I'm delighted, Fabio, to see you so humorous at
    such a moment.
FABIO: I'm always the same. *[FLÉRIDA comes forward]*
ARNESTO: What! You here, señora.
FLÉRIDA: Yes my troubles
    Have made me come down. What is happening?
ARNESTO: I went tonight to execute your orders,
    But as I could not keep him in his house
    By subterfuge, I have arrested him,
    And I have left him guarded in his house.
FLÉRIDA: Yes, certainly, he has been guarded well.
ARNESTO: I've scoured the countryside to try and find
    The man who waited for him, but in vain:
    I've only found his valet near the bridge,
    Who stood there with two horses; and not wishing
    To let him know his master was a prisoner,
    I thought to bring him home, and entered here
    By the postern gate of which I have a key.
FABIO: Have I offended anyone by holding horses?
ARNESTO: What do you wish, señora, should be done
    With Federico and with Fabio?
FLÉRIDA: Bring Federico here: my only aim
    Was to prevent misfortune, and now I know
    All that I need to know. Let Fabio go.
FABIO: A thousand thanks.
ARNESTO: I go to seek Federico.
                                                [Exit]
LAURA: Think what you're doing, señora; do not injure
    My reputation.
FLÉRIDA: Leave me, Laura.

    [Enter ENRIQUE]

ENRIQUE: Señora,
    If as a stranger I can ask for grace,
    I'd ask you to restore his liberty
    To Federico.
FLÉRIDA: There's no need to ask,
    For he is free. But tell me now, Enrique,
    Have you had letters from the Duke today?
ENRIQUE: I? No, señora.
FLÉRIDA: Well, I have.
ENRIQUE: *[Aside]*   How odd!
FLÉRIDA: And in this letter the Duke has written me
    That your affair is settled; and so, no doubt,
    You will return to Mantua tomorrow,
    Since you have nothing to detain you here.
ENRIQUE: It's true, señora, that I've not yet had
    A letter from the Duke, but I have had one

      From one of his best friends, who urges me
      Not to return so soon, because my hope
      Is not yet realized.
FLÉRIDA: Although your friend
      May tell you this, I tell you to return
      Tomorrow, for you're doing nothing here
      And you are needed there.
ENRIQUE: *[Aside]*   O heavens! The Duchess
      Dismisses me now with as much indifference
      As wit.

    [Enter LISARDO]

LISARDO: Give me your hand, señora, and allow me
      To kiss my Laura's hand. My happiness
      Is now assured. I have received this moment
      The dispensation which my love awaited
      So many centuries.
FLÉRIDA: *[Aside]*   His arrival's timely!
LAURA: *[Aside]* What grief I suffer!

    [Enter ARNESTO and FEDERICO]

ARNESTO: Here is Federico.
FEDERICO: What does your Highness order?
FLÉRIDA: That you give
    Your hand to Laura; for I'm more unselfish
    Than you supposed, and it is necessary
    The world should know it too.
FEDERICO: ⎱
                      What do you say?
LAURA: ⎰
FLÉRIDA: That I am who I am.
ARNESTO: But don't you see,
    Señora, that you are insulting me?
LISARDO: And that you do me wrong.
FLÉRIDA: It's necessary,
    Believe me, both of you.
ARNESTO: These words provide
    Another reason why I should refuse.
    Let it not be said there were secret reasons
    To make this marriage necessary.
FEDERICO: Señor,
    Whether these reasons are avowed or secret,
    You need not blush for me.
ARNESTO: I know it, señor;
    But I refuse consent.
FEDERICO: Yet you have promised
    To give me Laura.
ARNESTO: To you?
FEDERICO: Yes.
ARNESTO: When was that?

FEDERICO: In my own house, last night, when you declared
    That you would strive to make me give my hand
    To one who waited for me. That was Laura,
    And this ought to suffice you.
LISARDO: But not me,
    And rather than submit, I'll lose my life.
FEDERICO: I will defend my rights.
FLÉRIDA: What's this?
ARNESTO: I'll be
    Your second, Lisardo.
ENRIQUE: And I yours, Federico.
FLÉRIDA: *[Aside]* O cruel grief! But it is honor's part
    To heal love's sorrows. *[To ARNESTO and LISARDO]* If
      it's not enough
    For me to order it, know then that Federico
    Has for his second the Duke of Mantua.
ARNESTO: Who?
ENRIQUE: It is I
    Who came here to the palace incognito,
    That I might serve the lovely Flérida,
    I who protect Laura and Federico.
FLÉRIDA: And I, too, so that the world may learn
    My equanimity has conquered wrath.
ARNESTO: Upon my faith, Lisardo, since the Duke
    And Duchess are for them, I'll range myself
    On their side too.
LISARDO: I must console myself
    For what I've lost — although the loss is great —
    Seeing it's Federico whom she loves.
ENRIQUE: And now, señora, I implore you humbly
    To recompense my constancy and love.
FLÉRIDA: There is my hand. *[Aside]* I will perforce forget
    What I have been, so that I shall remember
    What I am now.
LAURA: Now all my prayers are answered.
FEDERICO: I've nothing more to pray for.
FABIO: Thousands of times I've been on the point of saying
    that Federico's lady was Laura. Now it's out at last,
    it is THE SECRET SPOKEN ALOUD. *[To the audience]* Ex-
    cuse our imperfections, for which in all humility we ask
    forgiveness.

ଈଈଈଈଈଈଈଈଈ

THE END

ଈଈଈଈଈଈଈଈଈ

No siempre
lo peor
es cierto

The exact date of composition of Calderón's *No siempre lo peor es cierto* remains to be determined. Its earliest known version is that published in the *Primera parte de comedias escogidas...* (Madrid, 1652). And H. W. Hilborn, for reasons of versification, assigned it to the years 1648-1650. Hilborn's methods of dating, however, have been seriously questioned by more recent critics of Calderón.[1] Moreover, there exists a document, dated 1651, which lists both new and old plays then in the repertoire of a Madrid theater company. One of the plays on the "old" list is *No siempre lo peor es cierto*.[2] Since the play was old in 1651, then it would have been written before 1644; for few, if any, secular plays were composed in Spain during the years 1644-1649, owing to the closure of the theaters for long periods of public mourning following the deaths of Queen Isabel and Prince Baltasar Carlos. The play might even have been composed in the 1630s; at least four of the five other plays on that "old" list were written in this decade. A more probable date, however, would appear to be 1640-1642. The work shows certain affinities with *El pintor de su deshonra*. There are, for example, verbal similarities between Don Juan's condemnation of the code of honor in act 3 of the tragedy and Don Pedro's comments on the same theme in *No siempre lo peor es cierto*. Don Juan's famous refrain, "Mal haya el primero, amén, / que hizo ley tan rigurosa," is repeated almost verbatim in Don Pedro's monologue: "Woe to the first who made so harsh a law."[3] It is unfortunate that the precise date of *El pintor de su deshonra* is also a matter of dispute; but most critics favor the years 1640-1642. Like many other plays by its author, *No siempre lo peor es cierto* was quickly to achieve fame and exercise influence outside Spain, notably in England and France. It was translated freely in the early 1660s by George Digby, earl of Bristol, as *Elvira; Or, The Worst Not Always True*. And Aphra Behn was supposed to have been influenced by it in *The Dutch Lover* (1673), though in her case the influence was probably indirect, through Digby's translation, or from the French adaptation by Scarron, *La fausse apparence* (1663).

At first glance, *No siempre lo peor es cierto* seems to be a very conventional cloak-and-sword comedy. It has a contemporary Spanish setting, in Valencia, which allows for traditionally topographical and topical references to real Spanish places, traits, customs, and social conditions. In typically striking contrast to the robust realism of the setting, there is the characteristically improbable plot, dependent on a most unlikely collection of coincidences. Carlos finds refuge for Leonor in the house of Don Juan. Don Juan's sister, Beatriz, happens to be the mistress of Don Diego, the man responsible for ruining Leonor's reputa-

tion. Don Juan happens to be the very person to whom Don
Pedro applies for help in restoring his honor and that of
his daughter, Leonor. Add to this the fact that Leonor is
in Juan's house under a false identity, that Carlos is hidden in a room in Juan's house, that Diego comes secretly to
Juan's house to visit Beatriz, and we have very much the
same effectively claustrophobic dramatic atmosphere and the
same breathless confusion of misunderstandings, overheard
conversations, concealments, discoveries and confrontations
so successfully managed by the dramatist in comedies like
La dama duende and *Casa con dos puertas.*

Yet closer inspection reveals that in certain important
respects *No siempre lo peor es cierto* is by no means a typical product of Calderón's comic talent. His heroine, Leonor, for instance, has more in common with the unfortunate
wives of his honor-tragedies than with the energetic and
spirited heroines of his best known cloak-and-sword plays.
For Leonor, unlike the dynamic and resourceful Ángela of *La
dama duende,* is essentially a passive character, dramatical-
ly interesting much less for what she does than for what be-
falls her. She is in fact strongly reminiscent of Serafina
in *El pintor de su deshonra:* the virtuous and almost blameless victim of other people's mistakes and wrongdoing and
of unfortunate combinations of circumstances. In Golden Age
terminology, Leonor is bedeviled by an adverse star. She
loses her reputation in the eyes of the world. She loses
the trust of the man she loves. She almost loses her innocent young life at the hands of her own father. And, spir-
itually overwhelmed by the weight of her misfortunes, she
comes close to losing her sanity. At the beginning of act
3 her mental state is very grave. As Juan informs Carlos:
"...she seemed to have lost her reason — / Her speech and
conduct did so much betray / Her trouble and confusion."[4]

Carlos for his part, the most important male character
in *No siempre lo peor es cierto,* also resembles a tragic
figure in the making. He reminds us to some degree of the
heroes of Calderón's honor-tragedies, particularly of Gutierre in *El médico de su honra.* Carlos's behavior toward
Leonor may be compared with that of Gutierre toward another
Leonor. Gutierre discovered a man in the house of his mistress; deeply concerned for his honor, he would not accept
her innocence. Carlos finding himself in the same predicament displays a similar attitude. Behind his stubborn refusal to believe that his Leonor might be innocent there
lies an extreme concern to safeguard his own honor from any
possible risk. Yet it must be said that Carlos is much less
ruthless than Gutierre. The latter deserts his unfortunate
mistress and marries Mencía instead, the wife whom he will
eventually destroy for his honor's sake. Carlos feels un-

able to marry Leonor, but he chivalrously protects her life,
and, wrongly supposing that she and Diego are lovers, he
even controls his own jealousy and tries to restore her reputation and happiness by arranging her marriage to Diego.
Also there can be no doubt as to the depth of Carlos's love
for Leonor. He is desperately unhappy in his belief that
for his honor's sake he must reject her and intends to go to
fight in Italy, hoping to end his unhappiness by dying on
the battlefield.[5]

The second pair of lovers in *No siempre lo peor es cierto,* Diego and Beatriz, make a much more typical duo for a
Calderonian comedy. Perhaps they are rather more frivolous
than is the norm, and they are certainly more unscrupulous;
but this means that they form a welcome dramatic contrast to
the extremely serious and worthy Carlos and Leonor. Calderón must depend heavily on the frivolous couple to provide
the comedy in his play. They are particularly amusing in
the first act. Diego visits Beatriz, fondly imagining that
she knows nothing of his activities while he was in Madrid.
But Beatriz had bribed Ginés, Diego's servant, to keep her
informed. And she is well aware that Diego spent his time
in the capital pursuing another woman, until he was attacked
by that woman's lover and left for dead. What is more, we,
the audience, realize that Beatriz knows the truth; for we
were present when she read Ginés's letter and were entertained by her indignant reaction. But now Beatriz plays a
waiting game. She allows Diego to deliver a flowery speech
protesting his great love and need for her. She sweetly
asks some apparently innocent and casual questions about his
stay in Madrid, which lead him into further extravagant un-
truths. Then she pounces and, in a witty tirade, which
likens Diego to a criminal, the lady in Madrid to his judge,
and the lady's lover to his executioner, denounces his disloyalty.[6]

In the first two acts this amusing pair are ably assist-
ed to entertain the audience by the two servants, Ginés and
Inés. Their roles, however, almost disappear in act 3: a
fact that strengthens our impression that *No siempre lo peor
es cierto* has a markedly serious emphasis and brings us
close to tragedy. Yet in the end Carlos does discover, as
the title indicates, that "the worst is not always certain,"
and accepts Leonor's innocence. So the outcome is a happy
one; more genuinely happy, perhaps, than that of many of
Calderón's lighter comedies. For we can feel assured,
since Carlos and Leonor deeply love each other, that they
will have a contented married life together. As for Diego
and Beatriz, whether their marriage turn out well or
badly, we are left with the feeling that they deserve each
other.[7]

Notes

1. See, for example, N. D. Shergold and J. E. Varey, "Some Early Calderón Dates," *Bulletin of Hispanic Studies* 38 (1961):274-75.

2. See C. Pérez Pastor, *Documentos para la biografía de D. Pedro Calderón de la Barca* (Madrid, 1905), pp. 189-90. The title is given as *Siempre lo peor es cierto [sic]*.

3. See below, p. 170.

4. See below, p. 183.

5. See below, p. 149.

6. See below, pp. 157-59.

7. For notes to the text of *The Worst Is Not Always Certain*, see pp. 285-88.

The Worst Is Not Always Certain

꣠꣠

DRAMATIS PERSONAE

Don Carlos　　　　　　　　　　　*Fabio, servant to Don Carlos*
Don Juan Roca　　　　　　　　　*Ginés, servant to Don Diego*
Don Diego Centellas　　　　　　*Doña Leonor*
Don Pedro de Lara, an old man,　*Doña Beatriz*
　father of Leonor　　　　　　　*Inés, servant to Beatriz*

The scene is laid in Valencia

꣠꣠

ACT ONE

Scene 1: A Room in an Inn

[Enter DON CARLOS and FABIO, in traveling dress]

CARLOS: Have you delivered my letter?
FABIO:　　　　　　　　　　　　　Yes, señor.
　　He seemed delighted and is coming promptly
　　To seek you at your inn.
CARLOS:　　　　　　　　And Leonor?
　　Has she arisen?
FABIO:　　　　　　No, she has not opened
　　Her shutters yet.
CARLOS:　　　　　　　Knock at her door. I wish
　　To acquaint her with the plans that I have made
　　To assure her life and honor — less for her
　　Than since I owe it to myself. Call her:
　　It's time that she awakened.

　　[Enter LEONOR]

LEONOR:　　　　　　　　　　Yes, Don Carlos,
　　You could talk thus if I were still asleep;

But one like me who tastes the bitter bread
Of hostile fate, who suffers every moment,
Cannot take any rest. What do you wish?
CARLOS: To inform you of the means which my affection
Would take for your protection in your plight,
Since I am not allowed to love you still,
Know then...
LEONOR: Stop there. Whatever you desire,
Whether it's fair or not, it is enough
For me to know it to submit to it.
Though in my sad position it is hurtful
To see you more solicitous to fulfill
A gentleman's duties than a lover's, yet
Your will is law to me, and I will blindly
Submit to it. Why should you urge me more?
CARLOS: Ah! lovely Leonor, how this submission
Would touch my heart, if only it proceeded
From love and not necessity.
LEONOR: The man,
Like you, who lets himself be taken in
By false appearance, is not easily
Redeemed from error, especially when he makes
Such feeble efforts to assure himself
Whether he's right or wrong.
CARLOS: Do not attempt
To justify yourself — that is impossible.
LEONOR: Grant me one favor: it will be the last
My love demands of you.
CARLOS: Whatever it is,
You can count on it. What is it you desire?
LEONOR: Listen to me at least, then if you must,
Refuse to believe me.[1]
CARLOS: Then, on that condition,
I will consent. Speak. What do you ask?
LEONOR: Your attention only.
CARLOS: One moment. Fabio!
FABIO: Sir?
CARLOS: If the man arrives, on whom you called,
Come in before him, so that Leonor
Has time to hide.

                                        [Exit FABIO]

                    Speak now.
LEONOR: My dear Don Carlos...
But no, I begin badly. I wish to speak
The truth, and I begin with something false.
You are not mine now any more, Don Carlos.
But oh, how much I love you, since the words
That cause offense to you are words of love...
You know I sprang of noble blood, and how

My family is held in high esteem;
You also know, Don Carlos, that this esteem
I've not demerited, though my misfortunes
Have soiled my reputation. Alas! I tremble
To approach this subject, feeling (to my shame)
The truth itself accuses me[2] — for who,
In seeing me wander in another region,
Accompanied only by a young gallant,
And treated by him with indifference,
So that I owe his care not to his love,
But merely to his sentiments of honor,
Who would believe that I had not deserved
Such treatment by my conduct? How explain
That the very man on whom I most rely
Is the same man to whom I give offense?...
But what does it matter, after all, that Fortune
And inauspicious stars conspire against me
With false appearances to ruin me?
One day the truth will triumph. As the sun,
Eclipsed for a moment, pierces with its beams
The jealous shades which covered up its light,
So will my virtue one day be victorious,
Emerging from the mists which tarnish now
Its natural brightness. Meanwhile I should use
The time you have allowed me and return
To my unhappy story. In Madrid,
My native city — and would to heaven, it
Had been my tomb! — one evening, Don Carlos,
You saw me: I went with several of my friends
To Saint Isidorus;[3] and you contrived
To accost us — the freedom of the promenade
Favoring your boldness then — you paid attention
To my beauty, I would say, if I supposed
That I possessed it; you were as gallant
As amiable; you had the art to hide
Your feelings underneath a courteous mask.
Then you began to haunt about my doors,
And sigh beneath my windows: night and day
You stood, a motionless statue, by my house,
Or dogged me like a shadow. You employed
The intermediary of friends and servants
To get, if not my thanks, at least my notice.
You know the time you spent, what pains, what art,
To make me read your letters, even one;
And in the end, persuaded your intentions
Were honorable, I listened to your vows —
Too easily, perhaps. But since you showed
Legitimate desires, I had my excuse:
Your noble birth, your conduct toward me,

Your qualities of mind. Once in accord,
We spoke together through my chamber-grille
In the silent night, our only confidant;
And soon, since we awakened the attention
Of those who will not mind their own affairs,
I agreed to see you in a servant's room
Where we were able to converse unseen —
A mad precaution, cause of all my woes,
Which freeing me from fears of those without,
Opened my doors to danger. One night you came
Later than usual; I will not ask you now
If keener pleasures had delayed you then,
I rather ought to thank you that you came
No sooner, since you came to your misfortune.
You entered and, when my unquiet affection,
My fearful constance, assaulted you
With love's reproaches which, with mingled trust
And fear, oft render tenderness more plainly,
Seeking to hide it. Hardly had I begun
To speak with you, Don Carlos, when I heard
A noise in my apartment... I returned
To find out what it was... You thought it was
A trick to punish you for being late,
And so you followed me...then, then... O heaven!
O cruel memory!...my voice is failing!...
I saw a man enveloped in a cloak
Coming toward me...[4]

[Enter FABIO]

FABIO: Sir, the gentleman
    To whom you sent me has arrived.
CARLOS: *[To LEONOR]*   Go in.
    He must not see you yet.
LEONOR: Nothing is lacking
    In my misfortunes. I do not even have
    The opportunity of lightening them
    By telling what they are.
CARLOS: It is in vain
    You seek to justify yourself.
FABIO: Señora, quick,
    If you wish to hide...he's coming in.
CARLOS: *[To FABIO]*   Leave us.
    [To LEONOR] You'll hear our conversation.
                                      [Exit FABIO]
LEONOR: Ah! how much
    Could I complain against my fatal star!
                                             [Exit]
CARLOS: I've no less reason to complain of mine
    Since it has robbed me of the thing it gave.

[Enter DON JUAN]

JUAN: Carlos! Dear cousin!
CARLOS: Let us embrace, dear Juan.
JUAN: I should not; but it's vain for me to have
    The justest motive for complaint — I see you,
    And all's forgotten. You're in Valencia,
    Carlos, but you are not in my house.
    What is the cause? Wherefore this injury
    Both to my friendship and our ties of blood?
CARLOS: Thanks, Juan, for your amiable reproaches.
    But here I have good reason for my conduct.
    How are you?
JUAN: As a man disposed to serve you
    In every circumstance and in spite of all.
CARLOS: How is your sister, my beloved cousin?
JUAN: Flourishing — but I beg you to cut short
    All compliments. What brings you here? What news
    In Madrid?
CARLOS: What do you think? In vain I fly
    From my misfortunes — they pursue me here.
JUAN: The little that you tell me, all this mystery,
    Your sighs, increase my wish to know the cause
    Which brings you here.
CARLOS: Some time ago I saw
    A beauty, and I loved her; and this feeling
    Struck me so suddenly; I do not know
    Which was the start of it — seeing or loving.
    Passionate, I assiduously wooed her;
    Constant, I suffered scorn; tender, I earned
    Some favors; jealous, I would weep in torment.
    For even so are the four ages of love:
    He takes his birth in the cold arms of scorn;
    He grows under the protection of desire;
    He is maintained by favors and he dies,
    Poisoned by jealousy... Well, then, one night
    I was with her in one of her servants' rooms,
    Adjoining her apartment, when we heard
    A sudden noise. She went within, and I,
    Fearing it was her father, and not wishing
    To leave her in this peril, followed her.
    And thereupon we saw a man come forth
    Wrapped in a cloak, and moving stealthily.
    "Who's that?" she asked. "Someone" (he answered her)
    "Who only wished to see what he has seen."
    I did not speak: roused by my jealousy
    And by my lady's presence, I relied
    Upon my sword to speak for me. We fought,
    Both resolute to conquer or to perish.

Heaven — shall I say in mercy or in anger? —
Willed that my foe should fall, as I believed,
Mortally wounded, and at the selfsame moment
I was struck down by the affront. You'll think,
No doubt, this was the sum of my misfortunes,
And that for this cause I was obliged to come
To Valencia, to escape the rigors of the law.
But no — there still remains for me to tell
The strangest story one has ever read
In all love's annals. Hearing the clash of swords,
To my mistress's despair, her women started
To shriek, so that her father was awakened.
Behold me then, devoured by jealousy,
Exposed to an old and noble father's wrath,
And hemmed in by his servants, while I have
On the one side my swooning mistress; on the other,
My adversary lying at my feet.
Such was my situation when the lady,
Regaining consciousness, begged me to save her.
A woman in the wrong is well advised
To trust a noble heart; and so, despite
Her treachery — the outrage I had suffered —
Instead of vengeance, I thought but of her.
"Follow me!" I cried; and with my sword and body
Protecting her, we safely gained the street.
Fear lent us wings; and soon in the residence
Of an ambassador we found asylum.
I sent to find one of my mistress's servants,
Who, learning secretly all that had chanced,
Came to inform me that the wounded man
Was staying in Madrid but for a while,
Engaged in a lawsuit — his name I have forgotten —
He had been wounded in the head and fallen
Unconscious; but the blow, though dangerous,
Had not been mortal; that an officer
Had put him under guard and taken him
To a neighboring house; that I myself was known
As the aggressor; and that all my goods
Had been distrained. I learned at the same time
My mistress's father with the tact and wisdom
Suiting his age and his nobility
Had brought no charge, nor lodged complaint against me,
Remitting to his sword the task of vengeance.
Beset by troubles, and in duty bound
To save her who had caused them, I decided
To leave Madrid and fly to another town
Where we could shelter from the threat of justice,
And from her kinsmen's wrath. I thought of you,
And come to beg your help. I've brought the lady,

Thinking of her, and stifling my resentment.
When I have put her in a place of safety,
I'll leave this cruel woman whom I defend
As a man of honor, whom as a lover
I still adore, but from whom I must flee
Because she has wronged me. Yes — tormented by
Conflicting passions, uniting the sentiments
Of gentleman and lover, full of tenderness
I cherish her, and full of jealousy
I loathe her. Since we left Madrid — believe me —
I have not spoken with her till this morning.
I would not wish it to be said of me,
My courage had been less than my desires.
He is a man uncivilized, a man
Insensate, cowardly, and infamous,
A man enslaved to sensual appetite
And animal desires, who is contented
With the accessory, after having lost
The principal. See now, I beg of you,
How the said lady would be able to live
Here in Valencia, under another name;
In what house or convent, in what village,
I can place her safely. The little I could bring
I'll leave you for her needs. As for my own,
My sword suffices me: for when she's safe,
I'll flee from her and go to serve the King
In Italy: and then I shall pray heaven
To grant that the first shot shall pierce my breast.
How can I wish for better than to see
The sudden ending of so many fears,
So many pains and torments, and such anguish
Which Love has made me suffer, and which honor
Now forces me to flee.[5]

JUAN: Your tale's so strange
And your adventure so extraordinary,
That my astonishment can be expressed
Only by silence. Let us leave what's past,
Since there's no remedy, and concentrate
On present needs. A convent would be best,
But they would charge you for this lady's board,
And you have lost your goods and been reduced
To a mere pittance. As for me, Don Carlos,
My soul, my life, my honor, all are yours
But my affairs are in a sorry state,
And I ought not to offer you assistance
Which I may not be able to continue;
And so, I think, if you should place this lady
In my own home, where she will...

CARLOS: Do not finish.

I appreciate your offers, but I can't agree
To accept them, nor to give my cousin burdens
Of such a nature... I have too much respect
For her, to let my lady stay with her...
Who, by her birth, is worthy, it is true
To sit beside her; but yet such escapades
Will always cast an evil luster on
Ancient nobility.

JUAN: All can be arranged.
My sister recently has settled in marriage
One of her maids, and wishes to replace her.
I'm paying my addresses to a friend
Of Beatriz, who can be fully trusted.
I'll beg her now to send, as from herself,
The lady in question; and my sister thus,
Ignorant who she is, will welcome her
Without embarrassment. Although, no doubt,
It will be somewhat awkward for this person
To enter my sister's house in such a guise,
It can be borne: for she will be a maid
Only in public; in private she will be
Treated just as a lady. For myself,
I'll do what I can to please her.

CARLOS: That would be
The surest way, I know; but I admit
I'd never dare propose it; for Leonor...

[Enter LEONOR]

LEONOR: Stop, Don Carlos; it is for me to reply.
Don Juan, I will not merely be content
And flattered to be servant in your house,
You will have in me a slave your kindness bought.
And if I can, in the middle of my woe,
Feel any consolation, it will be
In having for a master one who is
Close to Don Carlos. And so, upon my knees,
I beg you to be kind enough to grant
This favor. And since, after what you have heard,
I must seem guilty, and I should be grieved
If you admitted to your house a woman
As light as I appear, lest there should be
The slightest doubt, may the wrath of God destroy me,
May heaven's gates be closed to me forever,
If to the man discovered in my house
I ever gave a motive for such boldness,
Unless he should have seen in my contempt
Encouragement of his temerity.

JUAN: Your beauty and intelligence, señora,
Must recommend you in the strongest manner;

And if I have indeed proposed a service,
It is no longer for Don Carlos's sake,
But for your own. Kindly await me here.
I'm going to my lady's house to beg
A letter you will carry to my sister.
I will return immediately.

[Exit JUAN]

LEONOR: And so you have accomplished your desires;
You're going to be delivered from my presence.
There's only one thing more which I would ask.
It is a favor which you'll add to those
For which I am indebted.
CARLOS: In heaven's name,
Do not speak thus. You'll rend my heart. It is
Only at the moment when I'm going to lose you
That I feel how much I love you. But yet, say
What you desire of me?
LEONOR: That if one day
You see you have suspected me unjustly,
You'll keep your word.
CARLOS: Ah! Leonor, to pay
For such a happiness, that would be little...
I'll give you then my soul, my life. But how
Can I relent thus? Are you not the same
Who kept a man concealed in your apartment?
No, I do not wish to be undeceived,
And do not count on it. My one desire,
Now that you are in safety, is to shun you.
LEONOR: Go, go; heaven will one day take care
To justify me.
CARLOS: Ah! did there not remain
That hope, I should have died.
LEONOR: Ah! Carlos,
Sometimes you speak to me with tenderness,
Sometimes with fury. Why should you believe
Evil rather than good? Is it impossible
For me to be innocent?
CARLOS: Alas! I fear,
That it is always right to believe the worst.
LEONOR: Well, I rely upon my innocence;
And one day you will doubtless be convinced,
That contrary to common prejudice,
The worst is not always certain.

[Exeunt]

Scene 2: A Room in Don Juan's House

[Enter BEATRIZ and INÉS. BEATRIZ is reading a letter]

INÉS: *[Aside]* What's this paper my mistress is reading? It
seems to torment her, and I'm dying to know what's in
it. Sometimes she crumples it and gazes up to heaven,
and sometimes she weeps and sighs.

BEATRIZ: Was there ever a crueler fate?

INÉS: *[Aside]* She's beginning to read it again. What's the
reason for these conflicting emotions? Is it by any
chance the first draft of a play she is writing?[6]

BEATRIZ: It's rightly said that the pen is a viper, full of
fury, and its ink is a black poison spreading over the
paper. I know it now better than anyone, since this
letter has killed me. Who would believe it?

INÉS: I would.

BEATRIZ: What! Were you there, Inés?

INÉS: I've just come in and I've seen all the different
feelings which are vexing you. What is it that has
moved you so strongly?

BEATRIZ: I'll tell you, if only to assuage my grief. You
remember that Don Diego Centellas has courted me these
many months?

INÉS: Of course.

BEATRIZ: You know that, grateful for his constant attentions, I responded to his love?

INÉS: Yes, indeed.

BEATRIZ: You know, too, that despite his noble birth, he did
not wish to broach the matter to my brother till he knew
the result of a lawsuit which he went to Madrid to settle.

INÉS: Yes, señora. What then?

BEATRIZ: Well, Inés, his servant, who has certain obligations to me, has written this letter, from which it is
clear that Don Diego has fallen in love in Madrid, and
that the suit which has called him to the city is a
love suit. But the letter will tell you better of his
treachery, and how I'm right to be upset. *[Reads]*
"Señora, to fulfill my promise, which was that I should
tell you all that passed, I have the honor to let you
know that my master has had a fight with another gentleman in the house of a lady of this town, that he was
wounded and left for dead; that he passed two days unconscious and in prison. Thanks be to God, he is better, he is free, and he is about to return to Valencia,
etc." I stop there, for, I confess, I'm choking with
rage.

INÉS: After that, señora, there's no need to read more of it.

BEATRIZ: That's the suit which called Don Diego to Madrid!
INÉS: It was only to be expected; everyone in Madrid has
    love suits.
BEATRIZ: I have no words to express my grief!
INÉS: What rogues these men are! They take their leave in
    a frightful state, weeping buckets of tears[7] — and the
    tears last only till they catch a glimpse of another
    pretty face! But all is well, gentlemen, we do the
    same, and at the end of the road, God knows, we find
    ourselves even with you, and owing nothing.
BEATRIZ: I'm dying of jealousy and anger.
INÉS: You have good cause.
BEATRIZ: And my rage will last until... But, hush! wasn't
    that somebody knocking?
INÉS: Yes, señora.
BEATRIZ: Well, see who it is.
INÉS: You'd catch it, my poor Ginés, if someone wrote and
    told me that you had insulted my honor, and that you had
    had your head split open in Madrid.
                                                  [Exit]
BEATRIZ: Alas! Since I have learned now to my shame
    How men can change, I would that I could lose
    Memory too, since I have lost all hope.
    What would I not give to see the woman
    Who could engage his heart to such a point![8]

[Enter LEONOR and INÉS, LEONOR poorly dressed in a
cloak]

INÉS: She's here. Enter.
BEATRIZ: Who is asking for me?
LEONOR: A luckless woman who, if you'll allow her
    To kiss your hand, could thenceforth defy
    Her cruel destiny, since she will find,
    Señora, a sure refuge in your kindness
    Against the storms of fate.
BEATRIZ: Rise, rise, my friend.
LEONOR: [Aside] How wounding is her condescending tone!
BEATRIZ: What do you wish?
LEONOR: Here is a letter which
    Will tell you all.
BEATRIZ: From whom?
LEONOR: From Violante.
BEATRIZ: Inés, how pretty she is!
INÉS: Indifferently...
LEONOR: [Aside] O cruel Fortune, to what extremity
    Have you reduced me? And yet, although the past
    Afflicts me, the future terrifies me more.
BEATRIZ: Violante tells me in this letter
    That, having learned that I have lately settled

> One of my maids in marriage, she beseeches
> That I should take you in her place.

LEONOR: Alas!

BEATRIZ: She is sure of your virtue and your reputation
> And guarantees that I shall find in you
> Nothing except to praise. Her testimony
> Suffices me.

LEONOR: I thank you once again.

BEATRIZ: Where are you from?

LEONOR: The neighborhood of Toledo.

BEATRIZ: What brought you to Valencia?

LEONOR: I came
> With one of the Vicereine's ladies. She has died
> And I must therefore find another post.

BEATRIZ: Her manners and her person please me well
> What did you do when you were with this lady?

LEONOR: I was her sewing maid.

INÉS: *[Aside]*   That's possible —
> But not a maid, I guess.[9]

LEONOR: I dressed her hair,
> And fancy I could please you with my skill
> In that respect. Spring has no flower so lovely
> I have not learned to imitate it; my flowers
> Will give your hair the loveliness of Spring.
> You'll have no need to purchase skirts and collars;
> Starching and ironing I yield to none;
> I sew in finest linen, make all kinds
> Of scallops with facility, embroider
> Tolerably, and work on tapestry.[10]

BEATRIZ: You are exactly the person that I need.
> Remain here from this moment. Since I desire it,
> My brother, who is ruler of the house,
> Will raise no obstacle.

LEONOR: I can rely
> Upon his kindness; noble as he is,
> He'll not refuse protection to a woman
> Unfortunate as I am.

BEATRIZ: What is your name?

LEONOR: Isabel.

BEATRIZ: Take off your mantle.

[Enter DON JUAN]

JUAN: Beatriz...

BEATRIZ: Well, brother...

JUAN: What are you doing?

BEATRIZ: Something which will please you.

JUAN: What is that?

BEATRIZ: I know that you, as a devoted lover,
> Would wish me to accede to the requests

Of Violante, from whom I've just been sent
This maiden.

JUAN: Many thanks for your politeness,
And even for your raillery. *[To LEONOR]* For you,
Señora, both for the person who has sent you,
And for yourself, you're welcome to my house.
You will serve the sister, but yet the brother
Will do his best to serve you.

LEONOR: Heaven reward you
For all your kindness, sir. You have in me
A faithful slave.

JUAN: *[Aside]*   What say you of my house,
And of my pretty sister?

LEONOR: *[Aside]*   That thanks to her
Fate stops pursuing me.

JUAN: I'd speak with you
In private, Beatriz. I wish to ask
A favor.

BEATRIZ: What you will. *[To INÉS and LEONOR]* You're
dismissed.

> *[DON JUAN and BEATRIZ retire to the back of the
> stage]*

INÉS: I present myself to Señora Isabel as her humble servant, her friend and comrade, who will be always loyal
to her. I ask only one thing.

LEONOR: And that is...

INÉS: Not to be too scrupulous if she notices a love affair
going on.

LEONOR: There are no longer any scruples nowadays: they have
been discarded like old fashions. And besides, to tell
the truth, I have, like you, some little concerns.

INÉS: Heavens! You don't say so! In that case you will
find in me more sister than friend.

LEONOR: And you will find me more than a friend, a sister.
[Aside] Alas! Could I have foreseen that I would ever
have such conversations!

> *[Exeunt INÉS and LEONOR]*

BEATRIZ: Carlos is in Valencia?

JUAN: Yes, he is.
But do not speak of it. He goes in secret
To Naples, and has therefore not come here.
But yet he has proposed to come and see us
At nightfall; so, out of your love for me,
You should prepare for him a little present.

BEATRIZ: I'll search my cupboards and see if I can find
Something to offer him. Although I'm caught
A little unprovided, I'd be surprised
If I have not some gloves, some lace, a purse...
I have a hamper which I hope will please him.

JUAN: You are delightful.
BEATRIZ: You can rely on me
   For that — and supper.
JUAN: Farewell. I will return.
BEATRIZ: *[Aside]* Ah! Diego, how shall I avenge
   Your perfidies?

[Exit]

JUAN: Don Carlos must be told
   Of the effect of Violante's letter;
   And then this evening, in spite of his desire
   Not to be seen at all, I'll bring him here.

[Exit]

Scene 3: A Street outside Don Juan's House

[Enter DON DIEGO and GINÉS, in traveling clothes]

DIEGO: It must be confessed, Ginés, that it is a great pleasure to see one's hometown once again.
GINÉS: Yes, sir, especially when one has been at the point
   of never seeing it again.
DIEGO: Scarcely had I recovered, and been set free — thanks
   to the fact that no one registered a complaint against
   me — than I hastened to leave Madrid. Thus I avoided
   the vengeance that Leonor's kinsmen would have wished to
   take.
GINÉS: You've done well, sir. It is disagreeable enough to
   die; but to die twice would have been too vexing.
DIEGO: Is not that Don Juan coming out of his house?
GINÉS: It is indeed.
DIEGO: It seems to me, Ginés, that today all should go well
   for me.
GINÉS: A plague on it! What treasure have you found?
DIEGO: Is it not lucky that Don Juan goes out, so that I can
   speak with Beatriz?
GINÉS: What! You still remember her?
DIEGO: I have never forgotten her beauty.
GINÉS: It seemed to me that you did forget it a little the
   day you received on the head such a blow — I don't know
   whether it was the point or edge of the sword — that you
   were never likely to visit those parts again.
DIEGO: Separated from one's lady, one can court another.
   That is permitted to the most faithful lover.
GINÉS: These ladies, it is true, do much the same thing.
DIEGO: Go now. Ask for Inés and tell her of my arrival.
   Above all, remember...
GINÉS: What?

DIEGO: To say nothing of my adventure to anyone...above all
   in Beatriz's house.
GINÉS: Who? me, sir? How can you think it! I swear to you
   that they'll hear no more from me today than they
   learned yesterday before we arrived in Valencia.
DIEGO: Go and knock at the door.

             Scene 4: Within the House

INÉS: *[Within]* Who is it?
GINÉS: *[Within]* Señora Inés, a humble servant who returns
   to your feet as faithful and as constant as when he left
   you.

   [Enter INÉS and GINÉS]

INÉS: My own Ginés! Aren't you going to kiss me?
GINÉS: Several times, for I'm not a mean fellow.
INÉS: Why have you come back?
GINÉS: You'll hear about it later. At the moment there's
   something more urgent — my master wishes to speak with
   you.
INÉS: Has he also returned?

   [Enter DON DIEGO]

DIEGO: Yes, Inés, I am anxious to see you and hear the
   latest news of Beatriz.
INÉS: She's very well; and when she hears of your arrival...

   [Enter BEATRIZ]

BEATRIZ: Who has kept you so long, Inés?
DIEGO: It is a traveler, long buffeted
   By the storm of absence, and whose ship of love
   Has long been tossed and battered by the waves,
   Until the seas were calmer and the heaven
   More merciful, and they have let him sail
   To harbor at your feet; and he is come
   To the temple of his love to consecrate
   The vessel which had nearly been his tomb
   To the idol of his heart.[11]
BEATRIZ: *[Aside]*   These men are liars!
   But let me not betray myself. *[Aloud]* In vain,
   Diego...no, I'll tell you later *[To INÉS]* Inés,
   See now that Isabel does not come in,
   I would not have her learn on the first day
   About my griefs.
INÉS: You're right. *[To GINÉS]* I'll see you
        soon.

GINÉS: I hope so: then I'll demonstrate the truth
    Of the old song: "Inés, I love you true."

[Exit INÉS]

BEATRIZ: Yes, Don Diego, it is quite in vain
    For you to exaggerate the pains of absence:
    Never could you express what I have suffered,
    An ever-faithful lover. *[Aside]* How hard it is
    To stifle my resentment.
DIEGO: *[Aside to GINÉS]*   God be praised!
    She does not know it.
GINÉS: *[To DON DIEGO]*   How do you think she could?
BEATRIZ: How did you find your sojourn in Madrid?
DIEGO: I was far distant from the one I loved:
    In absence there is but one pleasure left.
BEATRIZ: And what is that?
DIEGO: To think we'll see again
    The one we love.
BEATRIZ: *[Aside]* The traitor! I have a viper in my heart,
    A cord around my neck! *[Aloud]* How is your suit?
DIEGO: I've left it where it was — my state of health
    Has forced me to return.
BEATRIZ: You were ill then?
DIEGO: Yes, because I could not see you.
BEATRIZ: But in Madrid
    There are other things to see. Are not the ladies
    Friendly and charming there?
DIEGO: Not having seen any,
    I cannot give an opinion.
BEATRIZ: Any?
DIEGO: Ask
    Ginés. Is it not true that I have been
    A pattern of constancy?
GINÉS: Why! yes, señora,
    He has been so constant there, that I have seen him
    About to die of love.
BEATRIZ: That's possible —
    But die for whom?
DIEGO: For whom do you think it was?
BEATRIZ: Then you are not the gentleman who changed
    From the civil suit which brought him to Madrid
    To a criminal one, so that a long-robed judge —
    But not a man — passed sentence on you which
    A certain rival executed on you.[12]
GINÉS: *[Aside to DIEGO]* How could she know it? We're in a
       horrid fix.
DIEGO: *[Aside]* I'm lost.
GINÉS: Why do you look at me like that?
    I haven't said a word.
DIEGO: What do you think

         She meant by that?
GINÉS: It's your adventure
      To a T.
BEATRIZ: All is known, Don Diego.
      And since you know the reasons that I have
      To be offended by a treacherous, fickle,
      Disloyal, and caddish hypocrite, who seeks
      To cover his offense by paying me
      Some hollow compliments, see me no more.
      I warn you else that in Valencia,
      As well as in Madrid, there is a woman
      Who can bring vengeance down upon a lover
      Inconstant and disloyal.
DIEGO: Consider, Beatriz...
BEATRIZ: Consider, Don Diego, it is late;
      Now that you bring me sorrow, it is pointless
      To risk my reputation talking to you,
      Though once you brought me joy. Therefore, farewell.
DIEGO: Till you are undeceived...
JUAN: *[Within]*   Fetch me a light.
BEATRIZ: O God! It is my brother.
GINÉS: Her brother? How
      Could he have known?

      [Enter INÉS]

INÉS: The master has arrived.
DIEGO: What's to be done?
BEATRIZ: I do not know.
INÉS: I have it. Go with Ginés
      Into this room, and stay in hiding there
      Till you can come out safely.
BEATRIZ: Alas! Alas!
INÉS: Quick!
GINÉS: *[Aside]*   To get out of this, I would willingly re-
      ceive
      Two hundred strokes.
               [DON DIEGO and GINÉS hide]
BEATRIZ: Shut the door over there, Inés,
      So that they can't be seen.
INÉS: It's closed completely.
JUAN: *[Within]* It's strange the house should not be lit to-
      night.

      *[Enter DON JUAN and DON CARLOS. LEONOR enters by an-
      other door with lights]*

LEONOR: Here is a light.
CARLOS: *[Aside]*   In seeing Leonor
      Carrying torches, the light has blinded me.
      [Aloud] Permit me cousin, that I kiss your hand,

    If I am not unworthy of this favor.
    [Aside] Ah! Leonor! A servant!
BEATRIZ: You cannot soothe me
    With compliments, Don Carlos, or succeed
    In making me forget you have not deigned
    To stay with us.
CARLOS: Already I have tried,
    Señora, to justify myself with Juan;
    It is for him to make excuses to you.
    But if I've not the honor to stay here,
    I shall be here in thought, and you will have
    My life and soul to serve you.
JUAN: I have already
    Informed my sister of your reasons, Carlos,
    Why you could not stay longer.
BEATRIZ: Since our happiness
    Must be so short, I'll do my best to serve you.
    You are not comfortable here. Come to my room.
    Isabel, light my cousin. *[Aside]* Heaven, have pity!
                      [Exit BEATRIZ]
       [JUAN, CARLOS, and LEONOR talk, taking care
       not to be overheard by INÉS]
LEONOR: Don Carlos, since today I have to serve you,
    It is the sweetest pleasure.
CARLOS: Ah! Leonor,
    If I could only serve you as I'd like,
    You would not need to serve another thus.
LEONOR: It's more than I deserve, since by ill luck
    You won't believe my oaths and protestations.
CARLOS: Who ever would lend credence to vain words
    Rather than to the witness of his eyes?
LEONOR: More than one has done so.
CARLOS: He was wrong.
LEONOR: Take care, Don Carlos, you must control yourself,
    So that they don't suspect.
CARLOS: *[Aside]*   How difficult
    To control myself in seeing Leonor
    In the guise of Isabel.
                 [Exeunt, except INÉS]
       [DON DIEGO and GINÉS show themselves
       behind the tapestry]
GINÉS: Can we come out, Inés?
INÉS: No, they will see you on your way out.
GINÉS: What shall we do then?
INÉS: Wait till our guest has gone.
GINÉS: What guest is that?
INÉS: A cousin of the family. I'll return
    To let you out. And if, by chance, my master
    Should shut the door, as soon as he's asleep,

Drop from the balcony.

GINÉS: From where, did you say?

INÉS: From the balcony. It is not far to jump.

GINÉS: I never jump, even at a dance. And so
    Arrange my exit in some other way.

DIEGO: Do the best you can, Inés.

GINÉS: You are accustomed
    To break your head, sir; it will be all the same
    To break your leg.

INÉS: Conceal yourselves. Don't talk!

DIEGO: Who has ever been in such a situation.

GINÉS: I have, sir; and what is worse, without knowing why
    or how.

                                          [Exeunt]

INÉS: This is a pretty kettle of fish! Pray God that all
    ends well.

                                          [Exit]

ༀༀༀༀༀༀༀༀༀༀༀༀༀༀༀༀༀༀༀༀༀༀༀༀༀༀༀༀༀༀༀༀༀༀༀༀༀ

ACT TWO

Scene 1: A Room in an Inn

[Enter DON CARLOS and FABIO]

CARLOS: Is everything ready?

FABIO: Yes, sir; the linen, the valises, all is ready. Only
    the post-horses are lacking.

CARLOS: There's another thing that must be done.

FABIO: What's that?

CARLOS: To inform Don Juan that I'm leaving this morning, so
    that I can take my leave of him.

FABIO: Doesn't he know of your departure?

CARLOS: Neither he nor Leonor, for yesterday evening I had
    not yet decided.

FABIO: Then I'll go and tell him.

CARLOS: No, wait. It seems that he's guessed my intention.
    Here he is, although it's scarcely day.

[Enter DON JUAN]

CARLOS: So early, Juan? What made you rise so early?

JUAN: I could address the same question to you. Where are
    you going in such haste?

CARLOS: Yesterday evening, when I returned, I learned that
    two Italian galleys were anchored at Vinaroz, and it's a
    chance I ought not to miss. Otherwise I don't know when
    I could leave Leonor; for though the sight of her is a

kind of death, to be deprived of the sight is also a
kind of death. The wisest thing is to flee. And now
that I'm contented about her lot, with your permission,
Juan, I'll leave today.

JUAN: If this permission depended on me, Carlos, it would be
a great comfort in my troubles if I could keep you here
for a while.

CARLOS: How is that?

JUAN: You should remain here some days more. My repose, my
life depend on it.

CARLOS: Fabio!

FABIO: Sir?

CARLOS: When the horses arrive, send them back.

[Exit FABIO]

You see, Juan, that your wishes are commands for me.
What has happened?

JUAN: We are alone?

CARLOS: Yes.

JUAN: Please shut the door.

CARLOS: There you are! Well! What is it?

JUAN: It is, my dear Carlos, such a great misfortune, such a
great pain, that I would not confide in anyone else in
the world — only to you, my friend, whose soul is the
half of mine: to you who share the same blood. See how,
from one day to another, everything alters with the
wheel of fickle fortune. Yesterday, in your troubles,
you came to ask my help: today it is I who ask for
yours. Ah! What a pitiful misfortune is mine, since
she hastens to claim what is owing to her!

CARLOS: What can have happened since yesterday evening which
has upset you so much?

JUAN: Yesterday evening, after you had gone...
You did not wish to stay the night, and I
Thought that I should not press you. You refused
My offer to accompany you here...
Then, wishing to retire, I had examined
The doors of my house, according to my habit,
Not from suspicion that anything was wrong,
I went to my room, and somewhat agitated
By the day's happenings, I could not sleep.
All kinds of fancies came into my mind,
And scarcely had I closed my eyes, when sleep
Forsook me. For some time I lay awake,
When — I tremble to recall it — I heard a window,
Which overlooked the street, being opened. At first,
Thinking it was a servant of the house
Who wished to chat, I opened silently
A window in my room, to see who it was;
Intending if I distinguished who it was

To remedy the harm without a fuss.
No one was in the street, and disabused,
Driving my vain suspicions far away
I thought the wind had caused the noise I heard.
How easily hope vanishes! That moment
I saw a man leap from the balcony.
I ran to fetch an arquebus, — too late,
For when I reached the window I perceived
This man and another disappearing
At the corner of the street. At the same time,
I heard the window close, and so was robbed
Of the consolation that it might be robbers:
I knew the person who had shut the lattice
Was an accomplice of the fugitives.
I wished to pursue them, but I realized
This would be useless: they had the start of me
And ran with all their power. All I could do
Was to discover which woman in the house
Had not yet gone to bed: so, to this end,
I opened my door, and found my sister's closed.
There was nothing to be done. If I had knocked,
All the women would have been alarmed;
I would then have been liable to suspect
Even the most innocent; and the guilty
Would have been put upon their guard. It is
Unwise for a man who has been wronged to show it,
When he's not able to avenge the wrong.
So I'll not change the way my house is run,
Nor yet my way of life; I shall appear
As I have always been; and I'll contrive
To dissemble my suspicions and my worries.
But to achieve my aim, I need a friend
Who can watch without when I'm at home, at home
When I go out. Since, therefore I am forced
To confide in another, whom could I better tell
Than you who are, as I have said, the half
Of my own soul; and who as friend and cousin
Should be concerned in all that might offend me?
Please listen to my plan. In my apartment
I have a closet full of books and papers,
In which no servant ever comes. If you
Will hide there... *[Knocking]* Did I hear a knock?
CARLOS: Wait. Who's there?
FABIO: *[Within]*   It's me, sir. Open quickly.
CARLOS: *[Opening]* Why do you knock? You saw I was engaged.

   [Enter FABIO]

FABIO: Because there's news which you should know at once.
CARLOS: What is it?

FABIO: As I waited at the door
   I saw the father of Leonor arrive
   In traveling dress, to ask for a night's lodging.
   You'll realize that I could not delay
   To tell you this, especially as they answered
   They had a room for him — one next to yours,
   Where he will see you if you venture out.
CARLOS: This is the last straw. He doubtless comes
   To pursue me as well as Leonor.
JUAN: He knows you?
CARLOS: Certainly.
JUAN: *[To FABIO]*   Watch for the moment
   When we can venture out without being seen,
   And let us know at once.
FABIO: Now is the time:
   He has just gone into his room.
JUAN: Well, let's escape,
   And see what can be done.
CARLOS: Let's hurry, Juan.
JUAN: Come to my house. It's now to your advantage
   As much as mine for you to hide there.
CARLOS: What fears assail me!
JUAN: What cares afflict me.
CARLOS: Ah!
   Leonor! The pains which you have cost me!

                                         [Exeunt]

              Scene 2: A Room in Don Juan's House

   [Enter BEATRIZ and INÉS]

BEATRIZ: Say nothing, Inés. You only aggravate
   My grief.
INÉS: But since we had the happiness
   Last night to let Don Diego get away
   So stealthily that he was not perceived,
   Why are you so distressed?
BEATRIZ: My very grief
   Should demonstrate my passion. What does it matter
   That they should leave the house without being seen
   By Isabel or my brother, if, when they've gone,
   And I am freed from fear, I find myself
   A prey to jealousy? Have you ever seen
   Such impudence, Inés? Did you observe
   With what false affability and show
   Of hypocritical sadness, Don Diego boasted
   Of his fidelity — to me who knew
   The dangers that he courted in Madrid

                     For another woman.
INÉS: He cannot overhear us,
       So I can take his part.   What would you have
       A man to do who goes up to Madrid,
       Center of beauty, elegance and fashion —
       A young gallant who's very much in love,
       But fifty leagues from the lady of his choice?
       He has already paid for what he did,
       Since he returned (it seems) from his adventure
       With a cracked pate.[13]   And that is why, señora,
       In spite of your disposition to accuse him
       I think that separation may excuse him.
BEATRIZ: My jealousy is not extravagant.   I know
       That when one truly loves, one must forgive
       Those infidelities which do not involve
       One's honor;[14] and, to tell the truth, to see
       Don Diego clear himself I'd give, —
       I know not what I would give... I'm mad.   I'm dying.
INÉS: One moment, señora.   If such is your desire
       You shall be satisfied.   I can foresee
       Naught that can hinder it.   If he lingers here,
       There'll be no cause for alarm, since we know how
       He can escape.
BEATRIZ: So be it.   And yet, Inés,
       I would not have him think me so enamored
       As to forget his conduct and myself
       Seek for excuses for him.
INÉS: There's a way
       To fix it up.
BEATRIZ: How?
INÉS: Thus.   I'll tell him that
       You're vexed and grieved extremely by his conduct
       And that a thousand times you have forbidden me
       To receive from him a letter or a message;
       But yet, to please him, I can take the risk...
BEATRIZ: Of what?
INÉS: Of bringing him to a place where you can
              talk.
       In such a way that I will get three things:
       First, that he sees you; then, that you do not seem
       To make advances; and lastly, he's in my debt.
BEATRIZ: I'm jealous, Inés, as you rightly thought.
       I've said enough to you — do what you will,
       But speak no more of it, or Isabel
       Will soon begin to suspect.

       [Enter LEONOR, with a tray of artificial flowers]

LEONOR: Here, señora,
       Are the flowers you asked me for.

BEATRIZ: I'll see them later.
   At present, Isabel, I have no taste
   For anything.
LEONOR: I should not be surprised
   To be so unsuccessful in my efforts:
   Who serve under a malignant star.
BEATRIZ: And I
   Ought not to be surprised at my vexations,
   Who love beneath a star that's even worse.

[Exit]

LEONOR: What is the cause of Lady Beatriz's grief?
INÉS: Nothing, my dear; it's nothing but the mood
   Of a great lady. She is melancholy,
   Capricious to a degree, and apt to change
   Her mind each hour, or minute. If you wish
   Not to displease her, listen, look and then
   Keep your mouth shut.

[Exit]

LEONOR: I hear and see enough,
   And have enough on which to hold my tongue.
   Mad Hope, why do you wish to make me think
   That here, far from my country and my home,
   Far from my father, I can cease to fear
   Misfortune? It is still so near to me
   That I ought not to hope that at long last
   Carlos will see the truth; Hope is so distant
   That I should not rely upon the future
   To clear my name; For that unlucky man
   Was but too right, who, suffering the same woe
   As mine, declared: "Miserable is he
   Who trusts to time to heal his ills at last";
   For if the remedy is sensible,
   It is uncertain and so slow indeed
   That usually before it has produced
   The desired effect, the patient is no more.
   I find it difficult to hide my grief.
   Was ever situation worse than mine?
   But did I ever give to tyrant Fortune
   A cause to persecute me?

[Enter DON JUAN]

JUAN: Isabel,
   Where is my sister?
LEONOR: In her room, my lord.
JUAN: Then I'll address to you another question:
   What are you doing all alone here now,
   Beautiful Leonor?
LEONOR: The same as always;
   Complaining of my fate. Have you seen Don Carlos?

JUAN: Yes, I had to see him before he left.
LEONOR: Already! He has gone!
JUAN: Yes, Leonor.
LEONOR: And I've not seen him! How little he respects me!
JUAN: Come, Leonor, do not indulge yourself
    In new distresses. You are placed already
    Under my care, and you will find in me
    A faithful servant who would, if need arose,
    Venture his life and honor for your sake.
LEONOR: Generous and noble as you are,
    You lend your aid to an unfortunate woman;
    And so that you can see what confidence
    Your kindness has inspired, allow me now —
    Since I'm unable to control my grief —
    Allow me to relieve you of my presence.
    To show my sorrow to you would display
    A lack of gratitude; and if I weep
    It should not be before you.
                                        [Exit]
JUAN: That man was right
    Who said there was no difference between
    Suffering and seeing suffer. Nevertheless
    I had to say that Carlos had departed
    Though he was hidden in my study here.
    For it is quite essential for us both
    That no one knows his hiding place. They keep
    A secret best who do not know it. Besides
    Leonor's father being here, this course
    Is best for everyone. *[Knocking on door]* Carlos?

    [Enter DON CARLOS]

CARLOS: Are you alone?
JUAN: Of course. I would not come
    With other people.
CARLOS: Have you spoken yet
    With Leonor?
JUAN: Yes, and her grief and tears
    Appeared to me sufficient guarantee
    Both of her love and virtue. When I told her
    Of your departure, she displayed so keen,
    So genuine a grief that she convinced me,
    In spite of indications to the contrary
    That she was never guilty.[15]
CARLOS: I've been tempted
    To say as much myself. But though I long
    To think her guiltless, ought I to believe it
    Unless I prove it's true?
JUAN: I don't say that.
CARLOS: It's therefore useless to discuss it; for

> Jealousy always ends by dissipating
> Impressions of love that are too favorable.
> Have you informed her of her father's coming
> To Valencia?

JUAN: No, it would have been cruel to add
> This new vexation to her former woes.

CARLOS: You have done well. What orders have you given
> To Fabio?

JUAN: That he should quietly stay
> At the hostelry. No danger is involved,
> Since he's not known to Señor Don Pedro.
> I've ordered him to watch him carefully,
> And keep us well informed of all he plans.

CARLOS: That may be useless: for he will not speak
> About his plans to anyone.

JUAN: I don't agree.
> What is that noise?

CARLOS: *[Looking through the keyhole]* The worst thing that
> could happen.
> The man who's coming up — it is Don Pedro,
> Leonor's father.

JUAN: What are you saying?

CARLOS: 'Tis he,
> I recognized him plainly through the keyhole.

JUAN: Leonor's father!

CARLOS   He.

JUAN: Quick! Into the study!
> I will receive him and find out, I hope,
> What his intentions are.

CARLOS: I can't consent.
> When Leonor's father comes into the house
> Where she and I are hidden, I cannot, I should not,
> Leave you alone with him.

JUAN: Nothing will stop you
> From coming in if need be. Let us not
> Anticipate misfortune; it always comes
> Quite soon enough. And so, let us see first
> What he will say. Quick! Hide!

CARLOS: Well, I consent.
> But I'll observe what passes.

>   *[DON CARLOS hides: DON JUAN opens the door]*

>   *[Enter DON PEDRO in traveling attire]*

JUAN: What do you wish, sir?

PEDRO: Tell me, I prithee, if Don Juan de Roca
> Is now at home.

JUAN: I am Don Juan, sir.
> What can I do for you?

PEDRO: Let me embrace you.

For it is in your house that my misfortunes
Will find a haven of safety. I'll confide
All my afflictions to you, and despite
My baneful star, I know that I will find
Here in your house the many consolations
Which I am seeking here.
CARLOS: *[Aside]*   He could not be
  More frank.
JUAN: *[Aside]* He will have doubtless been apprised
  That Leonor and Carlos both are here.
  [Aloud] Señor, I render thanks to my good fortune
  For the honor that you do me. But, indeed,
  I know not how to answer, being ignorant
  Of whom you are and what you wish of me.
PEDRO: Will you sit down, señor? Here is a letter
  Which will inform you who I am, and also
  What from your kindness I expect.
        [Gives him the letter. They sit]
JUAN: The letter
  Is from my honored lord, Lord Denia.
  [Aside] I know not what to think.
PEDRO: Please read it first,
  And then I will explain.
JUAN: *[Reading]* "Señor Don Pedro de Lara, my kinsman and
  friend, is going to your town in pursuit of a man of
  whom his honor requires satisfaction. My indifferent
  health does not permit me to accompany him; but I like
  to think that my wishes will always be respected wher-
  ever you are. I confine myself to telling you that his
  injury is mine, and that I pledge myself to the satis-
  faction he requires. The Marquis of Denia."
  My sole reply is that I place myself
  At your disposal; and that I am ready
  To serve you in whatever way you like.
PEDRO: God keep you! For I know that after all
  That I have heard of you, and from what I see,
  That I've done well in coming to you now,
  Not to rely on other help or introduction
  But only on this letter. It is true
  The Marquis told me I should find in you
  A staunch supporter, by reason of the thanks
  And gratitude you owe his house.
JUAN: I avow
  Frankly the obligations that I owe him;
  I'll try to quit them with you; but, señor,
  I first must hear the motive that has brought you
  To Valencia. *[Aside]* I must swallow at one gulp
  The draft of bitterness.
PEDRO: I'll tell you then.

I'm noble, señor, and I've been insulted
In the highest degree. My foe is in Valencia,
And I am seeking him. That is enough
For me to tell you.
JUAN: Now I know as much
As you yourself.
PEDRO: Well, you are now forewarned;
And I will tell you later when I need
Your services. *[They rise]*
JUAN: One moment. One word more.
PEDRO: Concerning what?
JUAN: It's necessary, señor,
That you should know that I have friends and kinsmen
Here in Valencia: therefore, till I know
Who is your adversary, the Marquis cannot
Command me anything against my honor,
Nor can I promise anything which might be turned
Against myself.
PEDRO: An observation worthy
Of your nobility and of your prudence;
Far from complaining, I esteem you more
And thank you for it. And so, Señor Don Juan,
To do away with mystery between us,
What kind of relations do you have
With Don Diego Centellas?
JUAN: I just know him.
That's all.
CARLOS: *[Aside]* That's good! He is my rival.
PEDRO: Then,
You have no more objections.
JUAN: No, I've none.
PEDRO: This man, then — what it costs me to repeat it! —
Was left for dead one night within my house
In such a way that I could not take vengeance,
For it would have been base to stab a corpse;
I tended him — though if he had been standing
I would have given him a thousand deaths.
Justice arrived: but yet I did not wish
To make a charge, for such a man as I
Does not avenge himself with vain procedures.
My daughter disappeared 'mid this confusion —
To tell you is for me another shame.
Woe to the first who made so harsh a law,
A contract so unjust, a tie so impious,
Which deals unequally to man and woman,
And links our honor to another's whim.
In short, my daughter disappeared, and though
Two men have brought upon me this disgrace,
It's Don Diego I pursue — because

I do not know the other, and the first
I reach should be the first to feel my vengeance;
And next because, in all the wayside inns
I have been told a gentleman passed by,
Seeking to hide himself, accompanied
By a lady and a servant; and from descriptions
I know this lady is my daughter, and
It is to be presumed that, being recovered,
He has protected her in this her flight.
That is the reason I pursue him now
With unabated fury, to rebuild
The ruined structure of my honor, or,
If it's beyond repair, to raze with vengeance
The very ground where once it proudly stood.
And now since nothing
Prevents you from assisting my designs,
I will return to find you. At this moment
I leave to carry out another plan
Of which I'll tell you later. I owe you this,
As one who will be shortly my recourse,
My helper, and my refuge, not so much
Because of the recommendation I have brought,
As for the obligation that you feel
In seeing the sorrow of a gentleman,
An old man's tears.

                                              [Exit]

[Enter DON CARLOS]

CARLOS: Was ever a situation
    More cruel than mine?
JUAN: Let us consider, Carlos,
    All that has happened.
CARLOS: You have in your house
    The lady of a friend...
JUAN: Who is the daughter
    Of a man who's come to ask me for my aid.
CARLOS: This friend is also hidden in your house.
JUAN: To help me to avenge my wrongs.
CARLOS: The foe
    Don Pedro seeks is also mine.
JUAN: And I,
    Amid so many conflicting obligations,
    I know not what to do. I have a duty
    To Leonor because she is a woman;
    To you, because you are my friend and kinsman;
    To Pedro for the Marquis; and, last of all
    To my honor, for myself. What's to be done?[16]
CARLOS: Time will teach us. Let us therefore act
    According to events.

JUAN: 'Tis well. Let's wait,
   And we shall see. Till then, remain
   In hiding here, the watchman of my honor,
   While I go out as usual, and pretend
   That I have no suspicion.
CARLOS: Farewell, then.
JUAN: Farewell.
CARLOS: Kind heaven,
   Deliver me from griefs!
JUAN: O powerful heaven,
   Protect me from these dangers!
                    [Exeunt, each through a different door,
                    and CARLOS should be heard locking his]

Scene 3: A Street before Don Juan's House

[Enter DON DIEGO and GINÉS]

DIEGO: Come on. March!
GINÉS: I can't.
DIEGO: Why not?
GINÉS: Because I have the best reason for not doing so —
   I've broken or sprained my ankle.
DIEGO: God help you! You're a fine fellow!
GINÉS: God help me! That's a nice thing for you to say, and
   it reminds me of a witty tale. One day a Portuguese
   fell into a well. Seeing him a man exclaimed: "God help
   you!" To which the other, at the bottom of the well re-
   plied: "It's too late!" You see the application which
   fits my situation like a glove; for it's all the same
   whether one falls into a well or falls from a balcony.[17]
DIEGO: What about me? Didn't I jump too?
GINÉS: Well, you aren't breakable, and I'm as fragile as
   glass.
DIEGO: No — but you're very clumsy.
GINÉS: Not at all! What is good for one is bad for another.
   One day a friar, who was dying of hunger and very tired,
   arrived at an inn and asked the hostess what she could
   give him for supper. "Nothing," she said, "unless I
   kill a hen." "If you kill it now," said he grumpily,
   "would it be eatable right away?" "Don't worry," replied the hostess, "I know an excellent secret for making it tender." And, taking the hen before killing it,
   she singed its feet, after which the said hen appeared
   very tender to the reverend father, who perhaps attrib-
   uted to the operation what could have come from his
   appetite. After this he went to bed, but the bed was

hard, so hard that the friar could not sleep. Then he
remembered the secret and applied fire to the foot of
the bed. "What!" exclaimed the hostess, alarmed when
she saw the flames, "What's going on, Father?" "Hostess, the bed is hard, and I'm singeing its feet in order
to make it soft." Don't be surprised therefore, if the
same experience has not produced the same effect on the
two of us: you are the mattress and I am the chicken.[18]

DIEGO: It's no use your recounting such tales: You'll not
avoid going to see Inés.

GINÉS: Who? Me? Inés! That abominable woman who, after
having kept us cruelly in a corner, ended by throwing us
from the balcony! What a reward for two zealous servants like us, you of the mistress, I of the maid! Good
God! I never want to see her again![19]

DIEGO: As for me, I shall be eternally grateful for what she
did, for she has saved Beatriz's life and honor.

GINÉS: As for me, I'm not grateful. How could a *fallen* man
be grateful for anything?

DIEGO: Come, your humor is unbearable.

GINÉS: Eh! I've no room for being in a good humor when I
see that your love has made us turn head over heels.

DIEGO: Please, Ginés, I ask it as a favor.

GINÉS: All right — but I don't expect to have any success.

DIEGO: Why not?

GINÉS: Because I've the devil's own limp.[20]

DIEGO: I'll wait at the corner of the street.

GINÉS: If you only wish to speak to Inés, you haven't long
to wait.

DIEGO: How so?

GINÉS: If shape and garments don't deceive me, she's coming
out of the house now.

DIEGO: Yes, it's she indeed. But I don't want to speak with
her so near the house. Go and tell her softly that I'm
waiting beneath this porch.

[Enter INÉS, with her mantle]

INÉS: *[To herself]* I've seen Don Diego from the window, and
despite my fears, I'm going to speak with him. My mistress has sent me out in secret, as she counts on my
zeal and initiative.

GINÉS: What's the use of this veil, treacherous wench, if
your garments and airs betray you and reveal to the
passersby the flower — the cauliflower — of womanhood?

INÉS: What's up with you, Ginés?

GINÉS: I'm limping.

INÉS: So I see. But how did you catch this malady?

GINÉS: I got it from yourself, Inés.

INÉS: You lie, you lame creature.

GINÉS: Yes, I got it from your balcony, so my malady must be
   yours.[21]

INÉS: I would discuss that point with you if I wasn't forced
   to take a message to Doña Violante's house; and I
   wouldn't like anyone in our house to see me chatting
   here with a clown of your sort.

GINÉS: Good! Very good! But first have a word with my master who awaits you a few steps away, and then we'll let
   you go.

INÉS: That would be still worse. If my mistress knew that I
   had spoken with him, she would kill me.

DIEGO: [Approaching] Why so, Inés?

INÉS: She is so angry, so furious with you, that she has
   forbidden me to receive any message or note from you.

DIEGO: Is she so inflexibly against one who adores her?

INÉS: She feels like slapping you.

DIEGO: Me?

INÉS: You don't love her...and you pay your addresses elsewhere.

GINÉS: When an angry man threatens a gentleman in his house,
   saying "I'm going to get four valets to throw you out of
   the window" the threat's enough to cool him down; and
   yet your mistress retains her rancor against us after
   we've been literally thrown from the balcony by one of
   her maids, and so well thrown that my fortunes will ever
   after limp! What more does she want?

DIEGO: I would not have believed, Inés, that you too were
   against me.

INÉS: I wouldn't tell everyone, and God knows what I have
   already suffered from having tried to justify you.

DIEGO: Well, Inés, if you are indeed well disposed toward
   me, arrange matters, I beg you, in such a way that I can
   speak to her alone for just a moment.

INÉS: That won't be easy.

DIEGO: Count on my gratitude; my love will be generous...and
   to begin with... [He gives her a purse]

INÉS: Oh! I don't act from motives of self-interest.

GINÉS: That's understood!

INÉS: And to prove my devotion, I'll return to tell my mistress that I've performed her commission. It is night
   ...my master is out...I'm going to enter first...and
   leaving the door open...

DIEGO: Ah! Inés! You restore me to life.

INÉS: You can enter after me, and then come what may!

DIEGO: Splendid! I'll follow you.

GINÉS: Yes, Inés, you are indeed charming.

INÉS: Señor, I believe my purse has caught your eye.

GINÉS: O, yes! Put me down for a share of it.

INÉS: Hands off! I've no time for the likes of you. You

may have a gammy leg, but I know quite well where your
real weakness lies.[22]

                                                    [Exit]

DIEGO: Follow me, Ginés.
GINÉS: Me?
DIEGO: Yes.
GINÉS: Where are you going?
DIEGO: Come and you will see.
GINÉS: No, may the devil take me rather! Amen. You
    wouldn't want to see me shut up again? Are you propos-
    ing more jumps out of windows? If so, I'll wait for you
    out here. No more jumping for me!
DIEGO: I didn't think you were such a coward, and I see that
    I'll get on better alone.
GINÉS: My cowardice is merely prudence...and I'm off now.

                                                    [Exeunt]

              Scene 4: A Room in Don Juan's House

    [Enter BEATRIZ and LEONOR]

BEATRIZ: Isabel, kindly see that lights are placed
    In the other room, and then await me there.
    Meanwhile, for relaxation after work,
    I'll sit at the window.
LEONOR: It shall be done, señora.
    [Aside] It's sorrowful to serve, and sadder still
    When one's not trusted. Beatriz and Inés
    Are always hiding. One has just gone out,
    The other waits for her. But I will leave them
    To their little secrets. Clearly they expect
    A visitor; I used to do the same
    In my own house; trusting some servants, and
    Keeping the others in the dark.
    O memories! Cease to torment me. Since,
    Unfortunate Leonor, you're now a servant,
    Look, hear, and hold your tongue.

                                                    [Exit]

    [Enter INÉS]

INÉS: You will not say
    That I've been slow.
BEATRIZ: I wait you here to know
    What Don Diego said.
INÉS: I played my part
    Superbly. He is following me now
    Without suspecting you have sent for him.

You must pretend, señora, you are angry,
    Especially with me.
BEATRIZ: See who is coming.
INÉS: O God! It is a man!
BEATRIZ: Who dares presume...?

[Enter DON DIEGO]

DIEGO: A hapless man who, prostrate at your feet,
    Adorable Beatriz, offers you his life
    A thousand times.
BEATRIZ: How did this happen, Inés?
INÉS: Señora, I assure you that I closed
    The door most carefully.
BEATRIZ: You lie.
    It's yet another perfidy of yours.
    You shall not stay another hour in my service.
DIEGO: Do not blame Inés; it is I alone
    Who am the guilty one. Turn against me
    The whole weight of your anger; I shall be
    Happy if you should deign to avenge yourself
    On me alone.
BEATRIZ: You might have spared yourself
    This final madness. You ought to be convinced
    That from this time I will not show you favor.
DIEGO: I never hoped for it; I knew too well
    That my small merit could not raise so high
    Its vain pretentions.
BEATRIZ: That's true; and today
    Less than ever.
DIEGO: Why so, señora?
BEATRIZ: Because insults
    Are not titles to love.
DIEGO: Allow me to disperse
    All your suspicions.
BEATRIZ: That will not be easy.
DIEGO: Perhaps it will.
BEATRIZ: Don Diego, the hour is hazardous,
    The door is open; my fate is in the balance.
    You have cost me my happiness, but do not now
    Cost me my life as well.
DIEGO: No, no, I'll not let slip this opportunity;
    Please hear me first and then I'll go.
BEATRIZ: Inés
    Watch at the door. Since I must pay this price
    For his departure, I will listen.   *[Exit INÉS]*
DIEGO: Well,
    Lovely Beatriz, when I left Valencia...

[Enter INÉS, in a panic]

INÉS: Señora!
BEATRIZ: What is it?
INÉS: It's my master!
BEATRIZ: Oh!
    What a misfortune!
INÉS: Quick! Why are you waiting?
    Let us use the room where they were safe last night.
DIEGO: *[Hiding]* Was ever love so crossed?
BEATRIZ: Is there a star
    More baleful?
INÉS: Courage, señora. Have no fear,
    Don't worry: my master does not yet suspect,
    For instead of coming in this door, he's gone
    Into his study.
BEATRIZ: Ah! Inés! What a trial!

    [Enter DON CARLOS and DON JUAN]

JUAN: Yes, Carlos, as I told you, when I entered
    I saw a man go in the house before me.
    Please wait for me outside and watch the door
    And windows. Let nobody leave!
CARLOS: Don't worry.
    Rely on me.
                                           [Exit]

JUAN: Beatriz?
BEATRIZ: Yes, brother?
JUAN: What were you doing?
BEATRIZ: I was here with Inés.
JUAN: Well.
BEATRIZ: Where are you going?
JUAN: In my house.
    Can I not go where I please?
BEATRIZ: Of course. But yet,
    It's curious.
JUAN: Be off!
BEATRIZ: You speak to me
    In a tone to which you've not accustomed me.
JUAN: Go away!
BEATRIZ: What a horrible misfortune!
DIEGO: *[Aside]* He's coming here...but there's another door.
    I'll see if I can find a safer refuge.
                                           [Exit]
JUAN: This time I'll set my doubts at rest. *[Draws his
        sword]*
BEATRIZ: Alas!
    He's drawn his sword to go into that chamber.
INÉS: Someone will be killed.
BEATRIZ: The die is cast.
INÉS: We've lost the game.

BEATRIZ: I'm dying.
INÉS: It's not worthwhile...
    Flight would be better... If we could...
BEATRIZ: I've not the strength
    To move a step.
INÉS: Don Diego must have gone:
    Your brother's not encountered him...
LEONOR: *[Within]*   Alas!
    How unfortunate I am!
BEATRIZ: In going
    From one room to the other, he has come
    Where Isabel was waiting. Seeing him
    She will be frightened. She is running here.
    Let us retire into this corner.

    [Enter LEONOR, carrying a torch. DON DIEGO follows her]

LEONOR: Man,
    Or whatever you are, shadow, illusion,
    Ghost, what do you want of me? Is it not enough
    That you have made me leave my home, without
    Causing my dismissal from that of others?
DIEGO: Woman!
    Or rather, shadow, illusion, ghost! Have you not caused
        me
    Enough misfortunes? Must you bring me more?
    Do you wish a second time to kill me now?
    But no, this time I will escape![23]

    [Enter DON JUAN]

JUAN: No, no, although you hide at the earth's center...
    What! It is you, Don Diego?
DIEGO: Lower your sword,
    Don Juan... Though I doubtless have not had
    The respect I owe your house; but yet your honor
    Is not impaired; and all can be explained.
    Besides, with regard to vengeance, it is better
    Not to have cause...
JUAN: *[Aside]*   Don Diego Centellas...
    I surprise him with Leonor, so my suspicions
    Are proved wrong... O my soul! Rejoice! I feared
    Another shame indeed!
BEATRIZ: *[Aside to INÉS]* Why does he pause
    In seeing him? Let us listen.
DIEGO: In Madrid
    I loved this lady there...and in her house
    A dreadful thing befell me. On my return,
    Hearing she lived with you...
LEONOR: Alas! Unfortunate!
DIEGO: I dared to enter, so that I could speak
    With her.

BEATRIZ: *[To INÉS]* The excuse is apt, if Isabel
    Does not deny it. Make a sign to her
    To lend assent to it. *[INÉS signs to LEONOR]*
LEONOR: All that you've heard,
    Don Juan, is but too true. Yes, Don Diego
    Is cause of all my ills. Because of him
    I'm exiled from my country and abhorred
    By my own father, scorned by my promised husband...
    And in the end obliged to serve your sister
    Under a borrowed name and humbly dressed.
INÉS: *[Aside to BEATRIZ]* She's understood my signs.
BEATRIZ: She plays her role
    So well that I would be deceived myself.
LEONOR: But yet, that he should say that in Madrid
    Or here,...
JUAN: Be silent, Leonor...
LEONOR: I ever gave him
    A pretext...
JUAN: Do not try to clear yourself.
    [Aside] Poor woman!
INÉS: You should be very grateful to her,
    That for your sake, señora, she accuses
    Herself.
BEATRIZ: If only my brother will believe her
    We've nothing more to fear.
JUAN: *[Aside]*   What's to be done?
    I'm reassured myself. But Carlos!

    [Enter DON CARLOS. He stays behind the tapestry]

CARLOS: *[Aside]* I heard a noise as of a clash of swords
    And hastened here... But no, their arms are lowered.
    Let's listen here. Perhaps he will forgo
    His vengeance, and arrange things amicably.
DIEGO: Those are the wrongs
    Which I have done you. Your honor, sir, is safe.
    Decide upon your course; will you pardon me,
    Or fight me?
JUAN: Don Diego, your explanations
    Are in accordance with the things I've heard
    From Leonor.
CARLOS: *[Aside]* What do I hear? He named
    Leonor and Don Diego.
JUAN: I have
    One question to ask you. Is it the first time
    You've entered here by night to speak with her?
DIEGO: *[Aside]* There's an insidious question — nevertheless
    I must save Beatriz. *[Aloud]* No, Don Juan.
    I came last night and left by the balcony.
    In my confession, I deem it unnecessary
    To recount the circumstances.

JUAN: And yet to me
    They're most important.
CARLOS: *[Aside]*   Don Juan's suspicions
    Are being allayed to my cost.
BEATRIZ: *[Aside]*   I think that now
    He's been persuaded. *[Aloud]* How now, Juan!
    Do not mistrust your sister in this way.
    This is the servant you've persuaded me
    To take at your lady's hands. *[Aside to LEONOR]* For-
        give me, my friend,
    And please continue.
LEONOR: *[To BEATRIZ]*   What do you wish, señora?
    I do not understand you.
JUAN: That's not in question.
    It's true that Don Diego in some ways
    Has satisfied me; and that Leonor
    Was placed in my household by another person,
    But yet my name imposes obligations,
    Although this gentleman has come for her
    And not for you, I have the duty still
    To punish his audacity.
CARLOS: *[Revealing himself]* No, no!
    'Tis I alone who has the right to complain;
    And I alone to avenge me!
LEONOR: *[Aside]*   Whom do I see?
    Don Carlos! There was lacking only this!
DIEGO: And who are you, who come to take in hand
    This quarrel.
CARLOS: You should recognize me, señor.
    You have good reason to. I am the man
    Who left you for dead in Madrid, and who now comes
    To finish what he started.
LEONOR: How horrible!
DIEGO: I think, on the contrary, that you have come
    To give me my revenge.
JUAN: I'll stand beside you,
    Carlos.
DIEGO: Two against one! I'm not afraid!
GINÉS: *[Within]* Come, all of you! This is where they're
    fighting.

    [Enter GINÉS with OTHERS]

GINÉS and OTHERS: What's happening?
BEATRIZ: Quick, Inés! Put out the torch! It's the only way
    To avert the greatest misfortunes.
        [INÉS extinguishes the torch; the men fight]
GINÉS: Stay where you are, please, since you cannot see.
JUAN: Remember, all of you, you're in my house.
GINÉS: Kindle a torch, so that they can see where they are.

LEONOR: What a misfortune!
DIEGO: I've found the door; this is not flight, but merely
    to postpone vengeance to a better occasion.
                                          [Exit]
BEATRIZ: Troubled and filled with fear, I retire to my cham-
    ber.
                                            [Exit]
INÉS: We have managed our affairs so well, that good as they
    were, we're left without any resource.
                                          [Exit]
GINÉS: Where are you, señor? The surgeon awaits you.[24]
CARLOS: Die, traitor!
GINÉS: I'm dead. It's enough that you commanded it.
    [Aside] Why the devil should I stay longer, if I do I
    might end up dead indeed.
                                          [Exit]
A MAN: A man's been slain! Let's flee from the watch!
    Let's get out of here!
                                      [Exeunt]
JUAN: A torch, there, ho! I'll go myself to find one!
                                          [Exit]

LEONOR: How I tremble! I am overwhelmed
    With my misfortunes. I have not the strength
    To go away.
CARLOS: I stay here at my post.
    They fly in haste, one after the other.
    I should remain where I have drawn the sword.

    [Enter DON JUAN with a torch]

JUAN: Now we shall see.
LEONOR: Stay, Don Carlos!
JUAN: What!
    You two alone!
CARLOS: Why should you be astonished?
    I never turn my back upon a foe,
    So I'm confronting Leonor, although
    The surest victory would lie in flight.
JUAN: Stop!
CARLOS: Let me, please, flee from this enemy,
    And so pursue the other.
JUAN: There's no point.
    You could never catch him.
LEONOR: Ah! If I could tear
    My breast and show my heart for what it is.
    My heart would be a witness to the truth
    Of what I've said. Perhaps you would believe.
CARLOS: Your heart's deceitful...
LEONOR: No, my heart is loyal.
CARLOS: We had the proof tonight! Ah! Leonor,
    Since you've forgotten what you owe to me,

Could you not have remembered that you were
In Don Juan's house?
LEONOR: In what am I to blame
For a madman's follies?
CARLOS: Yes, I am wrong: let's end this useless talk.
My friend, my cousin, the motive which you had
To postpone my journey now no more exists,
And these events have turned against me only,
And so, farewell. I'm leaving...leaving Valencia
Dishonored: But I must go tonight. My foe
Will say, if he wishes, that I've fled. But now
What matters my reputation or my honor?
Farewell. This woman I have loved so much,
I recommend her to your friendship — not
To keep her in your house, but to permit her
To rejoin Don Diego... May they both
Be happy in their love... But I need say no more.
Farewell, Juan.
LEONOR: O Heavens! Carlos, wait!
CARLOS: What do you wish for now?
LEONOR: If I had known...
CARLOS: Enough!
LEONOR: That Don Diego...
CARLOS: Enough, I tell you...
LEONOR: Oh! Yes enough! I cannot speak. My voice,
My sight have lost their power...my heart is failing...
Dear God! *[She faints]*
JUAN: She's fainted in my arms.
CARLOS: Sustain her,
Dear Juan. Ah! Leonor you're killing me,
And I adore you... And I'm as afflicted
By your misfortunes as by your betrayal.
JUAN: She only sobs and moans. Wait for me, Carlos.
I'll carry her into my sister's room
And then return.
CARLOS: Yes, go. Care for her well.
No, rather let her die, since she'll revive
Only to love another.
JUAN: Wait for me.
We shall see then what it is best to do.
                              [Exit, carrying LEONOR]
CARLOS: A curse upon my cowardly devotion,
So base a passion, and a love so slavish!
The more I'm wronged, the more I love. The more
I'm outraged, I have greater tenderness;
The more I am betrayed, the more I trust.
Why should I be surprised? It can't be said
He really loves a woman who does not love
Even her very faults.   *[Exit]*

ᘰᘰᘰ

ACT THREE

Scene 1: Another Room in Don Juan's House

[Enter DON CARLOS and DON JUAN]

CARLOS: Is she recovered?

JUAN: Yes, but in such a way,
It would have been much better, in my opinion,
If she had never done so.

CARLOS: What do you mean?

JUAN: When she recovered consciousness, her grief
Was so acute, she seemed to have lost her reason —
Her speech and conduct did so much betray
Her trouble and confusion.

CARLOS: What did she say?

JUAN: That she was most unfortunate...not being allowed
To explain how she was innocent.

CARLOS: Alas!
For my fatal love!

JUAN: What have you decided?

CARLOS: O God! What shall I say? I have decided
Upon a project that I can confide
Only to one who knows as you do, Juan,
What love is. Would you have me confess
All the vain thoughts and all the foolish fancies
Which have besieged my mind, which flatter most,
From which I would derive the greatest pleasure
To see them realized.

JUAN: Tell me, my friend.

CARLOS: Don't laugh at me, since I confess my weakness.
Well, if I could obtain from Don Diego
That he was willing to repair the honor
Of Leonor, and she could find a way
To obtain her father's pardon, that for me
Would be the sweetest vengeance. I would take
A singular pleasure in giving what she wishes
When she despairs. For after what has passed,
There is no doubt that Don Diego loves her,
And she returns his love. What should I lose
By doing this? Everything and nothing.
Besides, in my troubles, this alone can give
Some satisfaction to me. Since I've lost her,
I would be happy just to win from her
Some show of gratitude.

JUAN: This resolution
Comes from a very generous man, and I

Would recognize you by it. It shows how fine
And noble is the passion which inspires you.
CARLOS: No, Juan, there remains to execute
This plan of mine. How is it to be done?
JUAN: I hardly know. If one of us should speak
To Don Diego, to propose this marriage,
He would refuse it for that very reason.
For, after all, however strong his passion,
A man will hardly deign to accept a wife
At the hands of his rival. We must therefore get
The intervention of another person.
CARLOS: Then could you not inform her father now
That Leonor's here? And by his intervention
All will be arranged.
JUAN: That plan involves
One inconvenience.
CARLOS: What?
JUAN: We might be compromised.
And then the credit would not go to you.
CARLOS: You are right. But whom
Shall we approach?
JUAN: Wait... I have it. All
The difficulties would vanish.
CARLOS: Who then?
JUAN: Beatriz.
She is a woman, and in consequence,
If the proposal comes from her, Diego
Need not feel insulted. She cannot do less
For a woman in her house, of whom she now
Has heard the birth and family.
CARLOS: A good idea!
JUAN: Hide, therefore, while I go to speak of it
With Beatriz.
CARLOS: Why should I hide?
JUAN: Don Diego
And Leonor's father should not see you, till
All is settled.
CARLOS: I cannot hide.
JUAN: You must.
There is no other way.
CARLOS: Oh, well! So be it!
But on condition that no one but you
Shall know of it.
JUAN: That's understood.
CARLOS: Farewell.
[Aside] Ah! Leonor, I hope my love will have done
Enough for you, ungrateful one! For a first wrong
I gave you life, and for a second wrong
I give you honor. *[He hides, locking himself in]*

JUAN: If I should succeed,
   It will be I who gain the most: for I
   Will quit myself of all my obligations,
   To Leonor, to her father, to Diego,
   And even to Carlos. I must do my best
   To further this design on which depend
   My peace and happiness.

   [Enter BEATRIZ]

BEATRIZ: Is Don Carlos here?
JUAN: No, Beatriz.
BEATRIZ: I came to see him here.
JUAN: When Leonor fainted, I left Carlos here;
   But did not find him here on my return.
   [Aside] Beatriz must be kept in ignorance.
BEATRIZ: Doubtless his bravery has driven him
   To follow Don Diego.
JUAN: I do not know
   Where Carlos can be found, so I have not
   Gone out to search for him. Why do you wish
   To see him?
BEATRIZ: I have come to beg him, brother,
   To have some pity on his lady, if not as a lover,
   At least as a gentleman. She is weighed down
   With her affliction.
JUAN: What does she say?
BEATRIZ: She says
   That one thing could console her — to see Don Carlos.
JUAN: He is not here. And since we are alone,
   Knowing your prudence, I'd confide in you
   An idea that's come to me.
BEATRIZ: I am surprised
   That you should want now to confide in me
   For yesterday you thought so ill of me,
   You burst into the house, full of suspicions.
   Is it not strange to join in such a way
   Trust and distrust?
JUAN: Your reproach is vain!
   You're well aware of how much I esteem you.
   Then, Beatriz, you only can prevent
   The perils which threaten us — Diego, Carlos,
   And I myself. For in this quarrel now
   I'm bound to intervene.
BEATRIZ: What do you wish?
JUAN: This: please listen. Knowing Leonor's family
   I ought now, more than ever, to protect
   Her name and honor. But if I should attempt
   To raise the matter now with Don Diego,
   I do not know whether he would agree.

Yet, once the matter's broached, we could not brook
Any refusal by him. So, Beatriz,
I beg you to accept the office. Women
Manage such things more pleasantly than we do.
Then since this woman's in your house, and since
Your brother and your cousin find themselves
In the same fix, I have good cause to ask you
To speak with him.
BEATRIZ: With whom?
JUAN: With Don Diego.
    You'll let him understand that you're offended
    That he has been so lacking in respect
    Unto your house. You'll show him all the perils
    To which this lady exposes him: you'll urge him
    To ward them off; and then you'll make him see
    A marriage would settle everything. All this
    Should seem to come from you alone — we others
    Must not be involved in it.
BEATRIZ: A perfect scheme!
    I'll do my best to aid you.
JUAN: I'm going to see
    If I can meet Don Carlos. If you return
    To your own room, take care to close this door.
BEATRIZ: I will not fail.

                                   [Exit DON JUAN]
                    How vexing to be forced
    To act as go-between which angers me
    And makes me jealous! How shall I behave
    In such a situation? Well, I shall profit
    By the occasion to find out everything;
    And since my brother offers me a meeting
    With Don Diego, I'll try at least to emerge
    From the illusions and the mysteries
    Which now beset me! Inés!

    [Enter LEONOR]

LEONOR: What do you wish?
BEATRIZ: Oh! It's you.
LEONOR: You called one of your women
    And naturally your most devoted servant
    Came at your call.

    [Enter DON CARLOS: he shows himself behind the tapestry]

CARLOS: *[Aside]*   I heard the voice of Leonor
    And come to see if she's recovered now
    From that sad accident.
BEATRIZ: Yesterday, Leonor,
    I did not know who you were. Better informed
    Today, I put you in your proper place

And look on you as a friend _[Aside]_ I ought to say
My bitterest enemy.
LEONOR: No, no, señora,
Ceasing to bear the title of your maid
I'll not be compensated for the good
That I shall lose, by the honor I shall gain.
Let me still stay here in the humble office
In which I have been placed — near you, señora.
Yes, if she who unintentionally has caused
Such trouble in your house is not unworthy
Of your indulgence, treat me still, I pray,
As you have done till now.
BEATRIZ: It cannot be.
Think, then, that at this moment, to discharge
The debt I owe your birth and owe my house,
I'm busy with your marriage.
LEONOR: Heaven reward you
For so much kindness. But you'll not succeed
In your design. Don Carlos would not wish it.
He is so jealous!
BEATRIZ: I am not referring
To him.
LEONOR: To whom then?
BEATRIZ: To Don Diego Centellas.
LEONOR: Renounce that fantasy. Better to die
A thousand times than marry Don Diego!
BEATRIZ: You do not love him then?
LEONOR: Love Don Diego?
An asp encountered in the midst of flowers,
A serpent in the fields, a ravenous tiger
Appearing in the forest, are less odious
Than he is to me.[25]
BEATRIZ: _[Aside]_   Softly, if you please.
I'm very glad that she disdains him now,
But not as much as this.
CARLOS: _[Aside]_   Perfidious one!
She must have seen me; otherwise she would
Have used another language.
BEATRIZ: I thought to please you.
I did not think you could detest a man
Who, in Madrid, had nearly died for you
And who has tracked you to Valencia.
LEONOR: You do not know, señora, to what point
I am insulted by the vain pretensions
Of Don Diego.
BEATRIZ: I shall know it soon.
For all of us must in the end emerge
From this perplexing labyrinth — he, you, I,
My brother, and Don Carlos.   _[Exit]_

CARLOS: *[Aside]*   Now she's alone.
   O God! She's weeping. But this means little. I see
   Her tears, and do not know for whom she sheds them.
LEONOR: *[Aside]* O Heaven! Have pity on me!
CARLOS: *[Aside]*   O cruel pain!
LEONOR: *[Aside]* You only hear my plaint!
CARLOS: *[Aside]*   Oh, perfidy!
LEONOR: *[Aside]* I am not guilty, as you know.
CARLOS: *[Aside]*   My love!
LEONOR: *[Aside]* Why then am I accused?
CARLOS: *[Aside]*   I would tell you why
   If my divided feelings would allow.
LEONOR: *[Aside]* What have I ever done that could deserve
   Misfortune, punishment, and such dishonor?
   When will the truth reveal my innocence?
CARLOS: *[Aside]* Never, alas, since all you say is lies.
LEONOR: *[Aside]* Alas!
CARLOS: *[Aside]* Everything today conspires against me.
   I cannot doubt she knows I'm listening to her;
   But, after all, it does not matter, since
   I don't believe her. The human voice is not
   Like gold or silver; whether words are true
   Or false, they sound alike. So if I listened
   For centuries, I should not learn the truth.
LEONOR: Ah! Carlos, if you heard me!
CARLOS: Ah! Leonor, if...[26]
     [Knocking on the door]
   But someone's knocking at the door. I'll go
   To shut up mine.
LEONOR: I cannot even speak
   To his imaginary form but someone comes
   To interrupt me. I'll see who it is.
   Perhaps I shall have then some privacy.
   Who's there?

    [Enter DON PEDRO]

PEDRO: Is Señor Don Juan at home?
   [Aside] O Heavens! What do I see.
LEONOR: He has just gone out.
   [Aside] O God! My father!
PEDRO: My soul! What an encounter.
CARLOS: *[Aside]* Fear nothing, Leonor, you have a refuge
   Here in my arms.

    [LEONOR enters study]

PEDRO: She's shut the door behind her.
   That will not save her. When I defend my honor
   I can confront the world and overturn
   All obstacles. I will break down this door

Till I am able to destroy her too
As she deserves.

[Enter BEATRIZ]

BEATRIZ: What is it?   What signify
These cries, this noise?
PEDRO: An anger, a despair
Which must be satisfied; a thunderbolt
Which will destroy all things that would oppose
Its fury.
BEATRIZ: What!   In my house, señor,
So much audacity?   What is the cause
Which can have driven you to such excesses?
PEDRO: A wretch is hidden there.
BEATRIZ: Wait!   Do you speak
Of Leonor?
PEDRO: Who else could move me thus?
BEATRIZ: *[Aside]* Good Heavens!   Carlos and Don Diego —
There only lacked a lover with white hair!
But yet he may be able to keep the peace
Between the others.   *[Aloud]* Whatever your motives,
    which
I cannot penetrate, whatever the injury
For which you would exact your vengeance, señor,
How have you dared to enter in this house?
PEDRO: My situation must excuse me, señora.
It would justify still more.   So pardon me
For not expressing to you more respect.
BEATRIZ: You are mistaken, señor, if you think
There is no man within this house who...

[Enter DON JUAN]

JUAN: What is this?
BEATRIZ: What is it, brother? — This old gentleman
Who comes in search of Leonor, he also,
And amuses himself in smashing all our doors.
JUAN: Soft, Beatriz.   You've no cause to complain.
Don Pedro's not at fault.   He is the master
Of this our house, and all is at his service.
PEDRO: Don Juan, truce to empty compliments.
I'm not and do not wish to be the master
In your own house.   I am a stranger who
Confided in you, and, coming to speak with you,
Found my daughter in your house — there — hidden.
Open the door, please, or I shall myself
Be forced to break it open.
BEATRIZ: It's her father.
JUAN: *[Aside]* What's to be done?   What say? since he has
        seen her.
PEDRO: Well!   What do you decide?

JUAN: Señor Don Pedro...
    [Aside] I shall be lucky to get out of this!
    [Aloud] Yes, certainly, you show me gratitude
    For my eagerness to serve you! Yesterday
    You told me of your troubles; so I hastened
    To find your daughter, bring her to my sister,
    With whom you have found her. And I hope that all
    Will be settled to your satisfaction,
    And that you will return content and honored.
    But if my conduct irks you, I will cease
    To interfere in your affairs.
PEDRO: Permit me,
    Don Juan, to embrace you, and forgive me.
    The anger that I felt on seeing my daughter
    Deprived me of my judgment. It is hard
    For an unfortunate man to think aright,
    And recognize good fortune when it comes.
    I was carried away by passion. But at your feet
    I now put everything at your disposal.
JUAN: What are you doing, señor? Rise.
PEDRO: And you, señora,
    Forgive the pain and trouble I have caused you.
    I'm noble, and I have received an outrage...
BEATRIZ: Had I known who you were, I would have tried
    To calm you otherwise.
JUAN: Have you yet sent
    For Don Diego?
BEATRIZ: Yes, Inés has just gone.
JUAN: Will you accompany me, Señor Don Pedro?
    We have an overture of great importance
    Which we should make together. Do not worry
    Concerning Leonor: she'll stay with Beatriz.
BEATRIZ: I'll answer for her, señor.
PEDRO: It is enough,
    That she'll be near you. O almighty God,
    Let me behold my honor reestablished,
    Then death come when it will.
JUAN: *[Aside]*   I don't know where
    The devil to take him. *[To BEATRIZ]* Speak to Don Diego
    During my absence...try to persuade him to it...
    My happiness depends on it.
                          [Exeunt DON JUAN and DON PEDRO]
BEATRIZ: His happiness!
    And my misfortune! Open, Leonor,
    I am alone.

    [Enter LEONOR]

LEONOR: Under that guarantee
    I will come out.

CARLOS: *[Aside to LEONOR]*   Do not tell Beatriz
   That I am here.
LEONOR: *[Aside to CARLOS]*   Agreed.
BEATRIZ: You've just escaped
   From a great danger.
LEONOR: In that room I found
   My safety.
BEATRIZ: It was lucky that the door
   Of the study was left open, since my brother
   Always removes the key.
LEONOR: The whole of my life
   Was in that narrow space *[Aside]* which holds Don Carlos.
BEATRIZ: Leonor, since your father has now come
   To increase by his presence the embarrassment
   In which we find ourselves — enough already —
   I'll take more pains than ever in the affair
   In which I'm engaged on your behalf.
LEONOR: Then I
   Repeat with greater emphasis what I said
   A little while ago.
BEATRIZ: Your conduct seems
   Like obstinacy.
LEONOR: And yours is like an insult.
BEATRIZ: Let us leave that. Let's come into my room
   And shut that one.
LEONOR: I'll follow you at once.
BEATRIZ: *[Aside]* Ah! Don Diego, with what fearfulness
   I await your visit.

                                               [Exit]

LEONOR: Carlos, since I have
   The chance to speak a moment, will you hear me?

   [Enter DON CARLOS]

CARLOS: Leonor, if chance has furnished me
   Some opportunities to do you service
   And if this is our destiny — for you
   To wrong me constantly, and as for me
   To oblige you constantly, what would you more?
   Leave me alone, until some new occasion
   Of a fresh outrage to me, or until
   I can again restore you.
LEONOR: I'll not offend you
   More in the future than I have in the past,
   But if you wish to save me once again,
   You now can do it.
CARLOS: How?
LEONOR: Know that your cousin
   To my misfortune wishes me to marry
   With Don Diego. You've protected me

      With so much generous unselfishness;
      And now, today, you can save my life again;
      You only need to speak to Beatriz.
CARLOS: What! I hit upon the idea of this marriage,
      And would you now oppose it?
LEONOR: You desire it?
CARLOS: Certainly.
LEONOR: It was you that planned it.
CARLOS: Yes,
      And that's why I consented to be hidden
      So that I should not meet with Don Diego
      Or with your father.
LEONOR: I cannot understand you.
CARLOS: Yet it's not difficult.
LEONOR: Please explain yourself.
CARLOS: My love's so pure, my tenderness so noble,
      My jealousy is so impersonal,
      That losing you, I wish at least to save
      Your honor.
LEONOR: Carlos, I have my honor still.
CARLOS: I don't wish to revert to what is past;
      But, quite apart from the Madrid affair,
      Has Don Diego not come here to see you
      In the house in which I placed you? Is it not known
      That one night he leaped down from the balcony?
      Another time, was he not here surprised
      Closeted with you? Well! I wish that all
      Should be repaired by marriage. That must be
      The final sacrifice for any lover,
      The tenderest and most devoted... Yes,
      To restore your honor now, despite my love,
      I wish to see you in another's arms.
LEONOR: My Lord! My soul! My life!
CARLOS: My hurt! My loss!
      My death!
LEONOR: If on the night of the balcony
      I ever saw him may a thunderbolt
      Destroy me! And if, when he spoke to me
      I knew...
CARLOS: All lies!
LEONOR: If that was not the truth
      I wouldn't have said to Beatriz what I said.
CARLOS: You knew that I was listening.
LEONOR: How could I know?
CARLOS: You must have seen me hide...the proof is this:
      That when your father entered, you ran at once
      For my protection.
LEONOR: It was the effect of chance...
      But let's suppose it was as you pretend;

Why, when you yourself would have me marry him,
  Would I still lie?
CARLOS: Ask that, if you will,
  Of all the countless women who deceive
  Two men at once.
LEONOR: I am not one of those.
CARLOS: You're all alike.
BEATRIZ: _[Within]_   Leonor?
LEONOR: Beatriz is calling.
CARLOS: If you'd oblige me, do not tell her, please,
  That I am here.
LEONOR: Don't worry. You will not
  Believe me, then?
CARLOS: No, for as the proverb says:
  "The worst is always certain."
LEONOR: I would change
  That proverb, and would say instead: "The worst
  Is _not_ always certain." Ah! Carlos, what you cost me!
                                        [Exeunt]

                  Scene 2: The Same

[Enter BEATRIZ and DON DIEGO]

DIEGO: What! Beatriz, to send in quest of me,
  And not to fear lest one should see me enter
  Your house in broad daylight, to guard your room,
  And meet me in your brother's! Strange precautions!
  Is it benevolence or treachery?
  Is it for my welfare or destruction?
BEATRIZ: Don't be astonished at this change of front,
  Nor that I can receive you at this hour...
  As for my brother's room, I've chosen it
  In preference to mine, because today
  I expect a visit soon from Violante,
  And don't wish her to see you. No, Don Diego,
  You've naught to fear from me; and far from wishing
  To impose my love on you, I rather wish
  To assist with all my power the love you feel
  For another woman. I would serve you now
  But as a friend, since I no more aspire
  To another title, which belongs of right
  To a happier lady.
DIEGO: When I received your note,
  I doubted... When I saw how you received me,
  New doubts assailed me; and your present words
  Give me still more. They multiply apace.
  I beg you to explain yourself.

CARLOS: *[Aside, at the door]*   What's this?
   Do they discuss my troubles or their own?
   I'll listen.
BEATRIZ: If you do not understand me,
   Señor, although I'm speaking very plainly,
   It is because you do not wish to do so;
   But so that in the end you understand,
   I'll tell you everything. Because of you,
   Leonor has left her father's house,
   Lost her dear father, her repose, her honor,
   Don Juan rightly can complain of you;
   Don Carlos is insulted; and you know
   That I could also offer you reproaches,
   Either because you left me, jilted me,
   Or for the insult you have done my house.
   Then, lastly, Leonor's father now
   Is in Valencia. Your life's beset
   With perils on all sides; and with so many
   Combined against you, you must now decide
   Either to perish, or wed Leonor.
   You love her, and she shares your sentiments.
   Though many are desirous of your death,
   Your marriage would save all. Do you understand
   At last?
DIEGO: After such speech, it would be hard
   Not to do so. But let me now reply.
BEATRIZ: Proceed.
CARLOS: *[Aside]* What is all this, great God! Diego
   And Beatriz love each other. But have I not
   Enough of my own troubles without going on
   To concern myself with other people's. Here,
   At least, there's no pretense: for certainly
   Beatriz would not have spoken of her secrets
   If she had known that I had hidden here.
DIEGO: I wish I had the power now to divide
   Myself in two, so that I could fulfill
   The obligations of a gentleman,
   And those of a lover at the self-same time.
   For they are mutually contradictory,
   And I know not how to answer from my heart,
   With such conflicting sentiments, which fight
   And divide my heart. If I should speak
   To you as a lover, you might not believe me;
   But think my tenderness was to deceive you.
   So I am going to speak to you, purely and simply
   As gentleman, since I was nobly born
   Before I was a lover. In addition,
   I beg you, Beatriz, to imagine now
   It is not I addressing you. Let me forget

Both my love and your jealousy. I want
To think of duty only and my honor;
And, on your side, suppose it is another
Who demands this of me, and to that other
That I reply.
CARLOS: *[Aside]*   These are most strange precautions!
DIEGO: In Madrid, then, I saw Leonor
And her beauty made enough impression on me
To draw me night and day into the street
Where she resided. I beheld, patrolled...
I wrote; but she replied to my advances,
Not merely with disdain, but rather scorn.
This wounded me; I found it difficult
To bear, that she had not accorded me
Even the light response which women keep
Even for those whose courtship they reject —
A charming art which makes disdain itself
Seem grateful. But Leonor did not
Employ this art with me. So, vexed to see
Myself repulsed, I had recourse at last
To the usual means — my lady's serving-maids.
And one of these, won to my interests
By a jewel I gave her, told me that the scorn
Of Leonor was simply due to this:
She had another lover. I grew jealous;
And here, in spite of the demand I made
When I began my story, I consent
That you should listen as your very self.
I'd have you know it was my sense of honor
That prompted me; for in love's rivalries,
It's infamous for one to see unmoved
Another have what one could not obtain.
The maid informed me, too, her mistress meant
To wed her lover; and in this confidence
She let him come at night into her house.
I, Beatriz, simply to take revenge,
Resolved to check on this, so as to tell her
I knew her secret, and would not permit her
To give herself the airs of a proud beauty
Who rejected all alike. Her maid arranged
That I should hide in a closet off her room.
From there I saw her go into another room.
I followed her in the hope of hearing words
Which I could afterwards repeat to her.
Here, Beatriz, it's not to you I speak;
Forget that ever I, to avenge myself
Upon a woman, could so abase myself
As to commit this outrage. Leonor
Heard me and retraced her steps: her lover

Followed, and you know what happened then.[27]
I need not now repeat it. In the end
I came back to Valencia; and I swear —
May the wrath of heaven blast me if I lie!
I did not know that Leonor was here.
Consider, to convince you, that I came
To see you on the night I was obliged
To leap from this balcony. Then Beatriz,
Anxious to dissipate all your suspicions
Regarding me, I came here last night
To try to speak with you. At the same moment,
Don Juan, whom my evil star appears
To excite against me, followed at my heels.
Wishing to hide, I encountered Leonor;
But yet, in spite of the surprise I felt
At seeing her, above all in such a costume,
I had the presence of mind to substitute
Leonor for yourself. Then in the midst
Of these events, Don Carlos, too, arrived.
Why, therefore Beatriz, since you know all this
Do you propose that I should marry one
Who always hated me; whose scorn has caused
All my misfortunes; who has come to Valencia
With another lover; whom I met in your house
Only because I came to seek you there?
Was it for you — for anyone — to make
Such a proposal? If, while I was absent,
You've given your heart to another man, more happy,
And that you use my adventure in Madrid
As a pretext to break with me, — well and good,
Cast off a man who loves you; but don't try
To marry me to another. Not from your hand
Would I accept a bride.

CARLOS: *[Aside]*   What have I heard?
Never was man so surely disabused.
Ah! Leonor, my dearest Leonor,
Your truths were truths indeed.

BEATRIZ: What do you hope to do
Against so many enemies?

DIEGO: Which are they?

BEATRIZ: Leonor, Don Pedro, and Don Carlos,
Me and my brother.

DIEGO: Of all these enemies,
You are the only one I fear.

BEATRIZ: Why me
More than another?

DIEGO: Because my greatest grief
Is to observe the energy with which
You occupy yourself in this affair.

[Enter GINÉS and INÉS by different doors]

GINÉS: Señor!
INÉS: Señora!
BEATRIZ: What is it?
DIEGO: What's the news?
INÉS: My master's here; I've seen him in the street
GINÉS: And worse than that, Señor Don Pedro's with him.
DIEGO: I must have been predestined at my birth
    For such predicaments.
BEATRIZ: It matters little
    If my brother sees you here. But for Don Pedro
    It's another matter.
GINÉS: They are the most punctual
    Father and brother I have ever seen.
    If anything happens, they are on the spot.
DIEGO: I'm going to hide a moment in this closet.
    [Makes for the room where CARLOS is hiding]
GINÉS: Do we have to go through all this again?[28]
CARLOS: No one must enter.
DIEGO: O Heavens! A man is there.
BEATRIZ: Who can it be?
GINÉS: Doubtless it is Abindarráez... He's come a day early
    To be sure of a lodging.[29]
DIEGO: Don't feign to be astonished. When you led me
    To your brother's house to offer me the hand
    Of Leonor, you wished to satisfy
    The rival hidden there, to show him how
    You tried to get me married. But, by heaven...
BEATRIZ: Stop, Don Diego.

[Enter LEONOR]

LEONOR: What is this noise, señora?
    What do I see?
BEATRIZ: *[To DIEGO]* I don't know who it is.
DIEGO: Well, I shall have the pleasure to inform you.
    Even if it means my vengeful foes
    Should cause my death, I must behold the man
    So prudent or so base as not to appear
    When he's defied before his lady's eyes.

[Enter DON CARLOS]

CARLOS: Here I am! I can avoid a duel
    For certain reasons, not through cowardice.
LEONOR: O Fate! When will you cease pursuing me?

[Enter DON JUAN and DON PEDRO]

JUAN: What's happening here?
PEDRO: What strange confusion?
    I seek an enemy and find two before me!

     Traitor, Don Carlos! Vile Don Diego!
     If I cannot divide myself in two
     To strike you separately, stand side by side
     So that I can strike you with one blow.
JUAN: One moment; before we have recourse to arms,
     Let's see if reason cannot settle things.
     Don Diego, has Beatriz spoken to you
     Of the easiest way to settle everything?
DIEGO: That way would be impossible for me —
     Namely, to wed Leonor. I will not do it.
PEDRO: Well, Don Juan, need I hear more than this?
     Back to my sword!
CARLOS: Stop!
JUAN: You defend him
     When he refuses to wed Leonor?
     What would you have?
CARLOS: Had he consented to it,
     I would have killed him.
JUAN: What's this?
CARLOS: In a moment
     All is altered, and my love insists
     On the happiness of wedding Leonor.
JUAN: But what of your complaints?
CARLOS: I'm satisfied
     You should be, too. Leonor, let us ask
     Forgiveness from your father.
LEONOR: Señor...
PEDRO: Say nothing,
     My daughter. Now my honor's reestablished,
     In gratitude for this good fortune, I
     Forgive your lapses.
JUAN: Will you not, at least,
     Tell me what's caused this...
CARLOS: If you will allow me?
JUAN: Of course.
CARLOS: *[Placing himself between JUAN and DIEGO]*
               Let me stand here.
BEATRIZ: *[Aside]*   He's going to tell him
     What he has heard.
CARLOS: Don Diego, will you give
     Your hand to Beatriz!
DIEGO: My hand and heart.
JUAN: Explain.
CARLOS: It must be so; and this should tell you
     Why I have changed. Beatriz and Leonor
     Dwell in this house; Diego came a-wooing;
     And since I'm marrying Leonor, it follows
     That he himself must marry Beatriz.
JUAN: I did have some suspicions; but thank heaven

        That I have seen the remedy before
        I knew the evil.
GINÉS: Everyone makes peace.
        Everyone's getting married. Let's do the same,
        Inés.
            [To the audience]
                After the example you have seen,
        Let no one distrust his lady, whatsoever
        The appearances; for despite the ancient saying:
        THE WORST IS NOT ALWAYS CERTAIN,
        Pardon all our defects. Ring down the curtain!

                    ᘉᘉᘉᘉᘉᘉᘉᘉᘉ

                    THE END

                    ᘉᘉᘉᘉᘉᘉᘉᘉᘉ

Dicha y
desdicha
del nombre

This play survives in no fewer than three seventeenth-century manuscript copies, all of them, unfortunately, un-dated, and in volume 18 of the *Comedias Escogidas,* printed in Madrid in 1662. The exact date of composition is un-known. H. W. Hilborn suggests a date of 1660-1661 and on this occasion could well be right.[1] The work resembles *Peor está que estaba* in several respects. For instance, most of the action takes place in Milan, which, like Gaeta, was un-der Spanish rule in the seventeenth century. The Governor of Milan does not figure in the plot, though he is alluded to; but his chief minister of justice, Serafina's father, fulfills much the same role as Lisarda's parent, the Gover-nor of Gaeta, in *Peor está que estaba.* Milan's minister of justice, like Gaeta's Governor, keeps a young man and woman under arrest, for reasons connected with an affair of honor. His residence becomes the center of the dramatic action, and is as well appointed with different rooms and exits as was the Governor's palace in Gaeta. But *Dicha y desdicha del nombre* is almost half as long again as *Peor está que estaba* and displays, too, other distinctive characteristics, such as its elaborate use of music and choreography, which indi-cate that it was composed at least twenty and probably as many as thirty years after the other comedy.

A note in one edition mentions a performance of the play before the king and queen in the royal palace. Calderón ap-parently wrote the work for just such a performance, because he addresses Philip IV in the final lines. With some in-genious wordplay on the title he asks pardon of the king, in this sanctuary of the royal palace ("en el sagrado vues-tro"), for the deficiencies of his talent. That first royal performance of *Dicha y desdicha del nombre* might well have formed part of the palace's reputedly spectacular carnival celebrations. Certainly the play, with its scenes of rev-elry and masquerade, was an admirably suitable piece for carnival time. Doubtless the performance was leisurely and lavish and made use of some of the splendid palace furnish-ings and furniture for the scenes set in Félix's luxurious room, whose tapestries, cabinets, bed, mirrors, bureaus and the rest so greatly aroused the admiration of Tristán at the beginning of act 2.[2] Calderón's comedy was probably per-formed often at the palace thereafter; though only one such subsequent performance is on record: that given in the Re-tiro in June 1686.[3]

In a brief preface to his text of the play,[4] A. Valbuena Briones praises its prodigious modernity. He maintains that it could be staged nowadays with little difficulty and that the result would be a highly successful production. There is a generous measure of truth in this assertion. A modern audience could not fail to enjoy the physical excitement and

pace of this drama, which in act 1 alone offers an attempted
abduction, a nearly successful murder and a violent encounter with the law. Also, nowadays there is considerable interest in symbolic drama; and Calderón's play with its
masks, music and its "madmen's dance" is rich in symbolism
of life's confusions and perplexities: symbolism that modern
stage techniques could ingeniously convey. Moreover, the
change of identities, undertaken lightheartedly by Félix and
César, yet productive of serious consequences until the situation is finally resolved, allows Calderón to discuss is-
sues that are still extremely relevant today. One such is-
sue is the question of friendship and what it should involve. Initially Félix undertakes to pretend to be César
purely out of friendship for the real César. But he comes
to appreciate that there are personal advantages to be de-
rived from his false identity. One advantage is that he is
housed in Lidoro's mansion and therefore has the opportunity
to woo the magistrate's beautiful daughter. César objects
strongly to the fact that Félix is using his name to further
an affair with Serafina. In a tense scene in act 3 he argues that Félix is no longer behaving as a friend should,
and that his conduct is jeopardizing his, César's, good
name. Felix, however, is by now obsessed with Serafina and
shows little inclination to put the demands of friendship
before those of love.[5] Another modern theme that preoccu-
pies Calderón concerns man's sense of personal identity.
César in particular comes to experience a considerable feeling of disorientation as a result of surrendering his name
to Félix. His unease reaches a climax in the scene in which
he argues with Félix concerning Lisardo's challenge. The
challenge comes in the form of a note addressed to César,
but Félix insists that he should fight the duel with Lisardo
because in Milan he, Félix, is César. In consequence César
feels deprived of more of his identity than he had meant to
lose, and exclaims in distress: "Although you have assumed
/ My name, it's strange that you should wish that I / Should
not be César too."[6]
    The two friends are not the only psychologically inter-
esting characters in the drama. There is Serafina with her
endearing desire to be loved for herself, not worshiped for
her beauty like "a piece of sculpture," and her spirited
determination not to yield to her problems of love, "uncertainties, fears, perils, griefs," but to fight them.[7] Not
least in importance is the vengeful, murderous, mentally
unstable Lisardo, surely one of the blackest characters of
Calderonian comedy. Left alive at the end, for this, after
all, is comedy, he is, justly, the only ultimately unhappy
person: "Everyone's contented, / Save only me, still unavenged and jealous."

Yet there are certain aspects that a modern audience might find less to its liking. Some of the speeches are unnecessarily long and repetitive, even by Calderonian standards. The translator, however, has tried to deal with this problem through some condensation where it seemed appropriate. The other main problem would concern the anecdotes. Seventeenth-century audiences had a special liking for anecdotes, which most of us would find difficult to appreciate. Besides, many of the anecdotes in Golden Age plays have a highly topical slant. Fortunately for us, most Golden Age plays contain only a few anecdotes. Unfortunately, the *gracioso* and *graciosa* of *Dicha y desdicha del nombre* are inveterate storytellers, with a seemingly inexhaustible supply of material. So addicted are they to anecdotes that even their own master and mistress lose patience with them: at the beginning of act 2 Félix threatens to crack his lackey's skull if he dares to tell him another story. Not that this threat has the desired effect. Twice in the course of the comedy Tristán and Flora are given the stage to themselves and indulge in a contest, in which each tries to tell more stories than the other.[8] In the play's final lines they nearly finish two further stories: the tale of the *dueña* and the dwarf, and the story about the female monkey. At earlier points in the comedy they had tried to tell these same anecdotes and had always been interrupted. Doubtless Calderón's audiences were disappointed, but modern audiences would surely be relieved that these two tales at least never do reach their end in *La dicha y desdicha del nombre*. Happily there is plenty of additional humor that would be acceptable to any period: Tristán's comic concern over the loss of his baggage, for example, and his difficulties in carrying the bags when he does recover them. Then there is his entertaining parody of César in debate with himself on a point of honor.[9] Above all, there stands out that brief but hilarious scene in which Lidoro, fondly imagining that he is addressing the son of a close friend, asks Félix questions about members of César's family to which Félix knows none of the right answers and is obliged to rely on his powers of invention.[10]

Notes

1. See H. W. Hilborn, *A Chronology of the Plays of D. Pedro Calderón de la Barca* (Toronto, 1938), pp. 66-67.

2. See below, p. 229.

3. See J. E. Varey and N. D. Shergold, *Teatros y comedias en Madrid: 1666-1687. Estudio y documentos* (London, 1975), pp. 157, 190. The performance was open to the general public.

4. See the Aguilar edition of Calderón, *Comedias* (Madrid, 1956), 2:1797-99.

5. See below, pp. 260-61.

6. See below, p. 262.

7. See below, p. 258.

8. See below, pp. 235-36, 259.

9. See below, p. 266, and compare pp. 263-64.

10. See below, pp. 231-32. For notes to the text of *The Advantages and Disadvantages of a Name*, see pp. 288-90.

The Advantages & Disadvantages of a Name

𖠋𖠋𖠋

DRAMATIS PERSONAE

Don Félix Colona
Don César Farnesio
Tristán, valet of Don Félix
Fabio, valet of Don César
The Prince of Urbino
Serafina
Lidoro, her father

Violante
Aurelio, her father
Lisardo
Libio, valet
Nise ⎱ maids
Flora ⎰
Musicians, servants, and
attendants

The first two scenes are in Parma, and the remaining
scenes in Milan

𖠋𖠋𖠋

ACT ONE

Scene 1: The Courtyard of the Ducal Palace

[Enter DON CÉSAR, DON FÉLIX, and TRISTÁN]

FÉLIX: You're very happy.
CÉSAR: How should I not be so
    When I obtain today my utmost wishes?
FÉLIX: How so?
CÉSAR: I'll tell you, Félix. You know already,
    Since you're my closest friend and we have but
    A single soul — you know how many cares,
    Vexations, pains, misfortunes have been caused
    By my unquenchable love for Violante,
    Since I attempted first with tears and sighs —
    Vain weapons of war — to breach those diamond walls,
    To break those rocks of steel, to penetrate

Those mines of stone, and cross those fiery moats.
One of my saddest memories, as you know,
Is that of Laurencio, her cousin's, death,
With whom I fought a duel, upon some pretext,
And whom I killed through jealousy, because
He sought her hand in marriage — a wretched fight,
In which we each obtained an equal share
Of fortune and misfortune: for fate decreed
That the favored suitor die, while myself, alas,
Remained alive. After this sad adventure,
You will remember that I quitted Parma;
But absence could not change my sentiments:
And that will show you that my chain is strong,
Since conquering Time that everything destroys
Was powerless to destroy it. After some time —
Seeing that no one took upon himself
Laurencio's cause: his brother Lisardo,
To whom that task belonged, who from his youth
Had taken service with the Emperor
In Germany, not wishing to pursue me
By way of law, but hoping, I believe,
To take a nobler vengeance — my lord the Duke
Was free to grant my pardon. I returned
To Parma, bringing back with me both love
And jealousy. For if love can forget,
A jealous passion never can. I found
That Violante, were it possible,
Was more intractable and yet more cruel,
As though my conduct had been so outrageous
That it increased her scorn. But now at last —
To repeat the same examples — as there's no diamond,
No steel, no stone, no fire which does not yield
(Diamonds are cut, steel fashioned, stone at last
Is hollowed out by water, and the wind
Abates the fire) so Violante too,
By one of the miracles that love has wrought,
If one may credit stories of the past,
Was moved at last by pity, and today
She has written to me —[1]

[Enter FABIO]

FABIO: My Lord;
CESAR: What do you want
    You idiot?
FABIO: The Duke awaits your presence.
    He ordered me to let you know at once
    That you should speak with him without delay.
CESAR: *[To FÉLIX]* I am unlucky, you see, for when I want
    To tell of my distresses and my torments

There's ample time; but when I'm going to tell
Of my good fortune and my joys, the time
Does not allow me. But I will finish
My story soon. Wait for me. I'll be back.
FÉLIX: There's no need to say more: for I perceive
That Violante now at last is willing
To give you love for love. The haughtiest beauty,
Despite appearances, is in her heart
Delighted to be loved.   [Exit CÉSAR]
TRISTÁN: You're quite right, my lord. When I went a-
courting, if you'll allow the expression, when I courted
a certain damsel, I found her very stonyhearted. A rock
in fact, and as, by the grace of God, I'm as fickle as
susceptible, I got tired of her: but as soon as she perceived it, she cried: "Rascal, wretch, villain! Since
you've begun to love me, you'll kindly continue, or, by
heaven, I'll cudgel you to death. You have been impudent enough to love me: but you had better not have the
impudence to stop."
FÉLIX: You're always the same, Tristán. You have a wretched
story for all occasions.
TRISTÁN: Once upon a time a poor hidalgo was mending his
breeches when a friend entered and asked him: "What's
new?" To which he replied: "Only the thread." And I
tell you the same; for if I set myself to patch up these
old ideas of love, the only thing new about them will be
the thread of my tales.[2]

   [Enter CÉSAR]

CÉSAR: Ah! Félix.
Is there a more unhappy man than I?
How quickly do my pleasures turn to griefs!
How my contentment soon gives place to sorrow!
I had good cause to fear that time would fail me
To savor my good luck.
FÉLIX: What is it now?
What's happened? Have you suffered some new grief?
CÉSAR: Yes, such a grief that heaven could not have sent
A greater one. For just as I began
To tell you Violante in the end
Had yielded to my constancy, and written
To inform me that her father would be going
Tomorrow to a neighboring village where
He has some property, and that at night
She'd give me entry to her garden — then,
At the very moment when I was so near
To attaining happiness, I have been foiled,
Flung far from happiness as I could be,
For a thousand obstacles rise up before me.

FÉLIX: What! César, such a sudden change?
CÉSAR: Yes, Félix.
    I envy your felicity, for you
    Are not in love. And so that you may know
    All my misfortune...
FÉLIX: Let me know.
CÉSAR: The Duke
    Has heard that the Prince of Urbino has arrived
    In secret in Milan. He's come, I imagine
    To take command of the imperial troops
    Against the Swiss. As he's a near relation
    And a close friend, he is sending me to him
    To bear this letter,
    To bid him welcome and congratulate him;
    And he has ordered me to leave at once.
    You'll easily conceive the embarrassment
    In which I find myself. If I don't go
    I'll lose, no doubt, the favor of the Duke:
    And if I go, I lose the opportunity
    For which I've longed so long; since Violante,
    Not knowing why I must absent myself,
    Might think I wish to avenge her former scorn,
    And so will cease to favor me, and instead
    Will hate me once again.
FÉLIX: I've only one thing to suggest; you could
    Without its being known, stay till tomorrow;
    And yet be able with swift post-horses
    To make up for lost time.
CÉSAR: Impossible.
    The Duke has ordered me to leave at once,
    And in a six-day journey to lose two
    Would be too much.
FÉLIX: Well, you can warn her,
    Expressing your regrets.
CÉSAR: I can do that;
    But that would not restore the chance I had,
    Thanks to her father's absence.
FÉLIX: What's in the letter?
CÉSAR: What do you think? The usual compliments.
FÉLIX: Does it mention you?
CÉSAR: Yes, following the custom,
    Under this formula: "César Farnesio, my cousin, goes in
    my name, etc. etc." It is the customary style, so that
    the person to whom the letter is addressed knows the at-
    tentions he should pay to the person who bears it.
FÉLIX: There's nothing more?
CÉSAR: No.
FÉLIX: Does the Prince
    Of Urbino know you?

CÉSAR: He has never seen me,
   And there is no one in his retinue
   Who knows me, for he's been so many years
   In Germany, in the Emperor's service.
FÉLIX: Well,
   If you will risk it, as I'm known in Milan
   No more than you, I'll be your substitute,
   So that you can stay in secret here,
   And satisfy your love. There's nothing there
   To offend the Prince of Urbino or the Duke.
   The one will have sent his greetings and the other
   Will have received them. All one has to do
   Is to leave, give the letter, and return
   As soon as possible with the reply.
CÉSAR: Although I doubt if it is quite so simple
   As you pretend, I am in such a fix
   That I would willingly run greater risks.
TRISTÁN: I'm sure I could suggest a better way
   Of fixing things.
FÉLIX: Shut up, you idiot.
CÉSAR: So you'll consent to render me this service?
FÉLIX: I am not one of those who give advice
   And then back out. I'll go instead of you.
CÉSAR: I'll be eternally grateful, and...
FÉLIX: Enough!
   Spare me your thanks. Between friends there's no need.
CÉSAR: But there is still a difficulty.
FÉLIX: What's that?
CÉSAR: I have to go to Lord Aurelio's house, —
   He's Violante's father — to collect
   A certain sum the Duke has granted me
   For my expenses. This will make them think
   That I am leaving; but, with the result
   That Violante will no more expect me
   Tomorrow evening.
FÉLIX: You can write to her.
CÉSAR: That is impossible. I can only send
   A message by her maid who visits me;
   And, thinking that I'm leaving, she'll not come
   So soon to see me.
FÉLIX: Well, you have your voucher
   For payment; and your valet can present it
   And use it as a pretext to deliver
   A message without risk.
CÉSAR: Do not believe it.
   For, since his nephew's death, Aurelio,
   Though heedless of my love and jealousy,
   Dreams still of vengeance; and if he beheld
   One of my servants in his house, I fear

That before asking what his business was
He'd offer violence to him.
FÉLIX: I've an idea.
We can send Tristán there, who with his prudence,
His wit, and usual tact will easily
Avert suspicion.
TRISTÁN: I could never do it.
FÉLIX: What are you frightened of?
TRISTÁN: One ought to fear
Suspicions of a man of honor.
CÉSAR: Be sure
Any offense that's done to you, I'll treat
As a personal affront that's offered me.
TRISTÁN: That's a good one. I have a story which fits the
case nicely. Once upon a time, a Police Inspector,
stinking somewhat, presented himself before the magistrate, uttering cries of anger: "A chambermaid did empty
a chamberpot at an unlawful hour. And while I was writing out a charge, another maid showed a similar contempt
for the law by emptying a second chamberpot over me. As
I was writing at your orders, she did it not to me but
to you." Upon which the magistrate replied in severe
tones: "Well, you fool, who permits you to be offended
by injuries done to me?" So, if I get cudgeled, and
come back half dead, as the injury will be yours, you
could make me the same answer.[3]
FÉLIX: Don't waste time. You're going to carry the letter,
and on your return you will accompany me to Milan.
TRISTÁN: That's good. I like that part of the plan.
FÉLIX: You're glad to make this journey?
TRISTÁN: Certainly.
As it's the time of carnival, and in Milan
Especially, a time of great rejoicing,
I shall enjoy myself just like a priest
When Lent is round the corner.[4]
FÉLIX: Let us be off then. *[To CÉSAR]* We'll get the horses
     ready,
And in the meantime write your note for Tristán
To deliver.
CÉSAR: Let us hurry. Now's the time.
FÉLIX: How so?
CÉSAR: That is Aurelio coming out.
And in his absence it will be easier
To deliver the letter.

[Enter AURELIO, reading a letter]

FÉLIX: He is quite absorbed.
CÉSAR: So much the better. He will not observe us.

    [To TRISTÁN] Come, I will tell you to whom you should
    deliver
The note. *[TRISTÁN stays watching AURELIO]*
FÉLIX: What are you waiting for, you idiot?
TRISTÁN: Leave me.
FÉLIX: What are you doing?
TRISTÁN: I'm weighing up
The old man's strength, to see how many blows
He could administer without drawing breath.
                [Exeunt FÉLIX, CÉSAR and TRISTÁN]
AURELIO: *[Reading]* "My noble uncle, I have arrived at the
court of Milan, concealing my name and my country. Al-
though I am anxious to return home, I do not wish to ap-
pear there until I have avenged my brother's death. And
since this misfortune affects all of us, please let me
know if Don César Farnesio is at Parma."
This is an honorable resolution
Lisardo's taken; but I'm not surprised
Since he is of my blood. What shall I do?
Vengeance is sweet to me since I retain
Beneath the snow of age the fires of youth
All ready to erupt; yet prudence shows me
The danger that's involved; I've reached the age
When one should rather hear the voice of prudence
Than of resentment. If I don't encourage
Lisardo to this vengeance, I am lacking
In what I owe myself; and if I do
I'm failing in my duty. It would be wrong
In me who have lost one nephew, to advise
The other to a course which may result
In his death also. I had meant to marry
My daughter to the one who's dead: Lisardo,
The head of his family now, can marry her instead,
And to expose him to the Duke's displeasure,
To whom Don César is both cousin and servant,
Would go against my plan by putting him
In danger of an everlasting exile.
What should I do, then, to fulfill with honor
This double obligation? Heaven, help me!
I will go in to answer him. I'll find
A way to hold him in suspense, until
I have myself decided. For which purpose
I must reread his letter.
"Let me know if Don César Farnesio is at Parma, and take
care to set spies on his proceedings. I'll arrange to
challenge him. When you reply to me, address your let-
ter to Don Celio, in the household of the Prince of
Urbino."
                        [Exit]

Scene 2: A Room in Aurelio's House

[Enter VIOLANTE and NISE]

NISE: My lord is coming home; and he is deep
    In papers he is reading.
VIOLANTE: O my dear Nise,
    Audacity is sometimes full of fear,
    And when it ventures most it's least courageous.
    Since I have written to Don César, Nise,
    Informing him how sensible I was
    Of his most constant and submissive love,
    I've been afraid of my own shadow.
NISE: Why,
    Madam?
VIOLANTE: It seems to me my breast is crystal,
    In which my father can behold my heart
    And all its motions. *[Aside]* Heavens! Here he is!

[Enter AURELIO]

AURELIO: Violante!
VIOLANTE: What is the matter, father?
    You have returned so soon and you appear
    Very preoccupied.
AURELIO: It's nothing much.
    As I was going out a courier brought
    A letter which demands a swift reply.
    But who presumes to enter unannounced?

[Enter TRISTÁN]

TRISTÁN: *[Not seeing AURELIO]* Since the old man is not at
    home, I must go and find Nise and give her the message.
AURELIO: Who are you looking for, sirrah?
TRISTÁN: *[Aside]* A plague on this encounter!
    [Aloud] You, my lord.
AURELIO: Me?
TRISTÁN: Yourself.
AURELIO: Could you not knock?
TRISTÁN: You see, I am afraid to make a noise.[5]
AURELIO: What do you want then?
TRISTÁN: To give this paper to you.
AURELIO: Whose is it?
TRISTÁN: Yours, since I have given it you.
AURELIO: You seem to have been studying the art
    Of being witty.
TRISTÁN: I'm only a sophomore.[6]
AURELIO: Who is your master?
TRISTÁN: Don Félix. Remember I'm Félix's servant
    For it is most important to the plot.

And, if need be, I'm willing to repeat it.
A hundred thousand times.[7]
AURELIO: I do not like
Vain repetitions.
TRISTÁN: But I dote on them.[8]
AURELIO: Let me read it. "To my Treasurer, Aurelio. From
the sums in your possession, kindly give to Don César
..." What does this mean? Since the order is in Don
César's name, why is it Don Félix who has sent you?
TRISTÁN: Because Don Félix wants this money and Don César
owes him a good part of it.
AURELIO: *[Reading]* "Five hundred ducats which I've granted
him for the expenses of a journey which he is undertak-
ing in obedience to my command."
VIOLANTE: *[To NISE]* Have you heard, Nise? Don César's
    going to leave.
Heaven help me! Doubtless he wishes to avenge
My former scorn by present scorn of me.
TRISTÁN: *[Whispering]* Nise, Nise!
NISE: This valet is making
    signs with a paper.
AURELIO: What is it?
TRISTÁN: Nothing.
AURELIO: What is that paper?
TRISTÁN: Another note — but this one's not for you.
AURELIO: Where is Don César going?
TRISTÁN: *[Aside]*   To hell, no doubt.
    [Aloud] I have no idea.
AURELIO: Wait for me here.
    [Aside] I'll see to this, in order to ensure
The absence of my foe.
O heavens! I wonder if the Duke has learned
Lisardo's at Milan, and that's the reason
He's made Don César leave.
                                              [Exit]
VIOLANTE: I don't know why
I do not stifle with resentment now!
That he should treat me so! That one so constant,
So faithful when I showed him but disdain
Should serve my kindness thus!
TRISTÁN: Now I can speak,
    Madam, listen to me, and you will see
That I, in coming here to get some cash,
Have come as well to pay you what you're owed.
Don César sends this note.
NISE: Take it, and quickly too!
    My master's coming back.
VIOLANTE: I fear he's seen it.
    I'm trembling, Nise.

[Enter AURELIO]

AURELIO: *[To TRISTÁN]* Take this and be off.
TRISTÁN: May heaven preserve you for an eternity of centu-
     ries — give or take a few! *[Aside]* I'm getting off
     much better than I expected; for I've delivered the
     note; and I leave *with* the cash, and *without* a beating.
                                                        [Exit]
VIOLANTE: *[To NISE]* If my father should have seen the note!
NISE: Impossible! He'd have shown he was annoyed.
AURELIO: Violante, as I've told you, I am going
     Tomorrow to the village.
VIOLANTE: *[Aside]*   I'm relieved!
     He suspects nothing, since he's thinking still
     About his journey.
AURELIO: A man must supervise his own affairs
     Or run the risk of ruin...that is why
     You're going to let me see the billet-doux
     You have just hidden.[9]
VIOLANTE: My lord? A billet-doux!
NISE: *[Aside]* Now we're in for it.
AURELIO: Yes, give it me at once. If I've allowed
     The valet to depart, although I saw him
     Hand you the note, I did not wish to take
     Revenge until I know the facts, nor noise abroad
     My personal griefs. So I have held my tongue.
     But now give me the note.
VIOLANTE: Do not believe,
     My lord...
AURELIO: You're wasting time *[He snatches the note]*
                                Go inside at once,
     Lest in my anger I should lose control.
     I want to know precisely what is wrong
     Before applying a remedy. Out of my sight!
VIOLANTE: O heaven! protect me! For I have no right,
     Nor words to defend myself.
                                                        [Exit]
AURELIO: Nise, you go too.
NISE: As you wish.
AURELIO: No, not that way — but this.
     But tell me first, to fix my line of action,
     Since the valet was Don Félix's, and the order
     In the name of Don César, from whom has come
     This letter?
NISE: *[Aside]* If I should say Don César, who's
     His foe already, it would make things worse.
AURELIO: Answer me, Nise. Who has sent this note?
NISE: I do not know, but it was not Don César.
                                                        [Exit]

AURELIO: She has said enough. *[He opens the letter]*

                        I tremble as I open it.
[Reads] "My dearest, There is no obstacle which can
prevent me from coming to see you." *[Speaks]* Alas! It
is right fitting that the paper is made of vilest mat-
ter, and the ink of poison. *[Reads]* "Therefore, take
it as certain that tomorrow, as soon as your father
leaves, I will turn up, despite all dangers, in the gar-
den you mentioned. Heaven keep you." *[Speaks]*
What do I see? Don Félix, under this pretext,
And seconded by his perfidious friend,
Is making an attack upon my honor:
There is no doubt that Nise spoke the truth.
The man insisted he was Félix's servant.
To warn my daughter that he brought a message.
What's to be done? O how can I decide
When I have just received a cruel wound,
And when I've lost all hope of carrying out
The marriage for my daughter I had planned?
Is it not strange that at the very moment
When I was anxious to prevent my nephew
From taking vengeance, something else occurs
Which forces me to take revenge? Ah, well!
Since it is so, and since a righteous anger
Has conquered prudence, I will take revenge
On these two traitors. I will write at once
To ask Lisardo to settle with Don César,
And, since the opportunity is offered,
I myself will secretly dispatch
Don Félix. I will lock this door, to stop
My ungrateful girl from warning him. Tomorrow,
I'll kill him in the garden, take his body...
But hush, no more! For Fame will tell abroad
The tale of my revenge; and future ages
Will hear of it and tremble.

                                                [Exit]

            Scene 3: A Room in Lidoro's House in Milan

MASKERS: *[Singing off stage]*
    Let us laugh and dance and sing,
        Putting off our care and sorrow;
    For the carnival should bring
        Follies we'll forget tomorrow.

[Enter SERAFINA and FLORA]

SERAFINA: Shut the window, Flora, and see that no one
    Opens the shutters.

FLORA: Please, madam, let me watch
   This troop of maskers, passing by the palace,
   And singing as they go.
MASKERS: *[As FLORA dances]*
   Let us laugh and dance and sing, &c.
SERAFINA: Do not annoy me.
   You can see that I'm displeased.
FLORA: Do you not hear
   What they are singing?
MASKERS: For the carnival should bring
      Follies we'll forget tomorrow.
SERAFINA: That's precisely why
   I want to keep my head.
FLORA: But on a day
   Of general rejoicing, is it possible
   You do not wish to see — or to be seen.
SERAFINA: Were there no inconvenience involved,
   I am not yet so old that I'm unable
   To enjoy the carnival with all Milan;
   Especially now displays of fireworks add
   Enchantment to the dancing and the music.
FLORA: Where is the inconvenience, apart
   From your melancholic humor?
SERAFINA: You know it well enough, though you pretend
   You do not know it. So I must remind you,
   That in this street, disguised, there is a man
   Who in the Prince's suite came to Milan
   Two or three days ago; and since he's made
   Advances to me, I would not let him think
   That I was standing at the open window
   Because of him, for his attentions bore me.
FLORA: Perhaps it is another gentleman there
   Whom you have taken for him.
SERAFINA: Improbable!
FLORA: Once upon a time a foreign count was paying court to
   a lady of the palace, and when the sun disappeared be-
   hind the horizon, he'd go to bed, leaving on the terrace
   a Moorish slave of his, wearing his cloak and hat. Now,
   one day, when it was raining and snowing, the lady,
   wishing to do him a kindness, opened the shutter and
   whispered, "Go away, Count!" Whereupon the Moor replied
   "It isn't the Count, it's Hamet." And so, madam, it may
   well be that the masked man you have seen may be Hamet
   and not the Count.
SERAFINA: You always have some story ready.
FLORA: That one is a chestnut.
SERAFINA: I'd deprive myself of better carnivals than this
   to show him scorn.

FLORA: Nothing better proves your cruelty which he is continually deploring.
SERAFINA: Take care, Flora, that you never speak to me of
   his love.
FLORA: Well, to speak of something else, if you don't want
   to stand at the window, I'll show you a way of seeing
   the whole carnival without anyone seeing you.
SERAFINA: How?
FLORA: Thus. You know, madam, that in the carnival ladies
   of the highest rank disguise themselves. Well, all you
   must do is to disguise yourself and go out by the garden
   gate. You will thus kill two birds with one stone — because in addition to enjoying the carnival, you'll punish the person who is pestering you, who will waste the
   whole night waiting here. See — a broad-brimmed hat, a
   cloak, a torch, a mask; you mingle with the first troop
   which happens to pass and no one can possibly recognize
   you.
SERAFINA: And if during that time my father happens to come
   home?
FLORA: There's no danger of that. My lord, being a magistrate, is visiting all parts of the town today; and,
   besides, all you have to do is to let it be understood
   as you go out that you're going with one of your friends
   and so you won't expose yourself to blame.
SERAFINA: The plan appeals to me: but I don't think I've
   courage enough to carry it out.
FLORA: Come, madam; it will be a means of mocking at this
   fool and it will enrage all the women who see your beautiful and elegant figure.
SERAFINA: No, Flora, don't get at me through my vanity; I'm
   quite as anxious as you to go out.
FLORA: Hurry up, then.
SERAFINA: If ladies' maids had never existed, I believe that
   more than one peccadillo...
FLORA: This isn't the moment to start moralizing. Do you,
   or don't you, wish to go?
SERAFINA: Yes; for it would be too sad if the persecution of
   this bore should keep me confined to the house all day.
   Come and dress me.
FLORA: Yes, madam; and I want you to be the most beautiful
   of all the women in the carnival tonight.
                                        [Exit SERAFINA]
   She has spoken ill of maids. Well, let me act
   In character. *[Calling through the window]* Tst! Tst!
      Don Celio!
VOICE: *[Without]* Who calls?
FLORA: One who wants to render you a service.

My mistress soon is going out disguised
By the garden gate: and you can speak with her,
As though by chance you happened to pass by,
Pretending not to recognize her. Hush!
Good-bye.

[Exit]

Scene 4: A Public Place

[Enter LISARDO and LIBIO wearing masks]

LISARDO: Thank you, Flora, for your timely help.
   The news you've given me crowns all my wishes.
LIBIO: What! Are you determined on it?
LISARDO: Indeed.
   And now that I've a chance to speak with her,
   My boldness will achieve the rest.
LIBIO: What, then,
   Do you intend?
LISARDO: I stand to lose all chance
   Of happiness. For as you know,
   I've come to Italy to kill a man,
   Whose name is all I know; and I have written
   To ask my uncle how to meet this man.
   You know, too, that in waiting for his answer
   I've fallen in love with an ungrateful beauty
   Whose scorn is killing me. And so I must
   Obtain a double satisfaction.
   From the woman I love and from the man I hate.
   On the day I am avenged, I will return
   To Germany; and since I must remain
   In exile, it befits a man of daring
   To win in love, even if he runs the risk
   Of losing all. To take the chance
   That offers, I am going to her gate
   And if you wish to render me a service...
     [Noise without]

[Enter a crowd of MASKERS]

A MASKER: Let us dance here. It is the house of the chief
     magistrate.
LISARDO: Come, Libio,
   I'll tell you what to do. Let's hope she won't
   Appear just yet.
LIBIO: I'd like, my lord, to offer
   Some good advice.
LISARDO: It's useless. I'm resolved.
   I'll never have a better chance than now.

The night, the noise of revelers, the disguise,
All serve my turn: together they may bring me
The happiness I seek. No, you have nothing
To say to me, nor I to hear. Let's go.
                                    [Exeunt LISARDO and LIBIO]
A MASKER: Yes, my friends, we can dance here, for the day is
        dedicated to folly.
MASKERS: *[Singing]* "Let us laugh and dance" etc.
        [They dance]

    *[Enter SERAFINA and FLORA, disguised, Flora's disguise
    being somewhat ridiculous]*

SERAFINA: We are unlucky, Flora: the first troop
    We meet is made up of fools.
FLORA: On the contrary, madam.
    We know already how to play the fool.
    We know their dance and shall not get it wrong.[10]
MASKERS: *[Singing]* Let us laugh, etc. *[They dance]*
A MASKER: Let's go somewhere else.
                                    [Exeunt MASKERS]
SERAFINA: Let us leave them, Flora.

    [Enter LISARDO]

LISARDO: One moment, if you please.
    I wish to dance with you.
SERAFINA: *[Aside to FLORA]*   How irritating!
FLORA: In vain we tried to escape him.
SERAFINA: Do you think
    He's recognized me?
FLORA: There's no fear of that.
SERAFINA: Who is that standing there?
FLORA: It's doubtless Hamet,
    Like in the tale I told you.
LISARDO: Don't go away
    Without replying. You ought to know the rules:
    The carnival obliges you to answer.
SERAFINA: You are quite wrong. A masker has the right
    To speak with any other, but not the right
    To force an answer.
LISARDO: It's enough, madam,
    For me to know that I can speak with you.
SERAFINA: Is it not foolish to desire to speak
    To someone who has no desire to hear?
LISARDO: I share that foolishness with many others.
SERAFINA: Well, over there, there is a dance of fools:
    Join them, if you're a fool.
LISARDO: True, I am foolish.
    But...
FLORA: *[Aside]*   I hope he won't let the cat out of the bag.

LISARDO: My foolishness
     Consists in following, driven by my star
     A lovely siren.
SERAFINA: Really! I'm not she;
     So goodbye, handsome visor, for it's rude
     To speak about another woman to me.
LISARDO: No, madam, for through you I'll have revenge
     For all her scorn.
SERAFINA: To that extravagance
     I could reply that when one is mistaken
     About the cure, one will not do much good
     To the disease — but I prefer to finish
     Our conversation there. Good-bye.
LISARDO: I mean
     To follow, for I see a gleam of hope.
SERAFINA: *[Aside]* I don't know what to say to him. *[Aloud]*
     What hope
     Are you speaking of?
LISARDO: Madam, it is...

     [Reenter the MASKERS]

MASKERS: *[Singing]* 'Tis you alone, my lady,
     Who'll bring me my revenge.
LISARDO: It's you alone who can alleviate
     My heavy load of grief; and one might say,
     These singers here had come at my request;
     For what I feel, they tell you in my name:
     "'Tis you alone, my lady, who'll bring me my revenge."
          [The MASKERS sing the words after him]
SERAFINA: Consider, sir. To try to recognize me.
     And follow me, against my will, will rob me
     Of all the safeguards of the carnival.
     So don't compel me, I implore you, sir,
     To ask for help and succor as a woman
     You have insulted. For all who come disguised,
     Will hasten, since it is their common duty
     To come to my defense.

     [Enter LIBIO and other men]

LISARDO: *[Aside]*   Is that you, Libio?
LIBIO: Yes.
LISARDO: I shall be interested now to know,
     How, angry madam, you'll escape from me.
SERAFINA: Thus. Hola, maskers! Stop this man
     From following me.
LISARDO: Hola, maskers! Seize this woman.
          [LIBIO and his fellows seize SERAFINA]
SERAFINA: Ah! Heavens! Treason! Help!
LIBIO: Don't shout!

LISARDO: Take her to the place I mentioned.
FLORA: *[Aside]* Isn't there some desperate man to abduct me
     too?
SERAFINA: Before you abduct me...
LISARDO: Come with me.
SERAFINA: You must
     Now tear me limb from limb.
FLORA: I must be very unattractive since no one wants me.
SERAFINA: O Heavens! Will no one come to aid a woman
     In dire distress?
FÉLIX: *[Without]*   It is an unfortunate lady,
     Calling for help. Dismount, Tristán.
TRISTÁN: *[Without]* There's nothing I'd like better, if the
     horse doesn't object.
LISARDO: Libio, what are you waiting for? Be quick
     And take her to the country villa.
SERAFINA: Will no one come
     To defend an unfortunate woman?

     [Enter FÉLIX and TRISTÁN]

FÉLIX: By all means, madam.
     The single title "woman" would suffice:
     That of "unfortunate" gives greater force.
LISARDO: Sir, if you are not anxious to receive
     A disagreeable invitation, go
     To the place from which you came.
FÉLIX: Even if I wished it,
     I could not do so.
LISARDO: One step more, you'll have
     A bullet in your heart.
TRISTÁN: And, when he shoots
     Our horses will shoot off too.
FÉLIX: Since I have taken
     The pains to intervene, I'll not retreat
     On account of fear. Fire, then, and do not miss me.
TRISTÁN: But I, on the other hand, beg you to miss me.
LISARDO: Your arrogance will have the punishment
     Which it deserves!
          [The pistol misfires]
                         The devil take it!
TRISTÁN: My horses have let me down too. Your gun didn't go
     off right, and my horses have no right to go off.[11]
          [SERAFINA and FLORA get behind FÉLIX and TRISTÁN]
FÉLIX: Now you will see, sir, how I punish those
     Who insult women.
FLORA: *[To TRISTÁN]*   Where does our Don Quixote
     Come from?
TRISTÁN: From Spain, and I'm his Sancho Panza.[12]
          [FÉLIX and LISARDO draw and fight]

VOICE: *[Off]* Torches! Torches! There's a fight in the
    street.

*[Enter a crowd of masked people, carrying torches and
musical instruments, and LIDORO]*

VOICES: Stop! What's happening?
SERAFINA: *[Aside]*   Heavens! What an adventure!
LIDORO: Lay hands on them, in the name of the King!
FLORA: We women can hardly do that.[13]
SERAFINA: *[Aside]* My father! It wanted only that to brim
    The cup of my misfortunes.
LISARDO: *[To LIBIO]* It's the chief magistrate.
LIBIO: What are you waiting for?
    Let's fly, and they won't find out who we are.
LISARDO: A curse upon the opportunity
    And on the hope which both are lost tonight!
                                  [Exeunt LISARDO and LIBIO]
LIDORO: *[To FÉLIX]* I arrest you and these ladies, who have
    caused you
    To draw sword upon a masker, when
    All are trusting to a mutual pact
    And go unarmed.
TRISTÁN: Except that they each carry two or three pistols.
SERAFINA: *[Apart to FÉLIX]* I pray you, sir, to whom I owe
    my honor,
    Now let me owe my life to you as well.
    If I am recognized, I shall be lost.
FÉLIX: You will excuse my ignorance, my lord,
    When I inform you that I've just arrived
    This moment from Milan.
TRISTÁN: Only just: our horses
    Have just this moment left us.
FÉLIX: These ladies here
    Are quite unknown to me. I drew my sword
    Only to guard them from unruly force.
LIDORO: That's not enough to make me set you free.
FÉLIX: As far as I'm concerned, I do not care.
    But I will not allow you to arrest
    These ladies.
LIDORO: How will you prevent it, sir?
FÉLIX: You'll see. *[To SERAFINA and FLORA]*
                    Will you retire? I'll cover your flight.
SERAFINA: I can hardly bear up.
FLORA: Come, madam, one has always strength enough
    To run away.
TRISTÁN: If you should meet two horses,
    Tell them to wait for us. *[Exeunt SERAFINA and FLORA]*
FÉLIX: No one shall follow them,
    So long as I'm alive.

LIDORO: Kill this madman!
ALL: Let's kill him!
                        [They fight]
FÉLIX: Now that they have got away...
TRISTÁN: Like our horses!
FÉLIX: Let us protect ourselves, Tristán, and use
    This gateway as retreat.

    *[Enter the PRINCE, followed by servants with torches,
    and, from the other side, LISARDO, in ordinary clothes]*

THE PRINCE: Lower the torches. What is happening here?
    How dare they drive a man into my grounds,
    Whatever his crime!
LISARDO: *[Aside]*   I shan't be recognized,
    Now I'm no longer masked. My presence here
    May avert suspicion *[Aloud]* My lord, what's this?
THE PRINCE: Hold!
LIDORO: My lord the Prince,
    No one has more desire than I
    To serve you; but events are often found
    Too strong for us. This man here has committed
    A serious crime, ignoring the old laws
    Of the masquerade; and, what is worse, he acted
    On behalf of a lady whom he doubtless recognized
    Beneath the disguise she wore. And surely she
    Must be his lady, since he risked his life
    To rescue her. But, in pursuing him
    To the threshold of your palace, I'd not thought
    Of the immunities which protect him there.
    Forgive me, sire; your palace will henceforth
    Be an asylum for him.
FÉLIX: One moment, sire.
    Since I have had the happiness to gain
    Your royal protection, I don't wish to appear
    Guilty before you, but rather to convince you
    That I am innocent. I do not know
    The lady who was here, and I am ignorant
    Of her connection with a man who took
    Advantage of the carnival's disguise
    To try and abduct her. If I intervened
    It was because I heard her fearful cries,
    And later that she said she could be ruined
    If she were recognized. You will believe me,
    When I confess I am a stranger here,
    And when you've read this letter, I'm instructed
    To give your Highness.
TRISTÁN: And if the letter isn't enough, you have only to
    ask our two post-horses, who have just disguised their
    whereabouts like a couple of maskers.
THE PRINCE: From whom's this letter?

FÉLIX: From the Duke of Parma.
THE PRINCE: I could have received it at a better moment
    But I propose to read it publicly,
    So that the truth may be displayed to all.
    [To servants] Bring the torches near.
    [Reads] "My cousin and lord, when I learned of your
    happy arrival in Italy I was not in a good state of
    health, and so I could not come in person to welcome you
    and to congratulate you on your success. That is why
    Don César Farnese"...
LISARDO: *[Aside]* What have I heard!
LIDORO: *[Aside]* I am delighted...
THE PRINCE: "my kinsman and secretary"...
LIDORO: *[Aside]* to hear this news.
LISARDO: *[Aside]* How infuriating!
THE PRINCE: "comes to visit you in my name"...
LISARDO: *[Aside]* I am enraged.
THE PRINCE: "and he will bring me the news I am anxious to
    have of you and of your family"...
LISARDO: *[Aside]* This Don César is my brother's murderer.
THE PRINCE: "God be with you. Your friend and cousin, the
    Duke of Parma."
LIDORO: *[Aside]* How pleased I am to see him!
LISARDO: *[Aside]* I am overcome at sight of him.
THE PRINCE: I'm very grateful to the Duke of Parma
    For his attention, and I'm flattered too
    That you have brought his letter.
FÉLIX: I could not hope
    For a more glorious favor than to kneel
    Before you.
THE PRINCE: You must be weary, and the quarrel
    On your arrival doubtless proved more tiring
    Than your journey here by post-horses.
TRISTÁN: Mine was worse
    than his. I'm almost glad to see the back of that lean
    creature, even though it has left me with no clean un-
    derwear.
THE PRINCE: Go, then, and rest. *[To LISARDO]*
                          Celio, see that Don César
    Is lodged near me.
LISARDO: *[Aside]*   That I should have to serve him
    Is the last straw. *[To FÉLIX]* Come, I'll lodge you in
        my house.
LIDORO: No, Don César will not go with you, Don Celio.
LISARDO: *[Aside]* Does he suspect? *[Aloud]* Why not?
LIDORO: Because if I
    Deserve the happiness I should be flattered
    If instead Don César would agree
    To come to my house. I would make amends,

For the vexation I have so far caused him.
He'd have in me a man whose one desire
Was to serve him. We have not met before.
But his father and I were friends,
And once I owed to him both life and honor.
I'd like, as far as it is in my power
To show my gratitude unto his son.
THE PRINCE: I am delighted, Don Lidoro, that
A man for whom I have such great esteem
Should be your guest.
FÉLIX: I cannot find words now
To express the honor that I feel.
THE PRINCE: Farewell.
We'll meet tomorrow.
FÉLIX: I implore your Highness
To dispatch me soon, lest I should be remiss
In the Duke's service.
THE PRINCE: I can't let you return
So promptly. Now's the time a sojourn here
Can give delight to strangers. If the annoyance
You suffered earlier has not put you off
Our carnival, you will enjoy yourself.
    [To servants] Light Don César and Lidoro home!
                                        [Exit]

LIDORO: Follow me, sir.
LISARDO: *[Aside]*   Unfortunate that I am,
    The man who killed my brother is the same
    As he who hindered me in my affair,
    And is to be the guest of her I love.
    But vengeance shall be mine!
                                        [Exit]
TRISTÁN: Wouldn't it be a good idea, sir, now we're set for
    this lucky adventure, to save trouble to others, by
    finding out what's become of our horses?
FÉLIX: What do you think has become of them, you idiot?
    The groom will have seen to them.
TRISTÁN: Provided he isn't too busy looking after our lug-
        gage.
    That's what worries me.
LIDORO: They'll be recovered tomorrow. There's my house,
    Which, from today, is yours *[calling]* Flora! Lights!
    [To servants] You can go: they are coming down to light
        me.
                                [Exeunt servants]

[Enter SERAFINA and FLORA]

SERAFINA: Welcome, my lord. I'm told there was a fight,
    And knowing you were involved, I was afraid.
    But who is this? I did not know that you
    Were bringing company.

LIDORO: Serafina,
   The gentleman you see is Don César
   Farnese, who's agreed to be our guest.
   I owe a thousand obligations to his father
   Which I'll remember always. I was lucky
   To meet him in the fight of which you spoke.
   He came to the defense
   Of some lady who had begged for his protection,
   For fear she would be recognized, perhaps,
   By husband or by father.
SERAFINA: There are women
   Who are born to stir up trouble: this adventure
   Might have had fatal consequences.[14]

                              [To FÉLIX] Welcome,
   My lord, to a house where all is at your service.
   I can but ask for your indulgence.
TRISTÁN: This is more like a prologue than the end of an
            act.[15]
FÉLIX: For me, now that I've met this beauteous lady,
   Misfortune turns now into happiness.
SERAFINA: What are you thinking, Flora — that my protector
   Is now my guest?
FLORA: I would like to tell you an appropriate tale about it
   — But it would be too long.
FÉLIX: *[To TRISTÁN]*   Have you ever seen
   A rarer and a more accomplished beauty?
TRISTÁN: Very often, sir; and I would prove it to you by a
   tale, if this were the time for it.
LIDORO: Open his room, Flora. *[To FÉLIX]* Come and see.
   You'll find the room is rather cramped and modest,
   But I would like it to be large and splendid.
   We're going to talk together of your father,
   God rest his soul!

                                              [Exit]
TRISTÁN: That will be a marathon talk!
FÉLIX: I'm pulled in another direction by a superior force.
SERAFINA: Come, Flora.
FLORA: Well?
SERAFINA: I'm still in a state of fright.
FLORA: *[To TRISTÁN]* Good Lord! They're dragging their feet.
TRISTÁN: If our horses had done the same, they would easily
            have been caught.
SERAFINA: Why don't you follow my father, sir?
FÉLIX: I'm waiting
   For you to leave first, as I do not wish
   To turn my back on you.
SERAFINA: I know that mine
   Is safe with you behind me.
FÉLIX: Such is the fortune

From my misfortune.

SERAFINA: Well, believe me, sir...
   But no, do not believe me. Good-bye.

FÉLIX: Heaven protect you!

SERAFINA: }
FÉLIX: }   What fortunate misfortune!

                                            [Exeunt]

ᘒᘒᘒ

ACT TWO

Scene 1: A Room in Lidoro's House

[Enter FÉLIX, who is dressing, and TRISTÁN]

TRISTÁN: Yes, my Lord, I maintain that there's nothing better for a man than not to be himself, but someone else.

FÉLIX: Why?

TRISTÁN: Because another's happiness is, or seems to be,
   greater than ours. You yourself are a proof of it. In
   spite of your name, which signifies happiness, the only
   time you are happy is when you are Don César! — Beautiful room! what galleries! what tapestries! what sheets!
   what cabinets! what mirrors! what writing desks! what
   cupboards! what linen! what beds! what sideboards! what
   tables! what food! what dishes! what vessels! what sup-
   pers! and, above all, what wine!

FÉLIX: Ah! Tristán, in this delightful hospitality, all
   that I have seen is a dangerous beauty whose presence or
   absence both makes me die.

TRISTÁN: For me this beauty is my horse, who made me die
   when I saw him too close and who also makes me die now I
   no longer see him.

FÉLIX: Must it always be impossible to talk seriously with
   you?

TRISTÁN: A duenna decided to bring up a dwarf; and one
   day...

FÉLIX: Shut up, I beseech you, and stop recounting your
        stories...
   If not, by God, I'll knock you on the head.

TRISTÁN: What! You don't want any more stories?

FÉLIX: No.

TRISTÁN: Then you'll have to live in a bungalow.

FÉLIX: You're a fool *[Knock]* Someone's knocking.

TRISTÁN: Yes, it's at this door which leads to the street.

FÉLIX: Who can possibly wish to see me?

TRISTÁN: It may not be for you.

FÉLIX: In that case, tell them to go round to the other en-
     trance.
TRISTÁN: Wouldn't it be better to open the door and find out
     who it is?
FÉLIX: Can you?
TRISTÁN: It's not very difficult since the key is in the
     lock.
FÉLIX: Open it, then, and see who it is.

                                        [Exit TRISTÁN]

     Unfortunate that I am, I would not credit
     The irresistible power of love till now.
     But now I shall not doubt it. They are right
     Who say love's weapons once were bows and arrows
     But now since guns were...

     [Enter TRISTÁN]

TRISTÁN: Good news, sir.
FÉLIX: What are they?
TRISTÁN: You have become a figure of romance,
     A real knight-errant. A woman in a mask,
     A tasty morsel from the carnival,
     Who bears a basket full of I know not what
     Has asked to see you.
FÉLIX: See me? But who in Milan knows my name?
TRISTÁN: She didn't say Don Félix, but Don César.
FÉLIX: That's hardly less surprising; but nevertheless,
     Whoever she may be, let her come in.
TRISTÁN: The lady hasn't waited for permission.

     [Enter FLORA, masked with a basket]

FLORA: *[Aside]* I hope to God my mistress's stratagem
     Won't land us in a mess.[16]
FÉLIX: Whom do you seek,
     Madam? *[FLORA nods]* Me? *[FLORA nods]* You cannot
          speak?
TRISTÁN: She can't speak, my lord... I'll take this rare
          masker for myself.
     [FLORA gives a letter to FÉLIX]
FÉLIX: You wish me to take this letter?...and to read it?
     And that I do not speak of it?... Listen...wait!
     Should you not take an answer? No. As you like.
     But though this is a hoax, permitted by
     The custom of the country at this time,
     I want to recompense you for your pains.
     Here, take this ring. *[FLORA refuses it]*
TRISTÁN: *[Aside]*   This woman is unique.
     She keeps her mouth shut, gives, and will not take.
     [Aloud] I see, sir, Don Lidoro's coming in.
FÉLIX: Lest he should find you here, I'll let you go.

TRISTÁN: I'll follow her, for it would be disastrous
    To lose so rare a woman. You object?
    You say there's someone who would injure me?
    And to me too you give a note.
    To keep it secret. *[Takes letter]* Didn't you know such
        secrets
    Weren't for the likes of us!

                                        [Exit FLORA]
                        She's vanished!
FÉLIX: Keep this quiet, Tristán. We'll discover later
    What all this means.

    [Enter LIDORO]

LIDORO: How have you passed the night,
    Don César?
FÉLIX: Being in your house, my lord,
    How could I fail to have a perfect night?
LIDORO: You flatter me, sir. To see you dressed so early
    Makes me afraid you are not satisfied
    With our hospitality.
FÉLIX: On the contrary
    It proves that it is so agreeable to me
    I'd not lose any of it. To sleep late,
    When one is happy is an insult to
    One's happiness.
LIDORO: You are very courteous;
    But that does not surprise me, as you are
    The son of a man who was courtesy itself.
    How happy he would be to see you now,
    As gallant as you are! Well, God be with him!
    I lost a good friend there.
FÉLIX: Of all I got from him,
    That title is the one I value most.[17]
LIDORO: I never shall forget our comradeship
    In the Burgundian wars; for in one action,
    I'd have been left upon the field of battle,
    But for him.
    Oh! how sweet are the memories of my youth.
    What's become of your uncle?
TRISTÁN: *[Aside]*   Now he'll catch it?
FÉLIX: *[Aside]* What shall I answer now? What shall I do?
    It doesn't help that I am César's friend.
    I'm ignorant of these details *[Aloud]* Of whom do you
        speak?
LIDORO: Of Don Alexander Farnese.
TRISTÁN: *[Aside]*   Do be careful.
FÉLIX: He is dead.
TRISTÁN: *[Aside]* Good! That settles him.
FÉLIX: In the war.

LIDORO: I do not understand. Don Alexander
   Was not a soldier. In my time he was
   A lawyer, practicing in Parma.
FÉLIX: Yes,
   But he was sent as advocate to Piedmont.
TRISTÁN: *[Aside]* Bravo! You got out of that very nicely.
LIDORO: And how is his wife now, Doña Laura?
TRISTÁN: She has become an abbess.
LIDORO: Where?
TRISTÁN: At Uclés.[18]
FÉLIX: Your pardon, sir; this humorist has the habit
   Of making wretched jokes. My aunt, Doña Laura
   Is still at Parma, and her health is good.
TRISTÁN: It's simply that I lose patience to see you chat-
   ting about trifles, when you should be trying to recover
   our horses — and luggage, since you are not suitably
   dressed to go to the Palace.
LIDORO: Well, I will make the necessary inquiries.
   But tell me how —

[Enter a VALET]

VALET: *[To LIDORO]* The Governor has sent me to request you
   to go to his house as soon as possible. The matter is
   urgent: it concerns a criminal who should be apprehended
   forthwith.
LIDORO: *[To FÉLIX]* You wouldn't believe how onerous are my
   duties.
   Forgive me that I have to take my carriage:
   And, as it is early still, please do not leave
   Till I return.

                                         [Exit]
TRISTÁN: If he is going to ask any more questions, let's
   hope he never returns.
FÉLIX: The worst of it is that this predicament may recur
   again and again.
TRISTÁN: A thousand times! But to return to our little ad-
   venture: what has the beautiful masked lady left behind?
FÉLIX: Let us first see what the note has to say. *[Reads]*
   "You will find here something to help you with your ex-
   penses, while you wait for the recovery of your horses."
   [Speaks] I was right to say it was a mystery. See
   What's in the basket.
TRISTÁN: *[Lifting the cloth]* Gloves, lozenges, handker-
   chiefs, and linen.
FÉLIX: One moment!
   There is still a box, and, inside is a jewel
   Surrounded with diamonds.
TRISTÁN: Diamonds! Faith, our horses
   Can fly away now, if they wish! Did I not tell you

That it is great to be another person.
Don César will be sorry he's not here.
FÉLIX: He has nothing to regret, for he is happy
   In love.   But who on earth has sent us that?
TRISTÁN: Who do you think it is, if not
   An angel in disguise who wants to show,
   As Lent approaches, that the three chief virtues
   Of woman are to hold one's tongue, to give,
   And not to take.
FÉLIX: Do you know, Tristán? This
   Will doubtless be the woman whom I rescued,
   Who wants to show her thanks.
TRISTÁN: How in her panic
   Could she have learned your name and lodging, sir?
FÉLIX: How should I know?
TRISTÁN: I know no more than you.
   But do not worry. The future will tell all.
FÉLIX: Conceal this basket for the present, so
   That no one sees it.
TRISTÁN: I think it's only right
   For me to learn what is my share of this.
FÉLIX: Your share?
TRISTÁN: Yes, haven't I also lost my horse?
   And didn't I have a note?
FÉLIX: What does your note say?
TRISTÁN: One moment! I am going to read it, sir. *[Reading]*
   "If you don't hear and see everything without breathing
   a word, your master will reward you with a hundred
   strokes."
FÉLIX: So that's what you get out of it.
TRISTÁN: My God!
   This slut, this hussy, this person who comes here
       masked.
   If she dares come again.
FÉLIX: Quiet! I hear music.
       [Music off stage]
TRISTÁN: Truly we've come to an enchanted forest.[19]
VOICE: "If by chance, you see my folly   *[Singing off]*
           Do not be unkind.
       Think it only my misfortune:
           To my faults be blind."
FÉLIX: The words are pleasing.
TRISTÁN: Unlike this note of mine.
FÉLIX: Leave it! There's someone coming.
TRISTÁN: I don't see
   Why people will say "leave it" when one has not
   Been given anything.

   [Enter FLORA]

FLORA: *[Aside]*   As my master has gone out, my mistress has
    sent me to reconnoiter the enemy camp, and see what they
    think of my previous visit.
    I'll pretend to be leaving.
FÉLIX: Stop her, Tristán.
TRISTÁN: Why are you going so soon?
FLORA: I thought that you had gone out with my master,
    And I came to tidy up.   But since you're here,
    I'll go.
FÉLIX: Must you leave so soon?
FLORA: If my mistress
    Knew that I talked with you, she would be furious
    And even kill me.
FÉLIX: Then it would appear
    That she is very strict.
FLORA: She is indeed.
    Beside her Anaxarete would be
    As tender as a little girl.[20]
FÉLIX: Since chance
    Has given you an excuse, stay now and tell me
    What she is doing now.
FLORA: This music should
    Inform you better than I can, that she's arranging her
       hair.
TRISTÁN: That's true,
    For music likewise requires arrangement.[21]
FÉLIX: If only there were some place where I could hide
    And catch a glimpse of her.
FLORA: When she's dressing her hair?   Impossible!
    A lady only does such things in private.
    But what on earth's that basket?   What are these jewels?
    They don't belong to us.   It would appear
    That someone has already brought you presents.
    I'll tell my mistress, so she can behave
    Accordingly.
FÉLIX: Don't tell her, please; for though
    I'd like to tell her who brought me this basket,
    I simply do not know.
FLORA: My mistress isn't curious.
FÉLIX: So I imagine.
TRISTÁN: It was a trickster.
FLORA: Oh.
TRISTÁN: A meddler, one who keeps quiet and gives without
    taking in return.
FLORA: What a monster!   How did she get in?
TRISTÁN: From the street here.
FLORA: You don't know who she is?
FÉLIX: Certainly not.
FLORA: But whom do you suspect?

FÉLIX: Doubtless it was the lady who engaged me
    In her defense.
TRISTÁN: I will make certain of it
    If she returns.
FLORA: Why are you vexed with her?
TRISTÁN: Because she'd reward my services with blows.
FÉLIX: Ignore this idiot, Flora: but tell me, please,
    If I might see her.
FLORA: Well, I might suggest
    You go down to the garden, and approach
    A window on the ground floor screened by jasmine,
    And in this way...
    But I don't dare to give you such advice.
TRISTÁN: No! No! Don't! It would be very naughty of you.
FÉLIX: Thank you for the information; and,
    For want of better, accept this ring.
FLORA: *[Aside]*   To take
    One out of two is not too much; and only
    The wretched player never gets the ring.   *[Takes it]*
    [Aloud] There's no need for that, sir.
TRISTÁN: No, there isn't;
    But you might earn it yet.
FLORA: We're not all fools! Some-
       one's started
    To sing again. *[Soft music off stage]* This will enable
    you
    To approach with little risk.
FÉLIX: Stay here, Tristán.
    Lead me not blindly, love: take off your bandage.
                              [Exit]
TRISTÁN: Listen, my queen.
FLORA: I can't for long.
TRISTÁN: Never mind, listen! One day, an officer passed in
    revue a batch of recruits...
FLORA: *[Aside]* Help! a story! By my soul, I'll make him
    pay for this!
TRISTÁN: And he told his assistant to keep a watchful eye
    for cripples and invalids. And as a one-eyed man passed
    by, he said: "Keep an eye for him!" But a cripple who
    came next, having overheard, replied: "Since you order
    him to keep an eye for a recruit with one eye, tell him
    to keep a leg for me." Well, since you help the blind
    love of my master to see, I'd like to court you even
    though I stumble.[22]
FLORA: A Biscayan served the priest of a village where the
    butcher was called David.
TRISTÁN: *[Aside]* She's paying me back in my own coin.
FLORA: One day, when he was going to preach, the priest sent
    to ask the butcher for a haslet on credit; and at the

moment when the Biscayan returned with the answer, he
found the priest already in the pulpit, citing all the
prophets and crying: "What does David say?" To which
the Biscayan said from the door: "Sir, he vows that if
I don't bring him some money, whatever you say or do,
you won't have your haslet." You understand, don't you?
If he who doesn't pay, shouldn't eat, he who doesn't
give should neither walk nor see.[23]

TRISTÁN: One day a witch was punished by the usual method of
being forced to wear a cone-shaped hat, or *coroza,* with
her various offenses inscribed on it. When she was
freed, she received an account, which included so much
for the paper, so much for the glue, so much for the
paints, and so much for making it up. Seeing which, the
old woman said: "At least let me keep it for another occasion; for these days a poor widow woman can't afford
to buy a new *coroza* every time she needs one." Well
then, if a *coroza* can now be made to serve more than one
occasion, look at it how you will, one ring ought to be
recompense enough for more than one favor.[24]

FLORA: A man, one day, had cracked his wife's skull; and
she, seeing what the cure cost, said to herself, very
joyful: "He won't do that again." But the husband, seeing her restored to health, settled his account with the
surgeon and the apothecary and in so doing paid them
double. Whereupon she said, "Eh! my love, don't you see
you're making a mistake?" "No, love," said he, "Half
this money is for today's, and the other half is for the
next time I crack your skull. It is because of my considerable foresight I pay double."

TRISTÁN: A duenna brought up a little dwarf...

VOICE: *[Off]* Flora!

FLORA: My mistress calls me. Stop there.

TRISTÁN: At what point?

FLORA: At the point where a duenna brought up a little
dwarf.

TRISTÁN: Well, good-bye, Flora, till the little dwarf has
grown.

[Exeunt]

Scene 2: Another Part of Lidoro's House

*[Enter SERAFINA and FLORA from one side, FÉLIX from the
other]*

SERAFINA: Flora!

FLORA: Madam?

SERAFINA: See who is standing behind the shutters.

FÉLIX: One who will not deny his crime, in which
    He has been found out, for he's proud of it
    And glories in it, and would scorn to justify it.
SERAFINA: In such offenses, admission is more guilty
    Than the actual deed.
FÉLIX: In offenses of this kind,
    Which flatter the very person they annoy,
    Denial is cowardice, not repentance.
SERAFINA: Insult,
    However gracious, is not less an insult;
    And when one has insulted anyone it's wrong
    To boast of it.
FÉLIX: I declare myself vanquished, madam.
    And not because I could not make reply
    But since I much prefer to let you win.
SERAFINA: You want me to approve of your surrender,
    As if from courtesy you do what you would
    Though you're compelled to do so.
FÉLIX: Well, since I must tell you,
    I came into the garden quite by chance,
    And then a siren's song enticed me hither
    And if that doesn't excuse me in your eyes,
    The words she sang would do so.
SERAFINA: In what way?
FÉLIX: She sang: "If, by chance, you see my folly,
        Do not be unkind:
    Think it only my misfortune:
        To my faults be blind."
SERAFINA: And if indeed these words could be applied
    To this occasion, how would they excuse
    Your boldness?
FÉLIX: In this way: chance and my pains
    Led me to where I was mad enough to offend you
    At the same instant as I had the good sense
    To look upon you. Without hesitating,
    I came here, saying when one wants to obtain
    A lady's love, one must expose oneself
    To her displeasure; that one often reaches
    Goodness through evil; and that, though you repulse me,
    I would have naught to fear, if my plaints reached you.
    No, for a single check, I won't despair;
    For even your sternness pleases me, and I
    Adore your scorn. And so the harm you do me
    Is, in my eyes, a blessing. If my boldness
    Offends you, blame yourself alone, who cause it.
    Since you compel my homage, don't repel it
    Because it comes from me.
                                              [Exit]

SERAFINA: To hear you talk so

Does not befit my rank. I am who I am.
[Aside] But no, alas,
What can I say to him? Why should I play
The hypocrite and reproach him, when he seems
Guiltless to me?
How vexing! And how feebly one is vexed
When one would not be so!

FLORA: Since you are grateful
To Don César for what he has done for you,
Why do you show yourself offended, madam,
That he should love you.

SERAFINA: Because I have within me
Two contradictory feelings, and that's why
You'll see me play two different parts with him.
In his presence — speaking to him — I wish
To show him only coldness and disdain;
But, out of his sight, remembering he saved me
Before he knew me, I want to render him
A thousand services without his knowing
From whom they come.

FLORA: Very well, madam,
But if your cruelty estranges him
From you, will you not be jealous of the lady
He falls in love with, thinking her to be
A different one from you?

SERAFINA: No! When he knows me
I'd have him love me for my beauty, and,
Not knowing me, to love me for my wit,
My inward qualities: then I'd not mind
Which one of me he loves.

FLORA: Once upon a time, a monkey and her friends...

SERAFINA: None of your fables now, Flora. And, to return
To what I said just now, I want to go
This evening, veiled... But who's this?

[Enter LISARDO]

FLORA: Don Celio!

SERAFINA: I don't know how I'm to behave with him.
I'm overcome, but know it would be wrong
To show it.

FLORA: Hide your feelings if you can.

SERAFINA: I fear my face betrays them. *[To LISARDO]* Whom
do you seek, sir?

LISARDO: *[Aside]* My courage fails me. But since she pre-
tends
She does not recognize me, I should do the same.
[Aloud] Madam, it is your guest I come to see.
My lord, the Prince, has sent for tidings of him.

SERAFINA: There is his room. *[She moves away]*

LISARDO: Pardon me, I'm mistaken.
It's someone else I'm seeking, begging her
Not to leave on my account: from my folly
She has nothing to fear.
SERAFINA: I know I haven't,
Since I know whom you seek.
LISARDO: I don't understand.
SERAFINA: Neither do I. Yet if my safety now
Depends upon the fact that you are looking
For someone else, it's easy to construe.
LISARDO: How stern you are! But you will not deter me.
SERAFINA: What do you mean?
LISARDO: I mean, madam...
SERAFINA: Go on.
LISARDO: That one day you'll avenge me on yourself.
SERAFINA: Now I don't understand you: and thank heaven
I don't, for if I did... But how absurd
Of me to be vexed. Go, sir, and since we both
Have need of Don César, go you and find him;
And it is he who will avenge me on you.

                                          [Exit]

LISARDO: When can my love obtain the victory
Over such harshness, Flora?
FLORA: Do you not blush
To speak to me, you traitor?
LISARDO: Do you, too,
Reproach me?
FLORA: When you carried off my mistress
Should you not also, out of mere politeness
Have kidnapped me? Even if I'd been black!

                                          [Exit]

LISARDO: "We both have need of Don César. Go, find him,
And it is he who will avenge me on you."
Serafina by those words betrays
Her feelings, and it seems accuses me
Of cowardice with regard to Don César.
Let me attempt to clarify my thoughts.
To avenge my brother I have had to assume
A false name and country. If I kill
Don César here and now, then Serafina
Will think I killed him simply for revenge
Because he rescued her, and she'll denounce me.
That is against my honor. In any case
She may denounce me for the attempt to seize her;
But that's unlikely, lest she compromise
Her own good name. So I must change my plan
For the sake of honor, and act more circumspectly.
I've learned this, thanks to her. But yet, by heaven,
I'll show him who I am — and soon enough —

When we meet face to face upon the field.
But here he is.

[Enter DON FÉLIX]

FÉLIX: To what do I owe this honor, sir?
LISARDO: My lord the Prince has sent me to inquire
How you have passed the night?
FÉLIX: I thank you, sir,
And I am going to thank him for the honor
That he has done me.
LISARDO: God be with you, sir.
FÉLIX: And you, sir.
LISARDO: *[Aside]* I'm resolved: and now I know
Where he resides, my vengeance is assured.

                                                    [Exit]

FÉLIX: What a strange call!

   [Enter TRISTÁN]

TRISTÁN: Sir! Sir!
FÉLIX: What's the matter? What has happened?
TRISTÁN: I bring the strangest news. You won't believe
      them.
   Don César's at the door and asking for you.
FÉLIX: Who did you say? Don César?
TRISTÁN: Him.
FÉLIX: Don César
   At Milan! Why?
TRISTÁN: I don't know. Go and see.
   I didn't want, by asking, to delay
   Bringing the news.
FÉLIX: You're right. It's he indeed.
TRISTÁN: Now we shall catch it! He has doubtless heard
   Of your good fortune under his name, and now
   He comes to share the fun.
FÉLIX: I hear him asking
   For me, and they are allowing him to enter
   My room.

   [Enter DON CÉSAR]

CÉSAR: Embrace me, Félix.
FÉLIX: Why are you here? Is it because the Duke
   Has found out somehow that you had not started,
   And ordered you to come?
CÉSAR: I would to God
   That were the motive for my coming!
FÉLIX: What
   Has happened?
CÉSAR: No one's listening?
                                 No one.

                                    [To TRISTÁN]   Stand
At the door as sentry.
TRISTÁN: But can't I be present?
FÉLIX: You shall know everything, but later.
        [TRISTÁN retires]   Well?
    What is it?
CÉSAR: The most incredible, the most cruel,
    And the most horrible revenge a woman
    Has ever thought of! Violante, whom
    Neither my constancy nor my sufferings touched,
    Arranged to meet me in her garden, only
    To make me perish there, as a serpent hides
    Beneath the flowers. After your departure,
    I let it be assumed that I had gone,
    And thus I passed the night and following day.
    But in the morning, from a spy I'd posted,
    I learned of the departure of her father:
    And so, on this assurance, when night fell —
    That fatal night, whose darkness Love prefers
    To the brightest sunshine — I went toward the garden
    And when I'd given the signal we'd agreed
    I saw her treacherous doorway open wide.
    At the same time I felt instinctively
    A kind of fear I fought against, but yet
    Which put me on my guard. This saved my life,
    Since it was not the maid whom I expected
    To let me in, whose voice now bade me enter,
    I shielded my face and called out "Who goes there?"
    Immediately, to answer my suspicions,
    There was a pistol-shot. But — God be thanked!
    The assassin missed me, though at point-blank range.
    The bullet struck my shield and then glanced off.
    Then I was set on by a gang of men
    And forced to retire to the corner of the street,
    Fighting at every step. Meanwhile the shot
    And the resulting clamor had aroused
    The neighborhood, and my assailants fled
    Afraid of being recognized. So I
    Withdrew, took horse, and rode away from Parma.
    Why, you will ask. This, Félix, is the reason.
    The wretches who attacked me know my name
    But won't reveal it lest they should expose
    Their plot to murder me. So I, to avert
    Suspicion of the Duke and of the public,
    Thought it proper to present myself
    Here at Milan: and that is why I've come,
    Expecting I would join you here in time
    Before you'd been presented to the Prince.
    But on my arrival I was soon informed

        That you already had performed my mission
        And that you lodged here. So I came to give you
        An account of everything. Now it's for you
        To see what should be done, if there's a way
        Of setting things to rights.
FÉLIX: I've listened to you
        With great attention and I'm much disturbed
        To see such hatred and such ugly treason
        Lodged in a woman's heart. They say there's naught
        More dangerous than a woman roused. No more of that.
        I'm sure your move of coming here was right:
        Your absence should avert suspicion; but
        Unfortunately, after an adventure
        As strange as yours, but yet not tragical,
        I have indeed delivered the Duke's letter;
        And so we are compelled, while in Milan
        In carnival time, to be each other, you
        Don Félix, I Don César. Then we can
        Set off together, and once we have returned
        To Parma, no one will concern himself
        Which of us took the letters of the Duke —
        Don César or Don Félix.
CÉSAR: Well, meanwhile,
        I'm going to strive to tarnish the remembrance
        Of an ungrateful woman: despite her treachery
        She still obsesses me. But tell me, Félix,
        As by my reckoning, you arrived in Milan
        Yesterday evening, how does it come about
        That you have called upon the Prince already?
        And how did you come to take up lodging here
        In the chief magistrate's house.
FÉLIX: It is important
        You should know all the facts. Listen, then, César,
        And you will see that my adventure is
        As strange as yours. We scarcely had arrived
        In Milan even before we had dismounted
        When scares and cares beset us.²⁵

        [Enter TRISTÁN]

TRISTÁN: Here
        Is Lord Lidoro.
FÉLIX: I will tell you later.

        [Enter LIDORO]

LIDORO: Tristán, your luggage is at the Star Hotel.
        You have only to ask for it.
TRISTÁN: Yes, indeed, sir.
        I'll go at once, for all my goods are there,
        While here there's no one thinks of me at all.
                                                        [Exit]

LIDORO: Forgive me, sir, for being so late. The Governor
     Sent for me urgently — an affair of honor —
     Which has prevented me from coming sooner,
     And which compels me to depart at once.
     I have to arrest a man that I would like
     To set my hands on, even at the cost
     Of all I have, and am, although I know
     Only his name.
FÉLIX: We can go out together,
     For I must go to the Palace.
LIDORO: Who's this gentleman?
FÉLIX: One of my friends, sir, who has come to Milan
     On business, and who, knowing I was here
     Has come to see me. Will you approach, Don Félix.
LIDORO: What have I heard! His name is Don Félix?
FÉLIX: Yes, sir.
CÉSAR: Forgive me that I did not greet you first,
     Before I was presented.
LIDORO: *[Aside]*   I must do my duty.
     [To FÉLIX] What is the surname of your friend?
FÉLIX: Colona.
LIDORO: Don Félix Colona?
FÉLIX: Yes, sir. What's the matter?
LIDORO: I am very sorry to have heard him named.
CÉSAR: What! You do not like me having this name?
LIDORO: No, I would have given much before to find you:
     But at this moment I would give as much
     Not to have found you.
CÉSAR: What's my name to you, sir?
LIDORO: *[To FÉLIX]* I don't know how to tell you that my
          duty,
     My life, and honor demand that I arrest
     Your friend; and is why I'm very sorry
     To find he is your friend and in my house.
FÉLIX: You want to arrest Don Félix?
LIDORO: Yes.
CÉSAR: But why?
LIDORO: Do not pretend to be astonished, sir,
     For you know well you climbed into the house
     Of an old gentleman and after killing
     His groom, you ran off with his daughter. Now
     The Duke of Parma's written to the Governor
     To arrest you with the lady, Violante,
     Who's Lord Aurelio's daughter. *[To FÉLIX]* So you'll
          see
     I can't do otherwise than arrest your friend.
CÉSAR: *[Aside]* How extraordinary! That he should be look-
          ing
     For Félix and not me.

FÉLIX: *[Aside]*   How was it I
    Who loved Violante?
CÉSAR: *[Aside]*   Is it not to destroy me
    That she accuses me of abducting her?
FÉLIX: *[Aside]* How can I possibly have done this deed?
LIDORO: What do you say?
CÉSAR: My lord, I say that I
    Did not abduct a lady, and that you
    Are misinformed.
LIDORO: I would rejoice to find it so.
    Surrender now, and without any danger
    You'll be my prisoner.
FÉLIX: Think, sir: it's by an error
    That he has been accused.
CÉSAR: Someone's mistaken
    The name.
LIDORO: Are you Don Félix Colona?
CÉSAR: Yes.
LIDORO: Is there another gentleman in Parma
    Of the same name?
CÉSAR: No.
LIDORO: Well, it is you
    Who have been accused. Fear nothing. It's enough
    That you're Don César's friend for me to treat you
    In the best possible way, compatible
    With duty. We will settle the affair
    As amicably as possible. For although
    I'm the chief magistrate, I am not less
    A gentleman, and I know well those faults
    Are generous, which love makes us commit.
    So tell me where this lady is, and I
    Will go and find her. I will offer her
    My house as an asylum, and I hope
    My intervention will provide a means
    To bring about your happiness.
CÉSAR: There is no one
    In whom I would more willingly confide,
    And if I knew the lady's whereabouts,
    I swear, my lord, that I would let you know.
    But, I repeat, you are in error; Félix
    Had no adventure of this kind.
LIDORO: Well, sir,
    If there's an error, as you say, I must
    Give way. But although it would be wrong
    To arrest you, you will quite appreciate
    I cannot set you free. Wait for me here,
    Both of you. *[To FÉLIX]* I entrust your friend to you,
    And you shall be responsible for him.
    I'll spread the news abroad that he is here,

And set my spies to work; and by this means
I'll soon track down the lady.

[Exit]

CÉSAR: Do you understand
What can have happened?
FÉLIX: I should be quite proud
Of my sagacity if I understood.
CÉSAR: That I have gone into Aurelio's house
In pursuit of his daughter's true enough;
But that I am Don Félix, and that I have
Abducted Violante — that's beyond me.
FÉLIX: And it's beyond me why I'm treated well
Under Don César's name, while you're arrested
As me.
CÉSAR: What! Is it on my account
That you are treated so well?
FÉLIX: Yes. That is why
He was determined I should be his guest.
CÉSAR: And thinking I'm Don Félix, he'd arrest me.
FÉLIX: Come in, where we can talk more freely of it,
And try to puzzle out why I've been well treated
Under your name, while you have been arrested
Because you were under mine. It must derive
From *The Advantages and Disadvantages of a Name!*

[Exeunt]

Scene 3: An Inn Yard

[Enter VIOLANTE and NISE in traveling dress]

VIOLANTE: Where has Fabio gone?
NISE: I expect, madam, he has gone to all the inns
To inquire about Don César.
VIOLANTE: O my griefs!
So great in number that I cannot count them,
When will you cease to multiply? Who could
Foretell that in one day I'd leave my home,
And lose myself, my honor, my good name,
And nearly lose my life. Would to God
My heart had never passed from hate to love,
That I had never agreed to meet Don César,
And that my father had remained in ignorance,
Or else that, knowing all, he'd struck me dead!
Unhappy night in which
After his supposed departure, he awaited
Don César; in which Fabio, full of pity,
After the dreadful tumult, let me out,
And I left home to escape my father's anger,

And find Don César to beg his protection.
I wish that I had not been told that he
Had come to Milan for I cannot find him
And from this day the Star Hotel will be
An ill-starred dwelling, since I've come to live here.
NISE: For whom is your story? Don't I know your griefs?
VIOLANTE: It's for myself. And don't be astonished, Nise,
For only in itself does sorrow find
Some consolation.

[Enter TRISTÁN, carrying two valises]

TRISTÁN: Thank God, I've recovered my luggage.
And as for my master's he can thank me for it.
Let me see. How shall I best arrange to
Transport my belongings?
NISE: Look, madam, isn't that Don Félix's valet?
VIOLANTE: Yes it is he, and I begin to hope.
It's fortunate Don Félix should have come
Here to Milan, for he's Don César's friend,
And he will give me news. Call him...

                                        But no...
Stop!
NISE: Why hesitate?
VIOLANTE: I don't know.
I fear it will be useless. I'm afraid
Don Félix will not come; or if he comes
He will not greatly incommode himself
To be of service to me; for no man
Is keen to be of service to a woman
Who loves another...
TRISTÁN: This scene is like a farcical interlude.[26]
VIOLANTE: So it will be better
For him to learn that I am in the town
Only when he beholds me.
NISE: That is easy.
I'll follow his valet and return to tell you
His lodging, so that you can find him there.
VIOLANTE: Very well, Nise. But how can you follow him
Without arousing his suspicions.
NISE: Nothing
Is simpler than to cover up one's face
With a mantilla; and the Spaniards here
In the hotel will gladly lend me one.[27]
VIOLANTE: Come! Let us try to fight against my fate!
                              [Exeunt VIOLANTE and NISE]
TRISTÁN: These valises must go in one way or another, for,
without being Asturian or Galician, I'm a strong fellow
...How heavy is my master's valise! Not because it con-
tains more in it than mine, perhaps, but because even

the most loyal valet always finds that his master's
things weigh more than his own.

[Enter NISE, veiled]

NISE: *[Aside]* I'll dog his shadow all day.
TRISTÁN: I've noticed for some moments, my queen, that I
    drag behind me a third baggage in addition to the two
    I'm carrying.[28] What do you want? How can I help you?
    What do you think is in my two valises? *[Aside]* Is she
    the woman who gave us the jewel, and now having seen
    that we've got back our possessions, wants to take back
    her jewel.
NISE: Go on!
TRISTÁN: You can speak? You can't be the person I thought
    you.
NISE: *[Aside]* I'll continue to follow him.
TRISTÁN: Listen, princess. If, because I am a stranger, you
    imagine that my valises contain money, and that because
    of that you're on my trail, for goodness sake get that
    one out of your head. There are in my valises only
    clothes and linen; and all I could do for you is to give
    you one of my shirts — for you to wash. If you want
    anything else, you'll have to write to me. There's my
    house.
NISE: I'm glad to know it. Good-bye, my friend. *[Aside]*
    I must go and tell my mistress.
TRISTAN: *[Aside]* She only followed me to know where I
    lived, and perhaps to enjoy seeing a splendid chap like
    me carry so heavy a load.
        [He places the valises on the ground]   CURTAIN

                Scene 4: A Room in Lidoro's House

    [Enter DON FÉLIX and DON CÉSAR]

CÉSAR: Your story is amazing.
FÉLIX: All that's happened
    To me since yesterday.
CÉSAR: But up till now
    There's nothing to explain why you're suspected
    Of abducting Violante.
FÉLIX: Nor why she fled
    After her treachery to you?

    [Enter TRISTÁN]

    Tristán, where have you been?
TRISTÁN: I've just been having
    Loads of trouble... *[Knock]*

FÉLIX: Wasn't that a knock? See who it is.
TRISTÁN: Bad luck
    Will seize me if I open it.
FÉLIX: How so?
TRISTÁN: This door's supposed to bring relief but yet
    In letting in a hundred gifts for you,
    It will let in a hundred blows for me.
FÉLIX: Go on, Tristán; go and see! No nonsense!
TRISTÁN: One moment, Madam Mute!
CÉSAR: There are two ladies, veiled.

                                              [Exit]

FÉLIX: They're probably
    The ones I've spoken of.
CÉSAR: I'll go and wait
    In the next room, lest they should be embarrassed.

                                              [Exit]

FÉLIX: I'll shut the connecting door, for fear lest
        Serafina,
    Flora, or some other maid should learn
    That two veiled ladies have come in.

    [Enter SERAFINA and FLORA wearing veils]

SERAFINA: Although
    I did have news of you today by chance
    When I came by, I thought that I would like
    To see for myself how you were getting on,
    And so I've called.
FÉLIX: I thank you heartily,
    For your attentions.
SERAFINA: I owe you much, Don César,
    More than you think, more than I can repay.
FÉLIX: You owe me nothing, madam; for a man
    Must risk his life for a lady, and no thanks
    Are needed, since he does it for himself.
SERAFINA: I don't agree with you; for, while admitting
    You acted for yourself, it's I who've reaped
    The benefit, and ought not to consider
    The motives of your conduct, but my gains.
FÉLIX: Wit is compared to glass — now I see why.
    Your wit shines crystal clear; and you'll be quick
    To appreciate the danger you are in,
    For people may presume you're more discreet
    Than beautiful, unless you lift your veil.
SERAFINA: You are accusing me discreetly, sir,
    Of being ugly.
FÉLIX: I will beg forgiveness,
    If you will prove me wrong by your unveiling.
SERAFINA: It is not my way to enlarge a minor gaffe
    Into a point of honor.

FÉLIX: Permit me, madam,
   To repeat for myself the words you said
   When you came in. For not content with knowing
   About my welfare, you yet wished to see
   For yourself; and I, too, having heard you,
   Desire to see you too. Don't go away!
   Unveil, so I may see to whom I owe
   So high a favor. Only perfidy
   Is apt to hide her face.
SERAFINA: Sir, on the contrary,
   To do a service and remain concealed
   Adds to the benefit, for one does not ask
   For gratitude.
FÉLIX: I always will be grateful,
   But sorry too.
SERAFINA: How then have I offended?
FÉLIX: To send a man some valuable jewels,
   As you know well, is payment more than favor,
   And so I beg you let me give your maid...
SERAFINA: I'm still more pleased I did not show my face.
FÉLIX: Why?
SERAFINA: Because you do not see the blush that dyes
   My cheeks, to hear your words.
FÉLIX: I won't believe it,
   If I don't see it.
SERAFINA: I cannot offer proof.
   For though I am not uglier than most,
   I have good motives not to let you see me.
FÉLIX: What?
SERAFINA: You have seen the lady Serafina,
   Who's said to be a most accomplished beauty,
   And after her, I would be quite eclipsed.
FÉLIX: This is a most embarrassing position
   You've put me in.
SERAFINA: I do, sir? Why?
FÉLIX: Because if I admit she is as lovely
   As you suggest, it will not be polite
   To you, madam; and if I don't admit it,
   It would be very impolite to her.
SERAFINA: Well! Give your views on this another time.
TRISTÁN: *[To FLORA]* And you, my sweet, have you recovered
   the power of speech?
FLORA: Just a tiny bit.
TRISTÁN: We could make a happy mean out of you and a certain
   Flora who lives in this house...
FLORA: What do you mean?
TRISTÁN: As she speaks much too much and you don't speak
   enough, if the two of you were fastened together you
   would make a fine combination, a real bargain.

FLORA: Sir Tristán, women ought to guard their tongues for
 there isn't a worse vice than idle talk.
TRISTÁN: You're one to preach! You who came with your mistress to see us with all your tricks! It's like hearing
 a blind man singing the act of contrition and then offering the *Coplas de Calaínos* for sale at the top of his
 voice.[29]
FLORA: It's true that that is a little like the lady who
 said to a gentleman one day: "Bring me a sable to line
 this hair-shirt."
TRISTÁN: I'm coming to realize that you and Flora are two of
 a kind.
FLORA: And I to realize more and more that you and Tristán
 are two donkeys.
FÉLIX: It would appear that pressing supplications
 Have no effect on you.
SERAFINA: It seems to me
 You have no proper reason to complain,
 That I don't show my face.
FÉLIX: How so?
SERAFINA: Because
 You protected a veiled woman: now you see
 A veiled woman. I think this fair. Good-bye:
 You'll see us once again in a short while,
 Perhaps today.
FÉLIX: Wait! You shall not go.
 I have to choose now, either to let you go
 And show myself a fool, or lift your veil
 And show myself a cad. Well! of two evils
 I'll choose the least and... *[Knock]*
LIDORO: *[Without]*   Open the door.
FÉLIX: Who is it?
SERAFINA: *[Aside to FLORA]* It is my father's voice.
FLORA: And how!...
FÉLIX: See who it is,
 Tristán.
SERAFINA: Wait till I am gone. Is there not
 Another door?
FÉLIX: You cannot go that way.
 For it would insult Doña Serafina,
 And I don't want to be reproached for having
 Abused the laws of hospitality.
TRISTÁN: *[Returning]* It's a bad business, sir. It's Lord
   Lidoro
 Who's knocking.
SERAFINA: I beseech you, let me go
 This way.
FÉLIX: No! It doesn't matter to me if a lady
 Is found here, but...

SERAFINA: What is preventing you?
FÉLIX: I don't wish to be lacking in respect,
    As I have said, to Doña Serafina.
SERAFINA: She will be grateful if you let me go.
FÉLIX: Prove it...
SERAFINA: *[Lifting her veil]*   There, look! Do you still
        wish that I
    Should here be seen?
FÉLIX: Heavens! Who would have thought
        it?
    Leave, madam, leave; and in the meantime I
    Will open to your father, and detain him
    So that he does not catch a glimpse of you.
SERAFINA: Come, Flora.
FLORA: Quick! He's coming.

    *[As they are going out, enter VIOLANTE and NISE also
    veiled]*

VIOLANTE: Will you please tell me if this is the apartment
    Of Don Félix?
SERAFINA: How should I know?
                        [Exeunt SERAFINA and FLORA]
VIOLANTE: That lady
    Seems to be upset.
NISE: There are people here
    Who can inform us.

    [Enter LIDORO]

FÉLIX: Why, sir, is it you
    Who are making all that noise at your own door?
LIDORO: Yes, for I'm treated like a stranger here;
    Not only was the door not opened for me,
    But also I've a serious complaint
    Against the man I've treated with such kindness.
FÉLIX: How have I disobliged you?
LIDORO: In many ways.
FÉLIX: *[Aside]* Alas! He knows everything: and Serafina
    Has not yet had the strength to flee, or else
    Has not been able to open the door.

    [Enter DON CÉSAR]

CÉSAR: What is this noise, sir?
VIOLANTE: Nise, there's Don César!
NISE: Go and speak with him.
VIOLANTE: I dare not do so
    Before these witnesses. Hush! Let us listen.
LIDORO: Have I not every reason to complain
    When you both treat me with so little frankness?
    I begged you see in me a gentleman,

Rather than magistrate, and to inform me
Of where the lady was, to let me settle
Your little affair as amicably as I could.
You've obstinately denied that she was here,
And rather let her learn by seeking you
Throughout the city that her lover was
A prisoner in my house.
VIOLANTE: *[Aside]*   A prisoner!
FÉLIX: *[Aside]* None of this would have mattered, if Sera-
    fina
Had managed to escape.
LIDORO: One of my spies informed me she was told
Of where Don Félix was. So I have set
A guard outside, and she will not escape me.
But isn't it her I see?
FÉLIX: My lord, this lady
Is not the one you think. She entered here
By chance.
LIDORO: You won't make me believe that ladies
Run after men as soon as they arrive,
And come by chance for them to my house too.
Come, madam, you are recognized. Unveil!
CÉSAR: *[Aside to FÉLIX]* He thinks it's Violante.
FÉLIX: *[Aside to CÉSAR]*   Softly, César,
The problem's bigger than you realize.
VIOLANTE: *[Aside]* What do I hear?
LIDORO: Are you not Violante,
Daughter of Lord Aurelio? Have you not come
To seek here for Don Félix?
VIOLANTE: *[Aside]*   What can this mean?
Who can have told him about me?
        [Unveiling]   Yes, sir.
    I'm Doña Violante.
FÉLIX: What do I see?
CÉSAR: Heavens! What's this?
VIOLANTE: Yes, sir. I came to seek
Don Félix in this house, where I discover
Don César, and where I hope for a protection
I beg for at your feet.
FÉLIX: *[Aside]*   What's this? What causes
This sudden change?
CÉSAR: What's this? How has she come here?
LIDORO: Well, will you now admit you have deceived me?
CÉSAR: I've not deceived you since I am amazed
To see her here. *[To VIOLANTE]* Ungrateful and perfidi-
    ous,
The cruel enemy of my life's blood,
How did you come here?
VIOLANTE: Why do you speak like that,

When for your sake I've been exposed to troubles,
   Fatigues, and perils?
LIDORO: You see, it's really her.
CÉSAR: Is it not enough, treacherous and beautiful,
   That you betrayed me there that you should try
   Once more to betray me here?
VIOLANTE: I have betrayed you?
CÉSAR: You know you have.
VIOLANTE: This, then, is my reward?
CÉSAR: What else do I owe you?
LIDORO: It is not the time
   To engage in explanations. Follow me,
   Madam, and though I owe it neither to Don Félix,
   Nor to Don César, I am who I am,
   And I will act in your best interests.
   [To CÉSAR] Wait for me.
VIOLANTE: I'll follow you, sir.
LIDORO: *[Aside]*   As soon
   As I have taken this lady to Serafina,
   I must lock you up.
              [Exeunt LIDORO, VIOLANTE and NISE]
CÉSAR: Violante here!
FÉLIX: Serafina in my lodging!
CÉSAR: She came to seek
   For Félix!
FÉLIX: And she braved all dangers for me!
CÉSAR: What does it mean, Félix?
FÉLIX: I do not know.
CÉSAR: Time will unveil the mystery for us.
FÉLIX: No doubt; and how I wish I could abridge
   And expedite the time!

                            CURTAIN

ꙘꙘꙘ

ACT THREE

Scene 1: Serafina's Room in Lidoro's House

[Enter LIDORO and SERAFINA]

LIDORO: You are very angry.
SERAFINA: Have I not good reason?
LIDORO: True; but why take things so much to heart?
SERAFINA: What! When you, my father, without consulting me
   Bring without warning a guest into my house,
   Quarter a woman, an adventuress, on me,
   And do not turn a hair...

LIDORO: Wait, Serafina;
    I'm going to satisfy you on those matters,
    Lest you should think you've cause for your complaints.
    This gentleman, I have already told you,
    Is the son of my best friend, to whom I owe
    No less than life itself. I thought he'd stay
    But for a day and it is not my fault
    That, when the Prince insisted, he agreed
    To see the carnival. As for the lady,
    Before I offered her protection, I
    Considered that she was of noble birth;
    And though love's accidents can sometimes stain
    The purest blood, a gentleman would be wrong
    To refuse his aid to any who implore it,
    Apart from that, the gentleman who comes
    To Milan with this lady is a friend,
    A close friend of Don César's; I was ordered
    To arrest the fugitives; by keeping them
    In my own house, I'm able to fulfill
    Both duties, — as chief magistrate and friend.
    And then if I must tell you everything,
    I've other motives for my wish to treat
    Don César well. He's of the highest birth,
    Possesses a large fortune, is greatly favored
    By the Duke of Parma, and he's won my affection
    As well as my respect. I've said enough
    For you to understand me. It could happen,
    Daughter, that one day the guest of the house
    Became its master.

                                                   [Exit]

SERAFINA: O, what do I hear!
    Rejoice, for now perhaps for the first time
    Evil is changed to good. I was afraid
    That he suspected me, and he himself
    Encourages my love. *[Calling]* Flora!

    [Enter VIOLANTE]

VIOLANTE: What is your will?
SERAFINA: I was calling one of my maids.
VIOLANTE: Am I not here
    To serve you?
SERAFINA: God protect you, Violante,
    But I won't allow you to demean yourself.
    You're here at home, and though I disagreed
    With my father when he took you in the house,
    I now rejoice at it; and touched to the heart
    By your misfortunes, I regard you now
    As a friend to whom I am indebted greatly.
VIOLANTE: How so? I only bring a bad example.

SERAFINA: Not as bad as you say! You don't suspect
   How very convenient was your coming here.
VIOLANTE: But how can I be useful?
SERAFINA: You have been,
   Already.
VIOLANTE: Well, madam, since you are so grateful
   For some unwitting service I have rendered,
   May I, in my turn, ask of you a service?
SERAFINA: If I can help you, I am at your service.
   What do you want?
VIOLANTE: The fault I have committed
   I will not seek to justify to you.
   After I'd treated with the greatest scorn
   A gentleman who loved me a long while,
   At last I fell in love with him, although
   He'd killed my kinsman in a duel. This man
   Your father keeps a prisoner in his house
   As well as me. Alas! the love I bear him
   Has been my ruin! It seems the heavens have made
   An example of me, to show that a change of heart
   From hate to love is difficult and painful.
   Forgive me for recounting
   My melancholy story: it's because
   I want to touch your heart, perhaps awaken
   Your generosity. I wrote to him to come
   One night to our garden to converse with me
   He wrote that he would come, though he was meant
   To leave, by the Duke's orders, for Milan.
   My father saw the letter...
SERAFINA: One moment... He was sent here by the Duke?
VIOLANTE: Yes, madam. Is there anything in that
   To annoy you?
SERAFINA: Not at all. I was absentminded
   And had not understood. Continue please.
VIOLANTE: My father saw the letter; and although
   He had no wish to show his anger to me,
   Yet soon he was transported by his fury
   And locked me in my room.
SERAFINA: Is this the gentleman
   The one who comes to Milan for the Duke?
VIOLANTE: Yes, madam. I perceive you're not attending
   To what I'm saying.
SERAFINA: It's simply that I'm sad,
   Preoccupied with...but do not worry.
VIOLANTE: I'll stop now if my story vexes you.
SERAFINA: No, please go on.
VIOLANTE: I fear me...
SERAFINA: What do you fear?
VIOLANTE: That as you take no interest in my sorrows

You won't do much to bring them to an end.
SERAFINA: You are mistaken. All my interruptions
    Are but to make things clear. So pray continue.
VIOLANTE: The fatal night arrived: I could not warn him
    That with a troop of men my father waited
    For his arrival.
SERAFINA: For whom? The one who was
    To come to Milan?
VIOLANTE: Yes, that was the tragedy.
SERAFINA: *[Aside]* She will have to name him now, though bad
      things come
    Quite unsolicited, this is an exception.
VIOLANTE: So he arrived...
SERAFINA: Who?
VIOLANTE: Don César, who they thought was absent.
SERAFINA: Don César?
VIOLANTE: Yes.
SERAFINA: *[Aside]* I wish she hadn't named him. Now I wish
    I had not so insisted. *[Aloud]* And then?
VIOLANTE: I don't exactly know what passed between them;
    I only know that when I heard a shot
    And the clash of swords, my soul was torn between
    My father and my lover. Then an old servant,
    Believing it was best, broke down my door;
    And then...
SERAFINA: Excuse me there is still one point
    I do not understand. If it was Don César,
    Why did you come here looking for Don Félix?
VIOLANTE: Because he is a friend and I presumed
    He would accompany Don César.
SERAFINA: I see.
    Continue.
VIOLANTE: Seeing myself placed suddenly
    In such a dreadful fix, I was beset
    By contradictory emotions; but listening
    Only to Fear, that wretched counselor,
    I took a fatal course. Instead of seeking
    Asylum from my kinsmen or my friends,
    I went to my friend's house, in the belief
    That no one else would succor me so well
    And sympathize more keenly. But alas!
    I did not find him.
SERAFINA: Pray excuse me,
    Why did you ask at my father's house for Félix
    Rather than César.
VIOLANTE: Because it was his servant
    I saw at the inn.
SERAFINA: Continue.
VIOLANTE: Then they informed me at Don César's house

He had just left for Milan. Desperate,
And terrified, and knowing I was guilty
Of indiscretion, I saw no way out
Except by further faults. I got his servant
To get a carriage for me, and...
SERAFINA: Why was it said,
When orders were sent out for your arrest,
That you were accompanied not by Don César,
But by Don Félix.
VIOLANTE: Who says so?
SERAFINA: I do.
And the proof is my father's prisoner
Is not Don César, but Don Félix.
VIOLANTE: [Greatly puzzled]   Madam,
I see you are preoccupied with your griefs,
And so, to cut a tedious story short,
Whatever happens, I throw myself at your feet,
Hoping for your protection, not alone
For my misfortunes, madam, but because
You are the one you are; and I implore you
To intercede for me, and ask your father
To deign to speak with mine, who without doubt
Will hasten to come here. So please arrange
Matters in such a way that when he comes,
He'll find me safely married to Don César.
Now, madam, I'll retire, to enable me
Freely to weep, and not to grieve you more
By the recital of my griefs.[30]

                                           [Exit]

SERAFINA: Indeed,
Her griefs are great, but no more great than mine.
And with the endless muddle of the names
Of Don César and Don Félix, I don't know
If she or I has most cause to lament.
My father told me that the guest of the house
Might well become its master and my husband
So I rejoiced, but suddenly this happiness
Vanished, and my joy was changed to sorrow.
But let me think. How can this Violante,
Since Félix is her lover and she sought him,
Pretend the man she loves is Don César?
And if it were Don César, why not say so
When she perceived them looking for Don Félix?
Which is the truth? In this uncertainty
What would I not give not to have been snared
By gratitude? But no one could avoid
This kind of fate, and after it has happened,
It's useless to complain. And should I not
Be grateful to this man for what he did

So nobly, without coming in disguise
To speak with him? But every handsome woman
Wants to be certain that she is not loved
Just for her beauty, like a piece of sculpture.
If I disguised myself, it could be said
The customs of our country are to blame,
For they allow for honor's sake the use
Of veils and masks. But no! Away with such excuses!
My vanity was the cause — or gratitude.
Ingratitude's a crime that's capital,
But it's my gratitude has struck me down.
What would I give
Not to have raised my veil? I'd have dissembled,
And hidden underneath deceitful ice
The Aetna of my soul. But now I've been
Revealed to him, I will not run away —
That would be cowardice; and it is good
For men to realize we women have
Our courage and our point of honor too.
[Calling] Flora!

[Enter FLORA]

FLORA: What do you want, madam?
SERAFINA: Kindly go
   To Don César's apartment; and tell him,
   As though from you, that I am in the garden.
   [Aside] Uncertainties, fears, perils, griefs,
   I do defy you, and I wait for you!
   If you do not accept the combat, I
   Will say you are afraid; and if you learn
   That I'm enraged by jealousy, no doubt
   You won't appear, for everyone would dread
   A jealous woman![31]

                                              [Exit]
FLORA: What does all that mean?
   But after all it is not my affair.
   Were I to worry about it, I'd be old
   Before my time.

                                              [Exit]

                    Scene 2: Felix's Apartment

   [Enter FLORA and TRISTÁN]

FLORA: Tristán!
TRISTÁN: O Flora! beauteous flower of Italy and Spanish
   floribunda, why do you want me?
FLORA: Is your master at home?

TRISTÁN: No, he isn't.

FLORA: In that case, good-bye.

TRISTÁN: Wait a minute; you're not going until we've reached
    an agreement.

FLORA: What about?

TRISTÁN: About how much you'll charge to lose your head over
    me for half an hour; for my part I'm dying for half an
    hour's lovemaking with you, and indeed that would prob-
    ably be the sudden death of me.

FLORA: What a novel idea!

TRISTÁN: It isn't new.

FLORA: Is it not?

TRISTÁN: Once upon a time a miser was dying...

FLORA: I can guess. It's the story of the man who called
    the sacristan and asked: "How much will you charge for
    burying me?" To which he replied, no doubt, "Twenty
    Reals." "Will you take sixteen?" said the man. "I
    need more than that," replied the sacristan. "Well,"
    said the sick man, "see if you can manage to bury me for
    seventeen; or else, I warn you, if it costs me a farth-
    ing more, I'm not going to die." In the same way you
    want to know what it will cost you to die making love to
    me. Well! since that was your tale, now hear mine. One
    day a monkey and her friends...

TRISTÁN: One moment, wench! To rob me of one story and in-
    flict another on me is too much. A duenna was bringing
    up a little dwarf...

FLORA: I began first.

TRISTÁN: But I'll continue with mine.

BOTH: One day

TRISTÁN: ⎫ The duenna...
FLORA: ⎬ The monkey...

[Enter FÉLIX]

FÉLIX: What's all this noise?

TRISTÁN: It's a long story. The devil take you for a
    duenna!

FLORA: And you for a monkey. [32]

TRISTÁN: I'm never allowed to finish my tale.

FLORA: Nor am I.

FÉLIX: What are you doing here, Flora? What is it?

FLORA: I wanted to tell you that my mistress is walking in
    the garden alone. I've come in secret, because she does
    not trust everyone, especially since this lady has come
    to the house. According to what happens I'll warn you
    with a song whether to approach or retreat. *[To TRIS-
    TÁN]* Good-bye. Think of me; and don't forget that it's
    my turn next to tell you a story.

TRISTÁN: I have two turns owing to me.

FÉLIX: How can I ever thank you, Flora, for this kindness?
                                        [Exit FLORA]
TRISTÁN: Have you yet told me, sir, who was the veiled phan-
    tom who was suddenly transformed into Doña Violante?
FÉLIX: Ass! You've not recognized her?
TRISTÁN: No.
FÉLIX: Well! What does it matter to you? But silence!
    Listen! *[Music off]*
FLORA: *[Singing off]*
    "The bee is flitting midst the flowers;
    Come, love, come now and meet her."
FÉLIX: She's summoning me. Wait here, Tristán.

    [Enter CÉSAR]

CÉSAR: Where
    Are you going, Félix, without telling me
    What has been happening?
FÉLIX: I'll tell you soon.
    We've settled with the Prince about your business.
    He has agreed that you, although a prisoner,
    Should stay here in this house. But, for the moment,
    I want to profit by a lucky chance
    To see the woman I love — for Serafina
    Is now in the garden alone, and this voice tells me
    To go and join her.
CÉSAR: Wait! Don't go!
FÉLIX: Why stop me?
CÉSAR: I have my reasons.
FÉLIX: Let me go.
CÉSAR: You'd better not.
FÉLIX: What's to stop me?
FLORA: *[Singing off]*
    "Stay your flight; for if you float
        Above a waterfall,
    You'll fall, fall..."
FÉLIX: She's warning me to wait. Speak, then, but hurry
    For if she calls again, I'll have to leave you...
CÉSAR: No! *[To TRISTÁN]* Be off!
TRISTÁN: They're hiding things from me. Well! I will hide.
        [He hides behind the arras]
CÉSAR: Please listen. You will easily believe me,
    When I assure you, Félix, that my friendship
    Desires your happiness.
FÉLIX: I do not doubt it.
CÉSAR: And are you not my friend?
FÉLIX: Assuredly.
CÉSAR: Well, I must ask a favor.
FÉLIX: I'm quite prepared.
    Of what does it consist?

CÉSAR: Do not abuse
    My friendship for you. Thanks to my name alone
    You're honored, feted, coddled by Lidoro;
    So I am shocked that you misuse my name
    And are insensitive to the great honors
    Accorded you. All that Lidoro does
    On your behalf is really for my sake,
    And not for yours. That being so, I feel
    It rests with me to ensure that what you do
    Does not affect his honor. When we leave —
    After you've been so fortunate, and I
    Unfortunate — it's only fair that we
    Should leave behind no stain on my good name.
FLORA: *[Singing off]*
    "The bee is flitting midst the flowers;
    Come, love, come now and join her."
FÉLIX: I'll give you an answer later.
CÉSAR: Why not now?
FÉLIX: Think, at this very moment...
FLORA: *[Singing]* "Come, love, come now and join her."
FÉLIX: The chance is slipping away.
CÉSAR: You would oblige me
    Greatly.
SERAFINA'S VOICE: *[Outside]* Stop singing now.
FÉLIX: You're very cruel.
CÉSAR: No, no, you shall not go.
FÉLIX: You're making me lose
    The finest opportunity...
CÉSAR: Wait! Someone
    Has thrown a paper through the window.
FÉLIX: Doubtless
    To reproach me for delaying.
CÉSAR: It's addressed
    To César.
FÉLIX: Show it me, since I am César
    So long as we are here. I'll read it to you,
    To prove... But this is not a woman's hand.
CÉSAR: From whom can it be?
FÉLIX: It's signed Lisardo.
CÉSAR: Lisardo!
    What on earth is this?
FÉLIX: *[Reading]* "Although I could have avenged with cer-
    tainty the death of my brother, Laurencio..." It's a
    mystery.
CÉSAR: This note might be addressed to me. Before
    You read it, we should settle first between us
    Whether you're the right Don César, sir.
FÉLIX: Don't strain yourself to crack a feeble joke.
    I am Don César here: the note is mine.

CÉSAR: We changed names for a plan which came to nothing.
  But when it's a question which involves one's honor
  We must resume our rightful names.
FÉLIX: Your honor,
  Will run no risk with me, your closest friend.
CÉSAR: I do not doubt it. But I can't have peace
  Till I have seen this note.
FÉLIX: I cannot show it.
CÉSAR: But it is clear Lisardo is demanding
  Satisfaction — and therefore I must know
  Where he is to be found.
FÉLIX: The note's addressed
  To me, and it's for me to meet with him.
CÉSAR: No! for it deals with matters which concern me,
  Not you at all, to whom I lent my name.
FÉLIX: Here I am César, and it was for me
  The letter was intended. A mistake
  May easily be made about the name,
  But not about the person.
CÉSAR: Was it not I
  Who killed Laurencio?
FÉLIX: Yes.
CÉSAR: Were you his foe?
FÉLIX: No.
CÉSAR: Then even though the note was sent to you,
  It was meant for me.
FÉLIX: Are you Don César here?
CÉSAR: No.
FÉLIX: Am I not?
CÉSAR: Yes.
FÉLIX: Then the letter is for me,
  Because the man who wants to meet with me
  Doesn't know you.
CÉSAR: Although you have assumed
  My name, it's strange that you should wish that I
  Should not be César too.
FÉLIX: It would be stranger,
  If, after having been an honored guest,
  Experiencing the kindness of an angel,
  And then, having profited from this good fortune,
  I should give up being César from the moment
  Troubles begin. No, it shall not be said
  That I'm Don César as long as things go well,
  And cease to be him as soon as things go wrong.
  And since I'm not a man to yield to fortune,
  Let me accept the disadvantages
  As well as the advantages of a name.
CÉSAR: Say what you like, but let me read the letter.
FÉLIX: It doesn't concern you.

CÉSAR: Don't be obstinate.
     I tell you, I must see it.
FÉLIX: What if I keep it?
CÉSAR: At least I'll...
FÉLIX: What?
CÉSAR: Stop you from reading it.
FÉLIX: How?
CÉSAR: I shall not let you out of my sight.
     I'll follow you like your shadow.
FÉLIX: How will you do it
     Since you're a prisoner?
CÉSAR: I'll take my freedom,
     And tell them who I am.
FÉLIX: And court dishonor.
     You will not extricate yourself, and we
     Shall both get into trouble.
CÉSAR: Well, let me see
     The note, and then we both can judge what both
     Should do.
FÉLIX: I'll tell you later of the contents.
     Good-bye.
CÉSAR: Let's go. I'm following you.
FÉLIX: You can't
     Go out.
CÉSAR: I'm going.
FÉLIX: But think...
CÉSAR: Think yourself.

     [Enter LIDORO]

LIDORO: What's the matter?
FÉLIX: Nothing, my lord. *[Aside]* I'll
          take
     This opportunity.
LIDORO: What is it?
FÉLIX: He will tell you.
                                           [Exit]

CÉSAR: Yes, I will, but while he's here; because
     I would not have you doubt me. Stop him.
LIDORO: Why?
     I shall believe you.
CÉSAR: *[Aside]*   Cruel situation!
     [Aloud] Let me go after him.
LIDORO: Kindly recall
     That you're my prisoner and that it's enough
     The Prince has generously permitted it,
     Without...
CÉSAR: *[Aside]* Alas!
LIDORO: Why do you wish to go?
CÉSAR: *[Aside]* What shall I say? If I reveal he's going

  To fight a duel, that would not be right.
  But it would be still worse were I to let him
  Go in my place. I ought somehow to stop him
  Just for today from fighting, and tomorrow
  I hope...
LIDORO: You seem upset.
CÉSAR: You will not call him?
LIDORO: No.
CÉSAR: Nor yet allow me out to follow him?
LIDORO: No.
CÉSAR: Then, I must speak, follow him yourself,
  For he's received a challenge.
LIDORO: Don César? Why?
CÉSAR: I do not know.
LIDORO: And where is the duel to be?
CÉSAR: I do not know that either.
LIDORO: Wait for me here.
  I'm going after him, but I must set
  A guard upon you first.

                [Exit]

CÉSAR: What will the experts in the laws of honor
  Think of me now? They will enjoy debating
  The rights and wrongs of it, and yet the matter
  Is clear enough. The duel was my affair,
  And by this means, I may be able still
  To fight for myself. For soon this masquerade
  Will be exposed, since Violante...

  [Enter VIOLANTE]

VIOLANTE: I come, Don César, in a lucky moment,
  While Serafina is walking in the garden;
  Hearing you speak my name; and I rejoice,
  Whatever your feelings, that you think of me.
CÉSAR: I have no need to tell you of my feelings;
  They are appropriate ones toward a woman
  Whose conduct has been so perfidious.
VIOLANTE: But how can you complain of me, Don César,
  When for your sake I have abandoned home,
  When full of fear I see myself a prisoner
  In another's house.
CÉSAR: Your treason having failed,
  You'd now persuade me that you weren't involved
  In that cowardly attempt upon my life.
VIOLANTE: But is it rational to think, that I,
  In order to pretend that I was blameless,
  Would leave my country and my father, and
  Expose myself to every kind of censure?
CÉSAR: How did it happen that Aurelio
  Awaited me in the garden? Why did he make

An attempt upon my life?   And who but you
Could have informed him?
VIOLANTE: My father seized the letter
Brought by the servant of Don Félix.
CÉSAR: Don Félix's?
VIOLANTE: Yes.
CÉSAR: One moment.   This gives me much to think of.
If it's not caused by an effect of passion
That subjugates me still.   Your father saw
The letter which Don Félix's valet was
Instructed to deliver?
VIOLANTE: Yes, and by this letter,
He was informed of everything; and so
He locked me up, pretending to depart.
CÉSAR: Doubtless from this has sprung the notion that
Don Félix caused the tumult at your house;
For you must know that I'm a prisoner here
Under the name of Félix.
VIOLANTE: What!   You are posing
As Don Félix?
CÉSAR: Yes so that I could stay
At Parma on that fatal night, I made him
Leave under my name for Milan.
VIOLANTE: And so
You are not known here under your true name?
CÉSAR: Precisely.
VIOLANTE: So that's why Doña Serafina,
Asserted stubbornly that the gentleman
Who was a prisoner here on my account
Was not Don César!   So we were both deluded
For just as you believed that...

[Enter NISE]

NISE: I have searched
All through the house for you.   Doña Serafina
Is asking for you.
VIOLANTE: Come!   She'll be annoyed
If she suspects that I've been here.   Think, sir,
Of all that I have said.
CÉSAR: Without your news
I'd have believed you.
VIOLANTE: Why?
CÉSAR: Because I wanted
That you should not be guilty.
VIOLANTE: Guilty of what?
CÉSAR: Ingratitude.
VIOLANTE: Ingratitude?   Toward whom?
CÉSAR: Toward the man who adores you.
VIOLANTE: In that case

What better reassurance than to see me
In my present state?

CÉSAR: There's still a better way
To reassure me.

VIOLANTE: What is that?

CÉSAR: To show me
Your favor once again, since it is clear
Our passion burns now brightly.

VOICE: Flora! Violante!

NISE: There's someone calling you.

VIOLANTE: Adieu!

CÉSAR: Adieu!

[Exeunt]

Scene 3: A Street in Milan

[Enter LISARDO]

LISARDO: It's some time since I threw my letter in
Don César's window; and he was at home,
If I am not mistaken. We shall see
If Doña Serafina will be avenged,
Or if I will avenge myself on both —
On him and her. I'm waiting for him here,
And when he comes, I'll follow him, for though
I trust him for his noble birth and courage
To act correctly and to come alone,
It does no harm to check.

[Enter FÉLIX and TRISTÁN]

FÉLIX: Go back!
I swear if you persist in following me,
Or if you speak, I'll kill you.

TRISTÁN: As you know,
I am a model of obedience,
Especially in cases of this kind.

FÉLIX: Be off, then; and look sharp!

TRISTÁN: *[Aside]* This is the point where I should invoke my
honor. What ought I to do, when I know very well that
he's going to fight in another's place — as if one could
now fight in the same way as one marries, by proxy. The
first thing I have to do is not to be present; the second is to tell what's happening to someone who can stop
it; and this will be the first time I've ever done my
duty.

[Exit]

LISARDO: *[Aside]* Now he's alone. I was wrong to doubt his
courage.

FÉLIX: To check the place where he's awaiting me,
    Let me reread the letter. "Although I could have
    avenged with certainty the death of my brother
    Laurencio..."

[Enter LIBIO and AURELIO]

LIBIO: Excuse me, sir. There is a gentleman
    Wishes to speak with you. I've come to find you.
LISARDO: What a nuisance!
LIBIO: *[To AURELIO]* Approach, my lord, this is Don Celio.
                                           [Exit]

AURELIO: Embrace me...
LISARDO: Though I do not have the honor
    Of knowing you, I eagerly respond
    To such politeness. *[Aside]* He must not get away.
AURELIO: You owe me as much.
FÉLIX: *[Reading]* "I wish to behave as generously as possi-
    ble; and, in order to see whether you are as lucky with
    me as you were with him..."
LISARDO: Inform me of all my obligations, sir,
    So that I can fulfill them.
AURELIO: I will tell you
    In a single word my name and why I've come.
LISARDO: That will please me, for I'm very busy.
FÉLIX: "I will await you behind the castle.
    Farewell."
AURELIO: Embrace me as Lisardo, not as Celio,
    For I know who you are.
LISARDO: That is enough.
    You can be only Lord Aurelio.
FÉLIX: *[Aside]* Behind the castle, he says. Which is the
        way?
AURELIO: Yes, and the shames that I have suffered make me
    Address myself to you for both our honors.
LISARDO: I am grateful you have done so.
    [Aside] No doubt he knows Don César is in Milan,
    And comes to warn me of it.
AURELIO: You know, my friend,
    That...
FÉLIX: Gentlemen, will you kindly let me know
    The way to the castle?
AURELIO: What do I see? *[Draws]* I'll
        rather
    Show you the road to death.
LISARDO: I wasn't wrong.
FÉLIX: This duel will prevent me from attending
    The other one.
LISARDO: *[Aside]* I can't allow it to be said
    That a man I challenged was then set upon

By me and another man. I must prevent it.
[Aloud] Stop, Lord Aurelio!
AURELIO: What! You take his side?
LISARDO: It's my affair. I must.
AURELIO: When I am fighting
   To defend my honor, which is also yours,
   You take his part?
LISARDO: Yes.
FÉLIX: I must thank you,
   Although I'm not in danger. Lord Aurelio,
   Reflect, I pray you, that you have received
   No injury from me.
AURELIO: Then are you not
   The traitor, Félix?
LISARDO: *[Aside]*   Félix! What do I hear?
AURELIO: And therefore I shall know...

   [Enter LIDORO and others]

LIDORO: I've come in time.
   Don César, I am at your side. Now tell me,
   What is it all about?
AURELIO: It is the vengeance
   Of an insulted nobleman. But since
   You also are against it, I'll await
   Another chance, when there'll be fewer seconds
   To interfere.

                                           [Exit]

LISARDO: *[Aside]* What shall I do?
   I want to follow him, but yet I cannot
   Lose sight of César — for although Aurelio
   Called him "Don Félix," I have challenged him
   And I must keep the rendezvous.
LIDORO: What is all this?
FÉLIX: I do not know.
LIDORO: Who was this gentleman?
FÉLIX: The father of the lady Violante.
LIDORO: What! Lord Aurelio? What's he to do with you?
FÉLIX: It's probably because I am the friend
   Of Don Félix.
LIDORO: Lord Celio, while I go
   To pacify Aurelio — since I'm lucky
   To have found you here — don't leave Don César.
                              [Exeunt LIDORO and others]
LISARDO: No sir.
   I will not leave him: it serves my interest
   To follow him.
FÉLIX: Excuse me, please, for I
   Must go alone.
LISARDO: That is not possible.

FÉLIX: Why not?
LISARDO: Because, Don César or Don Félix —
    For you've been called both names — I cannot let you,
    When I've been told to guard you.
FÉLIX: I know what I
    Already owe you for your noble conduct
    A moment ago; but —

    [Enter LIDORO]

LIDORO: I could not catch him up;
    But since he is the father of Violante
    Who's in my house...
LISARDO: *[Aside]*   What! Violante there!
LIDORO: We must arrange that he shall find her married
    With Don Félix, and all will then end well.
    Come now, Don César, let us settle that.
FÉLIX: Excuse me. I will follow you.
LIDORO: I can't leave you.
LISARDO: *[Aside]* My problems grow apace.
LIDORO: Come, Lord Celio,
    Adieu!
LISARDO: God be with you.
FÉLIX: Since there's no alternative,
    I must confess my secret. *[Whispers to LISARDO]* Lord
        Celio,
    After the kindnesses that you have shown me,
    I'm bold enough to ask another service —
    One that concerns my honor.
LISARDO: What can I do?
FÉLIX: A man awaits me now to fight a duel.
    Though I don't know him, I don't wish to fail him.
    He's named Lisardo; and the rendezvous
    Behind the castle. Will you kindly go
    And tell him of the fix in which I'm placed,
    As you can witness; beg him to excuse me;
    Tell him that we shall see each other later.
    Can I rely on you?
LISARDO: By all means, sir.
    You can be sure he will receive your message
    As if you'd spoken to him face to face.
FÉLIX: God preserve you!
LIDORO: Well, are you coming?
FÉLIX: Yes.
    [Aside] Thus, though my honor is not satisfied,
    At least it's in less danger.
                        [Exeunt LIDORO and FÉLIX]

LISARDO: What has been happening? How can I sum up
    These doubts and mysteries? I send a challenge
    To Don César; he comes to answer it;

Aurelio comes to find him, calling him
Don Félix! I believed that he had come
On my account, but yet it was to avenge
An insult to himself! Then Lord Lidoro
Says he has Violante at his house!
How if this gentleman is named Don César,
Did not Aurelio know it? And if Don Félix,
Why did Lidoro say he would discuss
With him the marriage of Don Félix? Time
Alone will make all clear. I'll join Aurelio;
For from henceforth I should be at his side
Until we are avenged upon this man,
Whatever his name — Don César or Don Félix.
Till then, great Heaven, grant me resolution
And wisdom.

                                              [Exit]

Scene 4: A Room in Lidoro's House

[Enter SERAFINA and FLORA, masked]

SERAFINA: What have you said to Doña Violante?
FLORA: That several of your friends have persuaded you to
    disguise yourself; and that you are going with them to
    a great feast.
SERAFINA: Come quickly then.
FLORA: Are you quite determined?
SERAFINA:
                                                      Yes.
    Since I learned from Doña Violante,
    Don César is the sole cause of her griefs,
    And as he did not take the opportunity
    I offered him, to speak with me, although
    You gave the signal twice, I must believe
    That it was not his aim to make her jealous.
    But this which she's been spared has seized on me;
    And that is why, since he refused to come
    And find me in the garden, I intend
    To go masked to his own apartment.
    There I will tell him all I think and feel,
    And when I've eased my heart I will avenge it
    By the disdain he well deserves. Come, Flora.
FLORA: And yet it's not the thing...
SERAFINA: Be silent, Flora.
    You're right, of course, but is there any reason
    That can outweigh the fury of a woman
    Who's been insulted. Neither thunderbolts
    Nor fiery Aetnas — But such comparisons
    Are pointless. Let us go.

                                              [Exeunt]

Scene 5: Another Room in the Same House

[Enter VIOLANTE and NISE]

NISE: Well, madam, what do you propose to do?
VIOLANTE: Ah! Nise, since Doña Serafina's gone
   This evening to the carnival, if I
   Might speak with Don César, and properly
   Convince him of my faith! And how I wish
   That Fabio would arrive here to support
   The truth of what I've told him! and how happy
   I'd be, if I persuaded him to marry
   Before my father came!
NISE: I can but advise you.
   If you should go to his apartment now
   You might be found there; someone might come.
VIOLANTE: There's one way of avoiding any risk.
NISE: What's that?
VIOLANTE: To disguise ourselves, as everyone
   Does in the carnival.
NISE: There's a servant here
   With whom I'm friendly who will give us all
   We need for that.
VIOLANTE: In that case, kindly warn her,
   And tell her if by chance an old man comes
   To ask for me, she should reply... But no,
   That can be settled later, for I see
   That Lord Lidoro and Don Félix now
   Are coming in, and I would not be seen!
   Stay here and keep them off my track *[Aside]* O For-
     tune,
   To thee I commend myself. Thou owest me
   Some compensation for thy cruel injustice!
                           [Exit]

[Enter LIDORO and FÉLIX]

LIDORO: What's Doña Serafina doing now?
NISE: She has gone out, I think, with two of her friends.
LIDORO: Leave us.
                         [Exit NISE]
         Now we need delay no longer
   To speak of Don Félix.
FÉLIX: I do not doubt
   That once he is assured that Violante
   Knew nothing of the ambush, he'll be eager
   To marry her; the first thing to be done,
   Therefore, is for Doña Violante
   To have it out with him.
LIDORO: Since in these cases,
   One's more at ease with a friend, than with a man

Of my age, kindly arrange for them to meet,
And come to an agreement. It's convenient
That Serafina's out.
FÉLIX: I'll gladly do this.
LIDORO: I'll leave you for a while.

[Exit]

FÉLIX: The business
Is going too swiftly. I'll have no difficulty
With regard to the Prince, nor yet with Lord Lidoro
About the exchange of names; but Serafina,
Seeing that I'm not César...

[Enter CÉSAR and TRISTÁN]

TRISTÁN: How pleased I am, sir, to see you safe and sound.
FÉLIX: Don't be silly!
CÉSAR: I am glad to find you
At Lord Lidoro's, as I assume from that
You have not been where you intended.
FÉLIX: Well
I am not glad to see you; I never thought
Our friendship could be strained.
CÉSAR: I'd no alternative.
FÉLIX: Leave this till later;
Now I must tell you Lord Aurelio
Is in Milan.
CÉSAR: Who told you? Have you seen him?
FÉLIX: I've even crossed swords with him, but luckily
No blood was shed. Now all must be resolved.
César, we've talked of Violante's marriage.
What do you say?
CÉSAR: I say she's satisfied me
On almost everything. Her father saw
The note that Tristán should have given her,
And so, no doubt, he took you for her lover.
FÉLIX: That's certain. *[To TRISTÁN]* When did you give the
       letter?
TRISTÁN: While he was counting the money.
FÉLIX: He was there then?
TRISTÁN: No — but in the next room.
FÉLIX: Apparently he saw everything and dissimulated!
TRISTÁN: What a damned old wretch!
FÉLIX: Since it is so... *[Knock]* But someone knocked, I
       think.
TRISTÁN: It'll be the phantom lady.[33]
FÉLIX: Open then!
CÉSAR: Don't open.
FÉLIX: Why?
CÉSAR: Because I can't allow
That you and Serafina...

FÉLIX: One moment!
    You do not need these scruples: I intend
    To tell her all the truth of our deception,
    And that, no doubt, will put a certain end
    To any feelings that she has for me.
CÉSAR: Upon that understanding you may open.
FÉLIX: Retire behind the arras and you'll hear me
    In courteous terms inform her of the truth.

[Enter SERAFINA and FLORA carrying their masks]

SERAFINA: *[To FÉLIX]*   It's not to express my gratitude, Don
        César,
    I come to see you now; but since you failed
    To keep the rendezvous, I only come
    To tell you of a project I have formed
    For your approval.
TRISTÁN: *[To FLORA]* And you, my darling, have you formed a
        project for me?
FLORA: Me! What on earth for?
TRISTÁN: I would have liked you to fall madly in love with
    me.
FÉLIX: What is this project, madam?
SERAFINA: Listen carefully.
FÉLIX: Speak, madam.
SERAFINA: I have been informed, Don César,
    By Doña Violante that you were
    The arbiter of her fate. I have been touched
    By her sincerity, her tears, her love;
    And come to beg you to have pity on
    Her noble reputation and her honor.
    Think what you wish me to say to her, but think
    It over; for whatever your reply,
    I shall consider it an insult; for
    If it is No, you won't do what I ask,
    And if it's Yes, you'll do what I detest.
FÉLIX: You ask me to say Yes or No, but warn me
    That you'll be hurt by either, and I fear
    That I must hurt you doubly by my answer.
    Yes, since Don César is the arbiter
    Of Doña Violante's destiny;
    And No, since it's not true that I am he.
    So I reply again contrariwise,
    Félix is not the arbiter of her fate.
    And Yes, I'm he.
SERAFINA: I do not understand you.
FÉLIX: I'm not surprised.
SERAFINA: Then speak more plainly, sir.
FÉLIX: I cannot.
SERAFINA: How is that?

FÉLIX: I dare not.
SERAFINA: Why?
FÉLIX: I am too much afraid.
SERAFINA: Afraid of what?
FÉLIX: Of losing your favor.
SERAFINA: Don César does not love
    Doña Violante?
FÉLIX: He does, as I have told you.
SERAFINA: And are you not Don César?
FÉLIX: No, as I told you.
SERAFINA: Who are you then?
FÉLIX: It was a stratagem,
    Devised by us, in which I have discovered
    The Advantages and Disadvantages of a Name.
SERAFINA: Speak more clearly.
FÉLIX: I would like to.
SERAFINA: You
    Have nothing to fear.
FÉLIX: What do you mean?
SERAFINA: If you
    Are not Don César, if he loves another...
FÉLIX: I will be frank too, you shall know that I...
VIOLANTE: *[Without]* O heaven, protect me!
AURELIO: *[Without]*   Die, you ungrate-
    ful child!
LISARDO: *[Without]* And may all who defend you also die!
SERAFINA: What is this noise?
FLORA: We're in a mess!
TRISTÁN: The house is in an uproar!
FÉLIX: While I go to see what's happening
    Please wait for me.
CÉSAR: *[Emerging]*   It's Violante's voice.
    I'm going.
FLORA: Fly, madam, fly!
SERAFINA: Open that door.
FLORA: I can't. It's locked on the other side.

    *[Enter VIOLANTE, disguised, through the door in ques-
    tion]*

CÉSAR: What's happening,
    Doña Violante? Why did you come here so?
VIOLANTE: I can hardly speak. I put on this disguise
    To come and see you, when a servant told me
    That an old man was asking for me; so,
    Believing it was Fabio, I went
    To meet him, but it was my father. Now
    He's coming in.
CÉSAR: Go into the next room
    While we detain him here.

FÉLIX: *[To SERAFINA]* Will you go too,
  So that you aren't seen here?
                    [Exit VIOLANTE locking the door behind her]
SERAFINA: Wait!
VIOLANTE: *[Within]*   Please forgive me!
  If I don't lock the door I should be frightened
  For my own life!
FLORA: She's given tit for tat!
        [SERAFINA and FLORA don their masks]

  [Enter AURELIO, LISARDO, and LIDORO, sword in hand]

LIDORO: What is the cause of all this uproar here?
AURELIO: There is no place that can give sanctuary
  Against the revenge of honor; and if I find
  My daughter or this traitor...
LIDORO: Desist, sir.
CÉSAR: *[Aside, mistaking SERAFINA]* Violante is still here.
FÉLIX: *[Aside]* Since Serafina knows the house, at least
  She got to safety.
LIDORO: *[Aside]*   What a lucky thing
  That Serafina has gone out today!
AURELIO: Let me pass!
CÉSAR: If you do not consider
  What house you are in, consider, Lord Aurelio,
  That it is I who defend it.
AURELIO: Do not intervene
  In this affair, for I regard you too,
  Since the death of Laurencio, as a mortal foe.
LISARDO: It was you who killed my brother? I am Lisardo.
  I demand satisfaction.
FÉLIX: It was I
  You challenged first, and you must fight me first.
AURELIO: Don Félix, is one duel not enough for you?
LIDORO: What have I heard? Just now he called Don Félix
  Don César, and he calls Don César now
  Don Félix!
SERAFINA: *[Aside]* Merciful Heaven! Have pity on me!
AURELIO: *[To LISARDO]* We have before us both our enemies.
LISARDO: Let us revenge, or die in the attempt!
FÉLIX: Then die you will!
LIDORO: One moment! Listen to me!
VOICE: *[Without]* Stop! Stop!

    [Enter the PRINCE and SERVANTS]

PRINCE: What is this noise? As it takes place
  Within your house, Lidoro, I did not wish
  To pass without discovering the cause;
  Especially as I see Don César now
  And Celio.

LIDORO: I'll tell you all about it,
     At least I'll tell you what I know. This lady
     Is Doña Violante, Lord Aurelio's daughter.
SERAFINA: *[Aside]* Unlucky that I am!
LIDORO: She has been brought here by Don Félix, sire,
     This gentleman who is Don César's friend.
AURELIO: Take care. You are mistaken. This is Don Félix,
     And this is Don César.
PRINCE: Now I've a grievance;
     I'll brook no lies from anyone.
LIDORO: My grievance too,
     Since I have given him hospitality.
FÉLIX: If you will listen carefully, my lord,
     You'll soon be satisfied. One is not blamed
     For being a true friend. Don César loves
     Doña Violante; he had a rendezvous
     On the very day he was commanded here
     With the Duke's letters; so I took his name
     And came instead. Meanwhile my careless servant
     Allowed a letter to fall into the hands
     Of Lord Aurelio, written to his daughter.
     As a result Don César had to flee,
     And Lord Aurelio thought that it was I
     Who had insulted him. It's not a crime,
     I say again, to oblige a friend like this,
     Especially when, as I trust, it may
     End in Don César's marriage, who, through me,
     Offers to marry Doña Violante.
CÉSAR: I consent
     With joy to this betrothal.
AURELIO: On this assurance,
     I'm satisfied.
LISARDO: But I am not. My lord,
     Although I'm of your retinue as Celio,
     I am not as Lisardo, so forgive me,
     I don't so easily renounce my vengeance.
PRINCE: Whether you are Celio or Lisardo,
     Once I have interposed, you'll pardon him,
     As I myself have done. *[To CÉSAR]* Give your hand
     To Doña Violante.
CÉSAR: With all my heart.
     [To SERAFINA] And, madam, since all is forgiven now,
     Will you unveil? Well, what do you fear?
LIDORO: Why hesitate?
FELIX: Yes, madam, lift your veil
     And kiss your father's hand.
SERAFINA: What! Do *you* advise it?
FÉLIX: Certainly.
SERAFINA: Very well; but you don't know

To what you have consented.   *[Unveils]*
LIDORO: What do I see!
  Ungrateful daughter!   What are you doing here,
  In that disguise?
ALL: Be calm!
LIDORO: Alas!   How can I?
FÉLIX: Follow now Lord Aurelio's example,
  And since she's pleased to offer me her hand,
  And I am not unworthy of the honor
  You can't refuse me.
LIDORO: I'll follow this advice,
  I'll make a virtue of necessity.
PRINCE: And where is Doña Violante?

  [Enter VIOLANTE]

VIOLANTE: Here
  At your feet, where I seek refuge, sire.
CÉSAR: Give me your hand.
LISARDO: Everyone's contented,
  Save only me, still unavenged and jealous.
TRISTÁN: What shall we do, Flora?
FLORA: We could tell each other the two tales of the Duenna
        and the Ape.
TRISTÁN: That will keep for another day.   At present
  We have only to ask pardon for our faults.
FÉLIX: And if *The Advantages and Disadvantages*
  Of a Name have led to the result you've seen
  May the luck of the playwright make up in your eyes,
  Sire, for the pitiful failure of his wit.[34]

                    ჩჩჩჩჩჩჩჩ

                    THE END

                    ჩჩჩჩჩჩჩჩ

Notes

From Bad to Worse *(Peor está que estaba)*

1. Gaeta belonged to the Kingdom of Naples in the seventeenth century and so, if not part of Spain, it did form part of the Spanish Empire. Small wonder, then, that we find some Spaniards in Gaeta, notably the Governor himself, Don Juan de Aragón, and his daughter, Lisarda.

2. Celia's comment that Flérida is "witty" is meant to be spoken with a decidedly sarcastic inflection. The word *bachiller/a* in Spanish has a derogatory meaning and often denotes a pseudointellectual who overindulges in displays of rhetoric and wit. Of course, by making fun of Flérida in this way Calderón is also smiling at himself: it was he, after all, who wrote the flowery speech that Flérida addressed to Lisarda. Calderón had a remarkably fine talent for creating elaborate images and ingenious conceits. But sometimes his very poetic exuberance carried him to absurdity. And he knew it! Hence his smiling self-criticism implicit in comments such as this one, which are to be found in many of his plays.

3. An important technique of Golden Age comedy is to break the dramatic illusion and satirize the very conventions on which such comedy depends. The *gracioso*'s comments here exemplify Calderón's use of this technique. Camacho thinks his master should have been soliloquizing, because love-sick gallants in Golden Age plays always express their self-tormenting thoughts of love in this way. In satirizing the traditional love-soliloquy Camacho alludes humorously to another kind of Golden Age play based on strict conventions: the *auto* or one-act religious play, with its allegorical figures such as the devil, memory, thought, etc., whose best exponent was, of course, Calderón himself. Camacho concludes his humorous dramatic allusions with a reference to *La dama duende,* suggesting that the mysterious masked lady who visits his master has ambitions for a new version of *The Phantom Lady* with herself in the title role.

4. "The wolf in the fable": in the original Camacho uses the Latin tag "lupus in fabula," by way of a warning to his master that the mysterious woman about whom they have been talking is in fact approaching and might overhear. Had Camacho chosen to give his warning in Spanish, he would have used the proverb "el lobo está en la conseja," the exact equivalent in meaning of his "lupus in fabula." The *gracioso* of Golden Age comedy has a fondness for Latin tags, often using or misusing them to good comic effect. In this case Camacho's reference to the "lupus in fabula" is much more humorous than the translation can convey. The lackey vaguely recollects that the proper name "Lope" derives from Latin *lupus,* and so decides that "lupus in fabula" must relate to something once said by Lope de Vega!

5. In his comic exasperation with Celia for refusing to lift her mantle and reveal her face, Camacho resorts to amusing verbal abuse. This abuse involves much wordplay with *manto* ("mantle"). In the interests of wordplay, Camacho distorts the name of Rodomonte, turning it into *Radamanto* ("Radamantle"). Rodomonte, a character in the *Orlando furioso,* is noted for the fury of his jealousy on discovering that his beloved Doralice is the mistress of another man. Hence the *gracioso*'s reference to "las furias de Radamanto." Camacho might also vaguely have in mind Rhadamanthys, a son of Zeus who became one of the three judges in Hades. *Garamanto* ("Garamantle") is doubtless another distortion of the name of a figure, evidently a giant, from chivalresque literature. Many such giants had names beginning with "Ga," for example, Gandalás in the *Amadís de Gaula.*

6. Cork shoes with extremely high soles and heels ("chapines") were worn by fashionable ladies in Calderón's day. Camacho insists that these cork shoes, unlike cork shields, had not been banned by law; but other extremes of fashion, for example, the farthingale, certainly were banned in Spain by various sumptuary decrees. The comedy here derives from the ridiculous mental picture Camacho paints for us of his wearing these very feminine accessories. The saying "¡Desdichado el enfermo, donde chapines no hubiere!" means that a sick man is soothed by a woman's presence and attentions. But the *gracioso* chooses to give it a much more amusing literal interpretation. For comments on the use of the chopine in Spain and elsewhere at this period see B. B. Ashcom, "'By the Altitude of a Chopine,'" *Homenaje a Rodríguez-Moñino* (Madrid, 1966), 1:17-27.

7. Petrarchan imagery of ice and fire is much used in Golden-Age drama. In this instance, Calderón might well have chosen such highly conventional imagery to suggest that Juan's extravagant love for Lisarda is not very profound. Lisarda's response to Juan's flattery is equally conventional. She likens him, with more politeness than conviction, to Mars and Adonis.

8. There was an abnormal interest in the seventeenth century in human freaks, giants, dwarfs, siamese twins, as some of Velázquez's paintings well testify. Monstrous births, of infants with two heads, etc., were reported in some detail in such seventeenth-century newspapers as the *Gaceta de Madrid.*

9. Camacho has a special fondness for allusions to the literature of chivalry. The figures he mentions on this occasion are all protagonists of Spanish novels of chivalry: Belianís, the hero of *Belianís de Grecia;* Esplandián, the hero of *Las sergas de Esplandián;* and Beltenebros, a name sometimes assumed by Amadís de Gaula, Spain's most famous chivalresque hero, apart, of course, from Don Quixote himself. Camacho's comments here form an excellent parody not only of the fantastic plot-content but also of the pseudomedieval style of the Spanish chivalresque novel (regrettably, the stylistic aspects of his parody are impossible to recreate in a verse-translation). Yet, the *gracioso*'s chief aim is not to mock chivalresque fiction but rather to warn his master against the world of absurd romance and fantasy, into which he is being led by his mysterious lady friend. César does not heed his servant's warning, though in the end both he and Lisarda are obliged to abandon their dreamworld of romantic happiness and accept life's realities.

10. Imagery of painting is used effectively here to illuminate César's complex emotional state and to motivate his marriage to Flérida at the end of the drama. The imagery reveals that César,

despite his sincere feelings for Lisarda, has not succeeded in for-
getting his first love, Flérida. To prepare us still further for
the denouement, Calderón deliberately reminds us in act 3 of the
imagery used in this second act by César. I refer to the scene in
which Camacho is questioned by Lisarda about the mysterious lady in
César's life. Not realizing that Lisarda is herself that mystery
lady, Camacho repeats, in his own more basic language, what his master had said: there was a first love to be "effaced" before this new
love could be "painted." Calderón makes important use of images of
painting in a number of works, of which the most notable is *El pintor de su deshonra (The Painter of His Own Dishonor).*
    11. Calderón breaks the dramatic illusion. The conventional
lackey of Golden Age drama is his master's constant companion. Camacho does not accompany César on this occasion and, therefore,
would like us to regard him as more than just an ordinary *gracioso.*
    12. Camoens alludes to changes in fortune in many of his poems,
so that I have been unable to identify exactly which poem Calderón
has in mind.
    13. Celia's cynical description of all men as "ladykillers" in-
volves the skillful use of double meanings, impossible to reproduce
exactly in English translation. She uses the word *baraja* both in
its ordinary sense ("pack of cards") and figuratively ("struggle,"
"quarrel," "trouble," "confusion"). Above all, the maid plays on
the word *matador,* which besides meaning "killer" or "ladykiller,"
is, like *baraja,* a term used in card playing. Specifically, *matador*
is the name given in Spanish to certain cards, three in number, used
in a card game called "juego del hombre."
    In the same breath Celia shows she disapproves of astrologers as
much as other men. Astrology was a highly controversial subject in
seventeenth-century Spain. It was much criticized by certain intel-
lectuals, not least by Calderón himself who satirizes astrology in
a number of his comedies, especially *El astrólogo fingido (The Fake
Astrologer).* In his more serious dramas, however, like *La vida es
sueño,* he finds it a most useful method of dramatic motivation.
    14. "Let's come in, / because it's raining": Camacho employs a
well-known Spanish proverb ("Entrome acá, que llueve") to make it
clear that he is an entirely uninvited visitor to Lisarda's house.
He comes out of extreme curiosity, eager to see for himself the face
of the woman whose beauty has so enthralled his master.
    15. Camacho uses the word *danzar* in two different senses. He
means that he is nimble on his feet, like a dancer; and he soon
proves his point, by the quickness of his departure when Lisarda
threatens to have him thrown out of the window. But he means too
that he is an inquisitive person (a traditional fault of the Golden
Age *gracioso*); for *danzar* also signifies "to spy or pry."
    16. Calderón gives a neat original twist to the conventional
ideas that love blinds and jealousy misleads. Ragamuffin boys acting as but indifferent guides to blind beggars were a common sight
in Golden Age Spain. The custom was immortalized in the *Lazarillo
de Tormes,* Spain's first picaresque novel, whose *pícaro* hero began
his "working" life as guide to a blind beggar. By including this
original "Lazarus" imagery in Juan's speech of apology to his
friend, César, the playwright suggests that Juan's feelings for his
friend are much more profound and genuine than his love for Lisarda.
It is a pity that the interesting relationship between the two men
was not more fully explored.

The Secret Spoken Aloud *(El secreto a voces)*

1. The translator has recreated the mood and sentiments of the original song. But it is impossible to reproduce the wordplay of the refrain, which depends on the fact that the Spanish word *razón* means "right" as well as "reason" or "reasonableness." Calderón often began his plays with a song, as a means of quickly suggesting the right tone and communicating the main theme to his audience.

2. In the Spanish text, the "mysteriousness" of his master's guest provokes a religious quip from Fabio, which, because of the nature of the wordplay, defies translation. The quip involves the use of the words *misterios* ("mysteries") and *sacramentos* ("sacraments") in both their secular and their religious meanings. The word *sacramento* is used secularly in Spanish in the phrase "hacer sacramento," meaning "to make a mystery of something" or "to talk mysteriously." This is one of the quips to which the Madrid censor took exception in 1642.

3. The kind of intellectual and rhetorical debate in which the Duchess Flérida and her companions indulge was in fact a customary form of entertainment in Calderón's day, at the Spanish court, among the noble classes, and in cultured and artistic circles. Poets, for example, used to form literary academies and debate all manner of subjects, serious and burlesque. Calderón himself apparently took part in such activities. The inclusion of this type of debate in a play was common in the Golden Age. Playwrights found it a useful means of providing the audience with information as to the different feelings and preoccupations of the main characters and so of motivating subsequent developments in the dramatic action. In the course of this particular debate on love, we learn a great deal about the thoughts and emotions of Enrique, Lisardo, Federico, Flérida, and, above all, Laura whose contribution to the debate is by far the largest.

4. Gallants in Golden Age plays are very eager to obtain some personal item belonging to the lady they love, a ribbon, a glove, etc. When a lady, either accidentally or on purpose, drops such an item, the result is often a duel between two gallants. Lisardo is surprised, but not displeased, that Federico is disposed to avoid a duel over Laura's glove by returning it to its owner. Unlike the audience, Lisardo does not realize that the glove that Federico gives to Laura is not the same glove that she dropped.

5. Almost every comedy written by Calderón after his very successful *Dama duende* contains a play of words on its title. Evidently an understanding grew between him and his audience that he would include such a reference, which became a kind of trademark, a guarantee that the comedy they attended was a genuine creation by the maker of *The Phantom Lady* (compare, for example, note 3 to *Peor está que estaba*). In this case, for good measure, Calderón also refers to his comedy *El galán fantasma (The Gallant Ghost)*, itself written as a follow-up to *La dama duende*. It says much for Calderón's ingenuity that Fabio's quip is amusing in itself, so that it could still be enjoyed by a modern audience despite its double load of topicality. Fabio cannot understand how his master could have received the love letter by any ordinary means. Accordingly he concludes that his master must be out of his mind, a "ghost" of his former self, and his supposed lady a mere "specter" of his imagination.

6. In the original, Fabio gives an additional meaning to the ordinary Spanish idiom "no ser cosa de buen aire" ("not to be in good taste," "not to be the right thing," "to leave a lot to be desired"). The lackey invites us to take the phrase literally for once: if his master insists on dying (of love's torments) then he will be a corpse, and a corpse is not productive of "good air."

7. Some fine military and political imagery reveals Federico's eagerness for day to give way to night, so that he might meet Laura. She betrays a similar impatience for their meeting in a parallel speech later in the act ("Ah! how the day before a longed-for hour / Is slow to disappear"). Federico's imagery might have an additional application. In several places in the play Flérida is likened to the sun. Federico in this speech suggests that the sun is a tyrant ruler who has "misconceived his rights" and usurps the nocturnal jurisdiction of the stars. The same could be said of Flérida, who misuses her political power to interfere unjustly in the private love of Federico for Laura.

8. In this very brief exchange with Flora, Fabio manages to mock no fewer than three overworked conventions of the *comedia*. In cloak-and-sword plays there is often an incident in which a mysterious woman asks a passing gallant for assistance, an occurrence often leading to a duel with another gallant. Fabio, like most *graciosos,* is cowardly; hence his first comment to Flora. He then alludes in quick and comic succession to two further commonplace happenings: the one where a gallant secretly follows his lady because he suspects that she is unfaithful to him; and the other, in which a gallant notices an attractive lady in the street and follows her, hoping to enjoy her favors, as it were, free of charge.

9. Fabio's words would be spoken with a calculated leer; they are full of double meanings. He is not simply offering his services in a general way, but making verbal sexual advances. He continues in this vein later in the scene. For example, when Flérida tells him he can have freedom of access to her chambers (to bring news of Federico) he understands her to mean that he can be her "gentleman of the chamber" in the fullest sense. The phrase he actually uses, "gentilhombre de placer," has a very ingenious double meaning, impossible to convey correctly in translation, indicating his desire to fulfill a double role within the play. He is already, as *gracioso* or wag, a "gentleman of pleasure" in one sense. He would like to be Flérida's paramour and therefore become a "gentleman of pleasure" in another sense. The fact that Flérida is supremely unaware of his ambitions in this direction and remains elegantly oblivious of his coarse insinuations adds considerably to the amusement of this scene. Fabio's grotesquely amorous delusions regarding Flérida may be seen as indicative of a development in Golden Age comedy, which culminates in the caricature-comedies written by dramatists such as Moreto and Rojas Zorrilla, Calderón's two most gifted disciples. In these caricature-comedies, or *comedias de figurón, graciosos* sometimes assume the roles of gallants and woo in monstrously comic fashion ladies of high degree.

10. Fabio mocks the "follies" of courtly lovers at Flérida's palace. But Calderón's intention is surely also to satirize excesses of the many lovesick courtiers with poetic inclinations who were to be observed at the palace of Philip IV of Spain.

11. This would be a very good scene in performance, full of emotional tension but also of physical movement, as the jealous Lisardo

attempts to catch and piece together the incriminating letter that
Laura has torn up and is attempting to trample beneath her feet.

12. Laura intervenes quickly with accusations against Lisardo,
before he has the opportunity to make any complaint against her.
This is the same technique as the one used by Lisarda in act 3 of
Peor está que estaba, when Juan finds her in his room, a technique
well summed up by the Spanish proverb used by Lisarda on that occasion: "hacer del ladrón, fiel."

13. Inevitably here, as in other scenes where the word-code is
used, the translator has had to move further from the original text
than he would choose to do in normal circumstances.

14. Ignorant of the secret code used by Federico and Laura to
communicate together, Fabio cannot understand how his master could
possibly have discovered that he gossips to Flérida. Like many
Golden Age lackeys he has a superstitious streak and suggests several times in the play that his master might have a familiar spirit
or demon in his service.

15. Most Golden Age plays contain some allusions, topical in
their own day and meaning little to us now. Fabio's comment might
be a veiled reference to the rebellions in Portugal and Cataluña,
which began in 1640, against rule from Madrid. Or it could be a
complaint directed against the many people in Calderón's time who
pushed their way into the public theaters to see performances without paying and who were in consequence being disloyal to "la villa
de Madrid." Since 1638 public theaters in Madrid had been wholly
administered by the municipality; and proceeds were used for the
upkeep of almshouses.

16. The comic anecdote, relevant or irrelevant to the main
action, was part of the *gracioso*'s stock-in-trade. Some of these
anecdotes would hardly amuse a modern audience, though they were
doubtless well received in their own day. This particular story,
however, did not regale the ears of Madrid audiences who saw *El secreto a voces* in 1642. For the censor had insisted on its deletion,
doubtless because it depends for its effect on a comic misunder-
standing of certain lines in the Preface to the Mass: "Nos tibi sem-
per et ubique gratias agere." The story of Agere and Macarandona
does have a certain dramatic importance. Fabio tells it to persuade
his master to "worship" two women at once. Federico is absolutely
loyal to Laura, but later in the play he is to pretend to pay court
to Flérida, to allay her jealous suspicions. The *gracioso* is full
of approval and, inviting us to recall his anecdote, describes his
master's behavior as "a fashion of Macarandon" (see p. 121).

17. Laura shows here that double meanings are not just the prerogative of the *gracioso*. In saying that she will wed the man most
desirous of being her husband she means Federico, but intends her
father to understand Lisardo.

18. The Cordovan whom Fabio has in mind is probably Séneca, who
was born in Córdoba and was a very important influence on Golden Age
writers. Whether he ever made the comment which the *gracioso* at-
tributes to him is another matter. The comment plays on the simi-
larity in Spanish of *secreto* ("secret") and *secreta* ("a privy").

19. A clever use of drama symbolism. Laura is compelled by
Flérida to assume the heroine's role in a play ("farsa de noche")
within the play. Ironically, the role she must assume is the one
she already performs in the real play, the role of Federico's secret
lover.

The Worst Is Not Always Certain *(No siempre lo peor es cierto)*

1. This bitter and desperate plea by Leonor serves to emphasize the firmness of Carlos's disbelief in her innocence. She no longer asks him to believe her, simply to listen to her.

2. "The truth itself accuses me": Calderón's words are "contra mí hasta la misma / verdad sospechosa tengo," which appears to be an allusion to Alarcón's well-known play, *La verdad sospechosa (The Truth Made Suspect* [1630]). Alarcón's work, about a liar who is believed until he begins to tell the truth, might have encouraged Calderón to dramatize an opposite case: that of a truthful person who is disbelieved.

3. Saint Isidorus (San Isidro) is the patron saint of Madrid. He was canonized in 1622, and Madrid celebrated the occasion with many festivities, including a literary contest at which Calderón won a prize. Leonor is apparently alluding to the hermitage of San Isidro del Campo, situated to the southwest of Madrid.

4. Calderón usually includes a long speech early in his first acts as a means of exposition and often interrupts it, as he does here, at a crucial point, as a method of creating suspense.

5. This second long speech of the act begins by dealing with events already related by Leonor. But on hearing Carlos's version of these events we are allowed useful insight into his character. Also we are given some important additional information in the final section. Despite its length, delivered by a good actor this speech could be impressive in performance: there is much drama and excitement in it.

6. Calderón has a fondness for quips that remind the audience they are watching a play. Inés thinks that her mistress is behaving just like a dramatist in the throes of composition. The comparison conjures up an additional picture for us: of Calderón himself, sighing, rereading, crumpling up papers, and gazing heavenward for inspiration, as he tries to compose a play, perhaps one called *No siempre lo peor es cierto*.

7. In the original, Inés's cynical comments on men's lack of sincerity in affairs of love depend heavily on wordplay which defies exact translation. Inés describes men as "potters of love" because like potters they manufacture "pucheros" and "cantarillas." *Pucheros* in Spanish are earthenware pots, but they are also pouts or tears. *Cantarillas* are pots of a different size. But the word *cantarillas,* like the variants *cántaras* and *cántaros,* can also be used metaphorically, usually in conjunction with verbs like *llover* or *llorar.* For example, the phrase "llorar a cántaros / cántaras / cantarillas" would mean "to weep large quantities of tears." Here, in the interests of the wordplay, the verb used with *cantarillas* is *hacer,* but the metaphorical meaning is still: "to weep buckets of tears."

8. A good example of a favorite dramatic device of Calderón. A character on stage asks a rhetorical question or expresses some special desire without expecting it to be realized; and another character comes on stage and unwittingly answers the question or fulfills the desire.

9. Inés is playing on the word *doncella,* meaning "lady's maid," but also "maid" in the sense of "virgin." She apparently considers the state of maidenhood to be much overrated. Her main intention, however, is to cast doubt upon Leonor's virginity.

10. In pretending to be a lady's maid, Leonor is following a well-established tradition. Many other heroines of Golden Age cloak-and-sword plays adopt a similar disguise.

11. Diego displays a talent for poetic untruthfulness worthy of Don García, the liar-hero of Alarcón's *La verdad sospechosa*. I have already mentioned this play as a possible influence on Calderón (compare note 2).

12. "...a long-robed judge — / But not a man": in the original, Beatriz's witty denunciation includes several ingenious puns involving legal terminology. For instance, "sala de competencia" can mean "court of appeal" but also, in this context, "chamber of rivalry," that is, the room in Leonor's house where Diego fought a duel with his rival in love. As for "en estrado, no en estrados": *estrado* was the name given to the room where ladies received their visitors; *estrados* were, and still are, the law courts or the judge's chambers.

13. "With a cracked pate": the original reads "sin venir de Zaragoza, / vino descalabrado." The Aragonese had the reputation of being rough, tough, and quarrelsome in the seventeenth century. Moreover, Calderón evidently wrote his play at a time (1640-1642) when the Aragonese and Catalonians were in revolt against the Spanish crown. The playwright himself took part in the military campaign to suppress this rebellion.

14. Calderón presents Beatriz's inclination to forgive Diego's real infidelity in ironic opposition to Carlos's inflexible attitude toward Leonor's apparent infidelity and in consequence reminds us of the different rules governing the behavior of men and women in seventeenth-century Spanish society.

15. Of the three principal male characters, Juan displays the most insight and compassion regarding Leonor's predicament. Unlike Carlos, he reveals an instinctive awareness of her innocence. Also Juan's profound pity for her contrasts markedly with Diego's unscrupulous willingness to compromise Leonor's good name for his own selfish ends.

16. A useful summing-up of the plot so far, managed naturally in this dialogue between the two dismayed friends.

17. The first of two anecdotes told by Ginés in quick succession, more to the taste of a seventeenth-century audience than to ours. This first story has an interesting anti-Portuguese slant, a helpful indication that the play was indeed written in the early 1640s, after the start of the Portuguese rebellion. A Madrid audience of this period would certainly have enjoyed the suggestion that the Portuguese were "down the drain" and beyond God's help.

18. Ginés's second anecdote also has a topical flavor. Spanish inns of the time were notoriously uncomfortable places and are much satirized in contemporary writings, prose and poetry as well as drama. The *gracioso* uses the word *gallina* in two senses, for it means both "coward" and "hen" in Spanish. Compare our use of the word *chicken*. *Graciosos* in Golden Age plays are often described as *gallinas*.

19. Another topical joke skillfully elaborated and applied in the original, but defying adequate translation, since it depends on the fact that the word *servidor* could mean "chamber pot" in Golden Age Spanish, in addition to "servant" or "suitor." Ginés complains that he and his master, suitors of Inés and Beatriz, respectively, have been treated like two chamber pots. Like the chamber pots of maid and mistress, they have been kept in a corner and then emptied

out of the window. The custom of emptying chamber pots into the
street was not confined to Spain; but Spain had the reputation of
possessing some of the dirtiest streets in Europe. Comic allusions
to this practice are numerous in Golden Age drama.

20. One of a series of jokes by the *gracioso* in this scene, alluding to his injured leg. Here he plays on various meanings of the
word *mal,* "unsound," "unhappy," "evil," associating his limp with
the devil, traditionally depicted as lame.

21. Ginés's remarks are an amusing parody of the syllogism. He
reasons: "I was hurt by falling from the balcony; it was your balcony; therefore you caused my injury." Calderón is parodying a form
of reasoning to which he was himself much addicted in his serious
plays (see, for example, *El mágico prodigioso*). Ginés's comments
might also have a more scabrous meaning. The symptoms of syphilis
include painful ulceration and bone changes, which can cause limping. In maintaining that his malady has been caused by Inés, the
lackey could be suggesting that Inés has infected him with syphilis.
This would explain the indignant vehemence of her denial: "mientes
como un cojifeo" ("You're lying, ugly shanks!").

22. Inés's comment plays wittily on the phrase "saber de qué pie
uno cojea." This is a well-used idiom in Spanish, meaning "to know
someone's weak spot"; but a literal translation would be "to know on
which foot someone limps." Ginés's real weak spot is his love of
money.

23. Diego's words, echoes of Leonor's horrified exclamations,
well convey that he is at first as shocked as Leonor herself by
their untimely encounter. He regards her with a superstitious dread
akin to her own. She seems to him like some malign spirit bent on
his destruction. An understandable reaction, for, as he reminds us,
his last meeting with her almost cost him his life. However, his
sense of self-preservation quickly sets his wits to work again, to
turn the situation to his best advantage.

24. Ginés cannot resist a jesting reference to the outcome of
his master's previous duel with Carlos.

25. Leonor's vehement expression of her hatred for Don Diego
adds a welcome touch of forcefulness to an otherwise passive person-
ality.

26. This type of scene, full of interrupted comments and asides
is commonplace in Calderón, but it would present some difficulties
for modern actors.

27. The fourth and final version of what happened on that fate-
ful night in Madrid. Diego's account throws interesting light on
his reason for visiting Leonor that night. Ironically, it seems
that Leonor herself, by rejecting Diego's advances so scornfully,
without trying to salve his hurt pride with so much as a kind word,
caused the resentment that sent him to her house, to extract a peculiar kind of revenge.

28. Through Ginés, Calderón indulges in mild self-mockery for
including so many scenes in which his characters are forced to seek
a hiding place.

29. The story of the noble Moor Abindarráez and his love for the
beautiful Jarifa was well known in Golden Age Spain. There are various versions in prose and verse. Montemayor, for example, includes
the story in his pastoral novel *La Diana.* Abindarráez is captured
by Christians. But their leader, Rodrigo de Narváez, generously
gives the Moor leave to visit his beloved Jarifa. He enters the

castle by a hidden door; Jarifa awaits him, made anxious by his delay in coming, and their love is secretly consummated. Ginés mentions Abindarráez in order to exaggerate, for comic purposes, the
number of lovers secretly concealed in Juan's house. He invites us
to suppose that even the traditionally tardy Moor could not risk arriving late at this overcrowded place and came early "to be sure of
a lodging." Another *gracioso* of Calderón who makes amusing reference to Abindarráez is Cosme in *La dama duende*.

The Advantages and Disadvantages of a Name
(Dicha y desdicha del nombre)

1. A typically Calderonian monologue, beginning with a series
of metaphors, whose main elements (diamond, steel, stone, etc.) are
then reiterated to bring the speech to its conclusion.

2. Tristán's remarks are addressed to the audience rather than
to his master and offer another example of Calderón's liking for
self-mockery. The *gracioso* warns the audience that the play they
are about to see is made up of well-worn material ("vejeces de
amor": "old ideas of love"), the only new stuff being his anecdotes.

3. See note 19 to *The Worst Is Not Always Certain*.

4. Satire of the clergy was commonplace in the Golden Age, in
prose as well as drama.

5. In the original the *gracioso* here indulges in a religious
joke, playing on the double meaning of the phrase "tener tibios los
llamamientos." "Llamamiento" can mean a knock on a door; thus "tibios llamamientos" are barely audible knocks on a door. But "llamamiento" also means a religious calling or commitment. Therefore
someone who has but "tibios llamamientos" would be a "mal cristiano"
("poor Christian"). The wordplay is impossible to render satisfac-
torily in translation.

6. For comments on *bachiller/a* in the pejorative sense of "witty," see note 2 to *From Bad to Worse*. As the *gracioso*'s remark indicates, *bachiller* also meant a graduate in the Golden Age (compare
our "Bachelor of Arts"). The servant's boast that he has attended
all the necessary courses, though without actually graduating, needs
to be understood in the light of the fact that at this period in
Spain servants usually accompanied their noble masters to the university and were allowed to attend lectures. The *pícaro,* Pablos,
accompanied his master to the university in Quevedo's *El buscón*.

7. "...it is most important to the plot": Tristán disrupts the
dramatic illusion again, a frequent occurrence in the *comedia*. The
lackey is, of course, right. It is important to remember that he is
Don Félix's servant because for a large part of the play most of the
other characters will be referring to his master as Don César.

8. In the original: the first of many puns on counting / recounting / accounting. *Cuentos* has to do with "numbers," "counting," but is also the normal word for "tales," "anecdotes"; and
Tristán is indeed an avid teller of stories.

9. Calderón is adept in the use of dramatic irony, one of his
favorite devices. In this case, however, he prefers the technique
of surprise. It comes as a shock to the audience as well as to Violante when Aurelio suddenly reveals that he had after all noticed
the letter which Tristán had contrived to give to his daughter.

10. Flora has a malicious wit. She suggests that she and her mistress will find this particular carnival dance easy to perform, for it is the "baile de los locos" or "fools' dance," and they have had plenty of practice in playing the fool.

11. The wordplay of the original defies exact rendering, because it depends on the fact that *postas* in Spanish are both "post-horses" and "pellets" for a gun.

12. A shortened version of Tristán's comment in the Spanish, which alludes to a well-known episode in Cervantes's *Don Quixote,* Part 1: the episode in the Sierra Morena, where Don Quixote, as Tristán says, imitates the behavior of Amadís de Gaula (or Beltene-bros, as he is also called) on the Peña Pobre. The knight does penance, imagining that, like Amadís, he has lost his dear lady's favor. So Tristán's remarks contain an allusion within an allusion (compare note 9 to *From Bad to Worse*).

13. More witty wordplay from Flora, difficult to convey in translation. Lidoro uses *favor* in the sense of "help" in the phrase "favor al rey." But the word can also signify a lady's favor, such as a ribbon. Flora mentions a lady, presumably of rather easy virtue, who on hearing the cry "favor al rey" was moved to offer the king a green ribbon as a mark of her favor (green being the color of hope). The witticism is not without an element of daring, if one remembers that the play was performed before King Philip IV, who had a notorious weakness for the "favors" of the opposite sex.

14. Serafina has a gift for playing the innocent which is worthy of Ángela in *La dama duende*.

15. Another amusing reminder to the audience that they are witnessing art, not life. The *loa* or prologue to a play in the Golden Age usually contained an advance apology from the playwright for the shortcomings of his work.

16. And yet another. In the original Flora plays on the word *tramoya,* "scheme" or "stratagem," but also "a piece of stage-machinery." She is afraid that her mistress's stratagem might work in reverse like faulty stage-machinery, which, instead of bearing the angel upward, sends him crashing to the ground. The elaborate contraptions used in performances of religious dramas were not always reliable, as contemporary sources reveal.

17. Félix means more than Aurelio realizes. He prides himself on being a "good friend" to César, for whose sake he is in Milan and in Aurelio's house.

18. Tristán makes comic efforts to assist his master to invent answers to Lidoro's awkward questions. Golden Age audiences doubtless enjoyed the absurdity of his assertion that César's aunt, the Lady Laura, member of the illustrious Italian family of the Farneses and normally resident in Parma, had become the abbess of a convent in the small Spanish town of Uclés.

19. The masked woman, the mysterious gifts, the haunting music serve to remind Tristán of the improbable adventures experienced by the heroes of chivalresque novels in enchanted forests and other such places. Compare the observations of the *gracioso* in *From Bad to Worse* (pp. 37-38).

20. The myth of the merciless Anaxarete, turned into marble by the gods, is often used by Golden Age writers in a serious context. Here Calderón makes good comic use of it. Flora's allusion in the original to "una niña de Loreto" is not entirely clear. There appears to be some topical or traditional saying involved. Loreto,

of course, as a renowned place of pilgrimage, suggests Christian goodness and compassion.

21. Flora and Tristán use *tocar / tocarse* in at least two senses meaning both "to play music" and "to dress one's hair." The wordplay cannot be rendered exactly in translation.

22. Tristán finishes his anecdote with a pun on the phrase "ver / saber de qué pie uno cojea." Inés uses wordplay involving the same phrase in *The Worst Is Not Always Certain* (compare note 22, p. 287).

23. In the original, Flora's anecdote plays on the phrase "echar el bofe / los bofes," normally meaning "to strive for all one's worth," "to put one's whole heart into something." But *bofe / bofes* in Spanish are also the "lights" or "lungs" of an animal. In Flora's story the priest puts his whole heart (and lungs) into his preaching; nevertheless he will have no "lungs" for his supper unless he pays the butcher in advance.

24. The wearing of the *coroza*: a form of punishment imposed by the Spanish Inquisition for a variety of offenses against the Faith.

25. Félix uses the same pun on "apenas llegar" ("scarcely to arrive") and "llegar a penas" ("to arrive / come to grief / griefs") employed by Rosaura in a well-known line from *La vida es sueño*: "y apenas llega, cuando llega a penas."

26. In the original Tristán names the particular "entremés" or farcical interlude that he has in mind: the *Entremés de la Ronda* (Quiñones de Benavente composed an *entremés* with this title).

27. That there are Spanish women lodging at the Star Hotel is understandable: Milan was a Spanish possession until 1706.

28. Tristán plays on the word *maleta,* which besides signifying a "bag" or "valise" can mean a "trollop."

29. *Coplas de Calaínos:* a ridiculous verse-romance about a Moor called Calaínos and his extravagant love for a Moorish princess of Seville, frequently recited by blind beggars in the Golden Age. By extension, it came to mean any nonsensical story, absurd thing, or pointless idea.

30. A scene rich in irony and feminine tensions. Violante becomes progressively more perplexed and inhibited by Serafina's interruptions; while Serafina grows increasingly anxious to discover whether or not Violante's lover and the man she, Serafina, loves are one and the same person.

31. Imagery of dueling, well used to convey Serafina's emotional yet determined state of mind.

32. The insults exchanged by Flora and Tristán are much more offensive than they might perhaps appear at first glance. *Mona* in Spanish means "copycat" and "drunkard" as well as "monkey." As for *dueña,* it was also used as a term of abuse, signifying an absurdly ugly, foolish, malicious, and hypocritical old woman. "Chaperons" were an unpopular group in Golden Age society and were almost as much satirized in literature of the period as were doctors and apothecaries. One of the most merciless, and memorable, Golden Age satirists of "dueñas" is Quevedo, in his *Sueños (Visions)*.

33. This is not the only occasion on which Tristán suggests that Serafina is a "phantom lady" (see p. 260). Compare also note 3 to *From Bad to Worse* and note 5 to *The Secret Spoken Aloud.*

34. The dramatist makes the traditional apology for his faults with a final masterly pun on *dicha* and *desdicha,* impossible to reproduce in translation.

Selected Bibliography

Editions

Obras completas de don Pedro Calderón de la Barca. II. Comedias. Edited by Ángel Valbuena Briones. Madrid, 1956.

No siempre lo peor es cierto, in *Cuatro comedias.* Edited with notes and vocabulary by John M. Hill and Mabel M. Harlan. New York, 1941.

No siempre lo peor es cierto. Edited with an introduction by Luis G. Villaverde and Lucila Fariñas. Barcelona, 1977.

"*El secreto a voces:* An Edition with Introduction and Notes of the Autograph Manuscript of 1642." By Dorothy Porter Cummings. Ph.D. dissertation, in *Ohio State University Abstracts of Doctoral Dissertations* (1933), 12:41-47.

El secreto a voces. Edited by José M. de Osma. Lawrence, Kansas, 1938.

Translations

Eight Dramas of Calderón. Freely translated by Edward Fitzgerald. London and New York, 1906.

Four Plays. Translated by Edwin Honig. New York, 1961.

Théâtre de Calderon. Traduit par M. Damas Hinard, avec une introduction et des notes. 3 vols. Paris, 1903-1906.

Criticism

Bergman, Hannah E. "'Acrostics' in Calderón." In *Studies in Honor of Ruth Lee Kennedy.* Eds. Vern G. Williamsen and A. F. Michael Atlee. Chapel Hill, N.C., 1977, pp. 33-44.

Maccoll, Norman. "Introduction" to *Select Plays of Calderón.* London and New York, 1888.

Sauvage, Micheline. *Calderon: Dramaturge.* Paris, 1959.

Varey, John E. "*Casa con dos puertas:* Towards a Definition of Calderón's View of Comedy." *Modern Language Review* 67 (1972):83-94.

Wardropper, Bruce W. "Calderón's Comedy and His Serious Sense of Life." In *Hispanic Studies in Honor of Nicholson B. Adams.* Eds. John E. Keller and Karl L. Selig. Chapel Hill, N.C., 1966, pp. 179-93.

Wilson, Edward M. and Moir, Duncan. *The Golden Age: Drama 1492-1700 (A Literary History of Spain,* vol. 3). London and New York, 1971.

Wilson, Margaret. *"Comedia* Lovers and the Proprieties." *Bulletin of the Comediantes* 24 (1972):31-36.

Wurzbach, Wolfgang von. "Eine unbekannte Ausgabe und eine unbekannte Aufführung von Calderons *El secreto a voces."* In *Estudios Eruditos in Memoriam de Adolfo Bonilla y San Martín* (Madrid, 1927), 1:181-207.